BUSINESS WITHIN EUROPE
Advanced GNVQ

A A Scott

Senior Lecturer
Bolton Business School

PITMAN
PUBLISHING

PITMAN PUBLISHING
128 Long Acre, London WC2E 9AN

A Division of Longman Group Limited

First published in 1994

© A A Scot 1994

A CIP catalogue record for this book can be obtained from the British Library.

ISBN 0 273 60475 9

Typeset by 🅰 Tek-Art, Croydon, Surrey
Printed and bound in Great Britain by Clays Ltd, St Ives plc

The Publishers' policy is to use paper manufactured from sustainable forests.

Please note the assignments in this book are not part of the BTEC designed
assignments published by BTEC which meet the full requirements of the
BTEC specifications. They will, however, provide opportunities for students to
produce useful evidence towards the full requirement.

10 9 8 7 6 5 4 3 2

BUSINESS WITHIN EUROPE
Advanced GNVQ

Contents

Introduction   ix

Part One THE EUROPEAN UNION
1   Institutions and decision-making   3
2   Policies and their effect on business   22
3   The Single European Market (SEM)   44

Part Two THE EUROPEAN BUSINESS ENVIRONMENT
4   Geography and communications   75
5   EC economies and markets   95
6   Business culture   111
7   Who's who in Europe   127

Part Three GETTING ESTABLISHED IN EUROPE
8   Going transnational   145
9   Marketing and selling   163
10 Marketing information   182
11 Innovation, quality and safety   194

Part Four BUSINESS SUCCESS IN EUROPE
12 Distribution and logistics   213
13 Administration and documentation   233
14 Risk and financial management   244
15 Human resource management (HRM)   253
16 Support services and funding   274

Part Five EUROPE IN CONTEXT
17 A wider and deeper Europe   289
18 Europe in a world context   305

Glossary   323
Index   331

Unit 14 Business within Europe
A Guide to GNVQ Level 3 coverage

Element 14.1 Collect business information about identified regions within the EU

Performance Criteria	Chapter
a. Sources of socio-economic information are identified and used	5, 10
b. Levels of economic activity are compared	5, 7
c. Social factors affecting business operations are identified	8, 9
d. Problems with using data are recognised	10

Element 14.2 Identify potential business opportunities within identified regions

Performance Criteria	Chapter
a. Established markets for specific products/services are identified	12, 13, 14
b. Developing markets for specific products/services are identified	8, 9, 10
c. Trends in chosen markets are identified and analysed	8
d. Opportunities and threats are identified	11, 14

Element 14.3 Investigate ways of gaining advantage from market opportunities within identified regions

Performance Criteria	Chapter
a. The range of supporting services and agencies are identified and evaluated	16
b. Channels of distribution are examined	12
c. Legal requirements are recognised and incorporated	3

Element 14.4 Evaluate alternative locations for production

Performance Criteria	Chapter
a. Factors affecting location decision are described	4, 6
b. The impact of local characteristics on the achievement of goals is explained	8
c. The costs and benefits of locally obtained resources are identified	15

Introduction

Why study European business now?

In recent years Europe has experienced change on a massive scale.

Within the European Union the implementation of the Single European Market has provided new business opportunities, and many organisations have taken advantage of them.

There have been heated debates about the future direction that the Union should take and the extent to which member states should co-operate in economic, social, defence and foreign policy. The Maastricht Treaty was implemented in November 1993 after a stormy passage through Parliament and two legal challenges in the UK, two referenda in Denmark (the first narrowly rejected the Treaty) and a slender majority in favour in the French referendum. The UK remains outside the provisions of the Social Chapter agreed by the other 11 countries. The period leading up to ratification was notable for the intense speculation about the consequences of the Treaty, and the small amount of factual information to support the views given by people indulging in speculation. Opinion polls in the member states indicate differing levels of commitment to European co-operation from country to country, but in general there is more enthusiasm for increased co-operation among the young, and the UK is no exception to this tendency.

The European Union is now a major economic power, and has considerable potential to be a world leader in the areas of social development, defence and foreign relations. Most of the countries outside the Union that we consider to be stable and independent – like Switzerland and Sweden – are thinking carefully about their economic, social and political status and how their relationships with the European Union should develop. Many countries in and around Europe have applied for membership of the European Union, or are showing strong interest in co-operation agreements. An example of such an agreement is that between the 12 EC countries and seven EFTA countries to form a 'European Economic Area' that embodies many of the principles of the Single European Market.

Around the boundaries of the European Union change is even more dramatic. We have seen the break-up of the USSR, increasing independence in the Baltic states, moves away from communism towards market economies in countries like Poland and Hungary, the splitting of Czechoslovakia into two countries, and a bloody conflict in the former Yugoslavia.

Principal trading countries like the USA and Japan recognise the importance of developments in Europe. Their governments and big corporations are developing strategies that aim to ensure that they benefit from the changes. In the GATT talks on world trade, attempts are being made to build a framework that reflects the opportunities and threats arising from these changes.

It is an exciting time for businesses based in Europe. More than ever before, they are likely to be dealing with suppliers and customers in other European countries, and possibly to have branches and employees elsewhere in the European Union. Therefore, it is important that those who are, or in the near future will be, involved in business within European countries develop a good knowledge and understanding of business within Europe. This book aims to help in developing that knowledge and understanding.

Adopting a logical approach to studying

The book is split into five parts, each covering an aspect of business within Europe, and arranged in a sequence that allows a logical progression, beginning with a study of Europe's business infrastructure, and moving on to the point where the reader can formulate business policies and plans that meet the needs of individual businesses in specific markets in particular countries.

Part One examines the nature and role of European Union institutions and the methods of decision-making. It summarises the Union's policies and their impact upon businesses, and summarises the consequences of the Single European Market.

Once an understanding has been gained of the framework in which European business operates, it is possible to consider the factors that condition the nature of business activities. This is done in Part Two with a study of the business environment – geography, communications, economies (of individual countries and the Union), markets and consumer behaviour, business cultures, and so on – and a brief survey of Europe's most important businesses.

Part Three is intended to address the issues that will be met by an organisation becoming involved in transnational trading for the first time. It considers the reasons for transnational trade and the methods of identifying and entering new markets. Key issues that will affect a business's chance of success are identified, including approaches to innovation, quality, and health and safety.

Developing a customer base in new locations is the first stage of doing business beyond the domestic market, but it is also vital that operations in these locations are cost-effective and profitable. Part Four considers the aspects of business activity that will, if properly planned and executed, contribute to business success. These include distribution and logistics, administration and documentation, risk and financial management, human resource management, and support services and funding.

Businesses need a strategy for evaluating change that will help to avoid threats and take advantage of opportunities. Such a strategy might well be based on categorising change according to whether it relates to current markets, prospects for new markets, or the impact of actions by non-European countries and organisations. Part Five considers the future of Europe using these three categories, examining possibilities for further co-operation between existing European Community countries, likely increases in membership, and the nature of trade between Europe and other parts of the world.

Who is the book aimed at?

This book is intended as a text for students undertaking the 'Business within Europe' option as part of an Advanced GNVQ in Business. On page vii a guide to GNVQ coverage indicates how the book's content relates to the range and performance criteria. The index may also be useful in locating relevant material.

The material contained in the book has also been used successfully with undergraduates studying for BA degrees in Business Studies and Business Administration.

Experience of providing training for owners and managers of SMEs (small to medium-sized enterprises) in conjunction with organisations such as the Chamber of Commerce, Training and Enterprise Councils, and Export Clubs suggests that their needs are very similar. The book is written with this clearly in mind.

Checking on progress

Within each chapter there are a number of activities. These should be tackled as they are encountered. They are intended to confirm that the reader has understood the topic just covered, and to encourage independent thought.

At the end of each chapter is an assignment. It is a good idea to read through the assignment before reading the chapter because it may add to the reader's understanding of the aims of the chapter. Assignments are intended to be significant pieces of work requiring the reader to to make use of knowledge and understanding from previous chapters, as well as from the current one.

Assignments are intended to provide suitable evidence for assessment of GNVQ elements.

Gathering data

It is important for a business to have up-to-date data when planning European business activities and a number of sources are identified in the text. Some of the information is freely available. However, most of the sources are organisations established to support businesses and depend on fees and subscriptions from businesses for their income, or have limited budgets. Consequently they cannot be expected to respond positively to an approach from an individual student and will be able to offer only limited help to colleges without making a charge.

Collecting data can be very expensive, and consequently market research organisations guard their data jealously.

The amount of available information varies greatly from country to country. There is a great deal on major industrial nations of the European Union, and a reasonable amount on the other Union countries, much of it gathered by the European Commission's Eurostat organisation.

Where information is gathered from a variety of sources, the student and business person must be careful to ensure that they are comparing like with like. There can be considerable inconsistencies in the definitions and classifications.

The accuracy and validity of information may also be doubtful. Data on the former communist countries, for example, may have been collected in circumstances quite different from the present ones, and it would be dangerous to make forecasts using such data.

Time management

Where the reader finds it necessary to acquire additional data, or make contact with an individual or an organisation, care must be taken to allow sufficient time.

It takes a surprising amount of time to get a response to a letter, particularly where the correspondents are in different countries, and where perhaps there is a language barrier to be overcome too. Telephone calls reduce delays but tend to suffer from misunderstandings arising from language difficulties. Fax messages are usually the most effective way of communicating transnationally.

Business terminology

It is anticipated that readers will be reasonably familiar with terminology used in business, but may be less comfortable with the language of international trade. Where terms are used that are likely to be unfamiliar they are explained when they are first used. A glossary is also provided.

Part One
THE EUROPEAN UNION

1 Institutions and decision-making

OBJECTIVES
1 To outline the development of the European Union (EU) and its aims and objectives.

2 To identify the principal EU institutions.

3 To distinguish between various types of EU legislation and describe the legislative process.

4 To outline the structure and function of the European Commission.

5 To describe the activities of the European Parliament and the role of Members of the European Parliament (MEPs).

6 To evaluate the role of the Council of Ministers.

7 To identify the function and powers of the European Court of Justice.

8 To identify the nature of interaction between business, experts and special interest groups, and the EU institutions.

Background to the European Union

The European Union is unique among international organisations because its member countries have agreed to share a degree of sovereignty in order to develop common policies where joint action offers benefits for all.

The Treaty of Paris, signed on 18 April 1951, created the European Coal and Steel Community (ECSC). This experiment in co-operation proved successful, and the member states decided to deepen and widen it, embracing their whole economies. On 25 March 1957 the Treaty of Rome created the European Economic Community (EEC) and European Atomic Energy Community (EURATOM).

It became clear that progress towards unified economies was made difficult by the barriers to the movement of goods, people and finance that were enshrined in the laws and practices of the member states. In order to achieve a market truly without barriers, it was recognised that progress was needed towards co-operation or union in many areas: technology development and transfer; progress towards economic and monetary union; strengthening of economic and social cohesion; improvement of the environment and working conditions; and a common approach to foreign policy. It was also felt that measures were needed to make the Community work more efficiently and more democratically.

These objectives were incorporated into the Single European Act (SEA), which was signed in February 1986 and came into force in July 1987. It amended and complemented the Paris and Rome Treaties. Its principal goals were to remove barriers to trade and create a Single European Market (SEM). At this time the European Economic Community (EEC) became the European Community (EC). Implementation of the SEA was to be completed by 31 December 1992.

Between 1986 and 1992 the UK Government, mainly through the Department of Trade and Industry (DTI), mounted a campaign to make businesses aware of the implications of the SEA and to help them prepare to operate successfully in the SEM. Only in 1992, when the EC was beginning to think about the next stage of European union, were the other aspects of the SEA – the social implications, sovereignty, European monetary union, and so on – widely discussed within the UK.

In February 1992 the foreign ministers of the 12 EC member states signed the Treaty of European Union (known popularly as the Maastricht Treaty). This document has profound constitutional significance for the UK and the future direction of the EC, which was renamed the European Union. As the Treaty moved through the ratification process in the 12 member states it was the subject of heated, even furious, debate.

ACTIVITY 1.1
What do you understand by the term 'sovereignty'?

EU membership

Six members formed the original Community – Belgium, France, West Germany, Italy, Luxembourg and the Netherlands. In 1973 Denmark, Ireland and the UK joined. In 1981 Greece was added to the list, and in 1986 Portugal and Spain brought the number to 12.

In October 1991 agreement was reached with the EFTA (European Free Trade Area) countries for the formation of the European Economic Area, the world's largest free trade area. This agreement gives the EFTA countries – Austria,

Fig. 1.1 EU and EFTA countries

Finland, Iceland, Liechtenstein, Norway, Sweden and Switzerland many of the business advantages of EU membership. However, many of the EFTA countries have applied for full EU membership.

Turkey and Morocco applied for EU membership in 1987. Cyprus and Malta have association agreements. Many eastern European countries would also like to be members, recognising the benefits of the common market. Hungary is best placed to receive a favourable response because it has been moving towards an enterprise culture and market economy for longer than the others.

The criteria for acceptance are mainly political and economic. Greece, Spain and Portugal were not accepted for several years because they were dictatorships. Turkey's application has not been accepted because its per capita income is only half that of Portugal, the poorest of the existing member states. There is a limit to the extent to which the existing states can support a poor newcomer. Old hostility and rivalry may also result in the veto of an application. Greece, for example, is quite likely to veto a Turkish application.

ACTIVITY 1.2

Why should successful applicants for EU membership be democracies with enterprise economies?

EU aims and objectives

The aims of the European Union, as set out in the Treaties and the Single European Act, are:

- To achieve an ever closer relationship between the peoples of Europe.
- Continually to improve the living and working conditions of its population.
- Steady expansion, balanced trade and fair competition.
- A reduction in the deprivation that some areas suffer as compared with others.
- The removal of restrictions on international trade.
- Support to developing nations.
- The pooling of resources to preserve and strengthen peace and freedom.

ACTIVITY 1.3

1 What do you understand by 'fair competition'?

2 Regional deprivation can be reduced by EU and national government intervention but this usually gives some businesses advantage over others. How can this be reconciled with the concept of 'fair competition'?

The Commission
Makes proposals

The European Parliament
Gives opinions and proposes
amendments

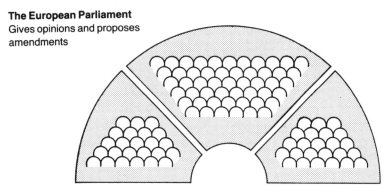

The Council
Decides

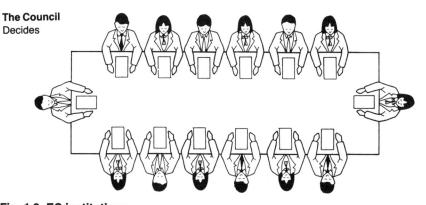

Fig. 1.2 EC institutions
Source: Department of Trade and Industry

To co-ordinate the actions that help to achieve the EU's aims, and to manage its activities, there are five main institutions: the European Commission; the European Parliament; the Council of Ministers; the Court of Justice; and the Court of Auditors.

Decision-making in the European Union

The European Commission is the EU's 'civil service'. It proposes EU legislation, supervises the day-to-day running of Community policies, administers EU funds, and ensures that member states comply with EU rules.

The Parliament considers the Commission's proposals, first in committee, then in the whole Parliament, and makes formal comments on them. The Commission is not obliged to accept the Parliament's comments, but it has to justify itself if it does not. The Commission may make changes to its original proposals after receiving the Parliament's comments. Revisions to the proposals must be reconsidered by the Parliament. The Parliament can block legislation by withholding its opinion; or it can refuse to accept the EU budget; or – as a last resort – it can dismiss the whole Commission (but not individual members).

The Council of Ministers is the body that takes the decisions to adopt proposals. When taking a decision on a proposal the Council will be attended by the appropriate member of each country's government. For instance, decisions on finance would be taken by the finance ministers from the member countries. Thus, although the Council does not always comprise the same people, there is always a specialist representative of each country present. To maintain fairness, each country has a number of votes related to the size of its population (for example, the UK has 10 votes while Denmark has only 3). As this book goes to press there is intense debate on changes to the rules of voting with the UK and Spain confronting the rest.

The Court of Justice comprises 13 judges, at least one from each member country, and interprets and applies Community law. The Court's judgments are binding on the member states and have primacy over national law.

The Court of Auditors is responsible for checking the soundness of management of the Community's finances.

Types of Community legislation

Regulations

These have general application and apply to all member countries. They do not have to be confirmed by national parliaments to have binding legal effect. If there is a conflict between a regulation and an existing national law, the regulation prevails.

Directives

Member countries are compelled to comply with directives within a stated period. The method of implementation is left to national governments.

Decisions

These are binding on specified member countries, companies, or individuals. Decisions involving financial obligations are enforceable in national courts.

Recommendations and opinions

These have no binding force, but merely state the view of the institutions that issue them.

ACTIVITY 1.4

Use your library to identify a directive that relates to a business you are interested in. Investigate how it was implemented in UK law.

The European Commission

Commissioners are appointed by the member governments for four-year renewable terms, and are based in Brussels. There are 17 Commissioners, two from each of France, Germany, Italy, Spain and the UK, and one from each of Belgium, Denmark, Greece, Ireland, Luxembourg, the Netherlands and Portugal.

Commissioners are not national representatives and must act in the interests of the Union as a whole. Sir Leon Brittan QC, for example, one of the two UK Commissioners, on several occasions was at odds with the British Government of Mrs Thatcher in the late 1980s, even though he had previously been one of her Cabinet Ministers.

One of the Commissioners is designated the president, and six are designated as vice-presidents. They hold their posts for two-year, renewable terms.

The Commission has 23 Directorates-General (DGs) – agriculture, transport, finance, external relations, and so on – and the Commissioners each take responsibility for one or more DGs. Sir Leon Brittan, for example, at the time of writing is a vice-president and is the Commissioner for competition policy and also for financial institutions. Bruce Millan, the other UK Commissioner, is responsible for regional policy.

Although the European Commission is a 'civil service' it is far smaller than the British civil service. Charged with setting up a vast amount of new legislation, administering EU policies and monitoring compliance with the legislation, the Commission comprised less than 15,000 people in 1990. This included nearly 2200 translators and interpreters, needed because the Commission has to work in all of the EU's nine official languages. This is not the 'vast bureaucracy' that some parts of the media would have us believe it to be. In fact the total number of employees in all the institutions (Commission, Parliament, Court of Justice, and so forth) was less than 23,000.

Each Commissioner has a personal staff, called a 'cabinet', of about 15 people. There are several other central departments, the largest of which are the translation and interpreter departments, employing about 2900 people. The rest of the Commission staff work in DGs. The largest are DG IX (Personnel and Administration) with about 2500 people and DG XII (the Science and R & D Centre) with just under 2500.

Most of the Commission staff work in Brussels, but the Commission is very much a multinational organisation. Every EU country is well represented amongst the Commission's employees, the largest groups being Belgian (3500) and Italian (2700).

DG I	External relations
DG II	Economic and financial affairs
DD III	Internal market and industrial affairs
DG IV	Competition
DD V	Employment, social affairs and education
DG VI	Agriculture
DG VII	Transport
DG VIII	Development
DX IX	Personnel and administration
DG X	Information, communication and culture
DG XI	Environment and nuclear safety
DG XII	Science, research and development
DG XIII	Telecommunications, information industries and innovation
DG XIV	Fisheries
DG XV	Financial institutions and company law
DG XVI	Regional policy
DG XVII	Energy
DGXVIII	Credit and investments
DG XIX	Budgets
DG XX	Financial control
DG XXI	Customs union and indirect taxation
DG XXII	Coordination of structural instruments
DG XXIII	SME (small and medium-sized enterprises) task force

Fig. 1.3 European Commission Directorates General

Because it is relatively small, the Commission makes great use of external organisations for expert advice. Amongst these is the Economic and Social Committee, set up under the Treaty of Rome, which advises the Commission and the Council, and comprises 189 members who represent employers, trade unions, consumer and other interests. The UK has 24 members on this Committee.

ACTIVITY 1.5

Identify the Directorates General that have a *direct* effect on business in the UK, justifying your choice.

The European Parliament

The European Parliament is a directly elected body of 518 members.

The Parliament's activities are split between three locations. Administration is mainly carried out in Luxembourg; full public sessions of the Parliament are held for one week each month in Strasbourg; and the meetings of its 18 committees are held during two weeks of each month in Brussels.

It is important for Members of the European Parliament (MEPs) to be accessible to their constituents. For this reason it is necessary to understand something of their routine and the how they may be contacted. The MEP normally spends one week in four in his or her constituency. He or she will usually be a member of at least one of the Parliament's 18 committees that meet in two- or three-day sessions once a month in the Parliament building in Brussels. He or she will also attend the full plenary sessions, lasting a week, which are held in Strasbourg. Between committees and plenary sessions the MEP will attend a two-day meeting of his or her political group where the group's policies and attitude to forthcoming legislation are decided. These meetings may be held either in Brussels or in other capitals or towns of the member states.

With such a complex schedule it is important that the MEP has good support services. In fact, both personal and office facilities for MEPs in Strasbourg are very good. There are good research facilities, and each MEP has a budget for secretarial and research assistants, and an allowance to run their constituency office. An MEP gets the same salary as the member of his or her national parliament, paid and taxed in the constituency country. In addition they receive an air travel allowance from their home addresses to Brussels, Strasbourg and the other meeting places, plus an allowance for expenses (e.g. hotel bills, meals, local travel).

It is generally possible to contact an MEP through the constituency office.

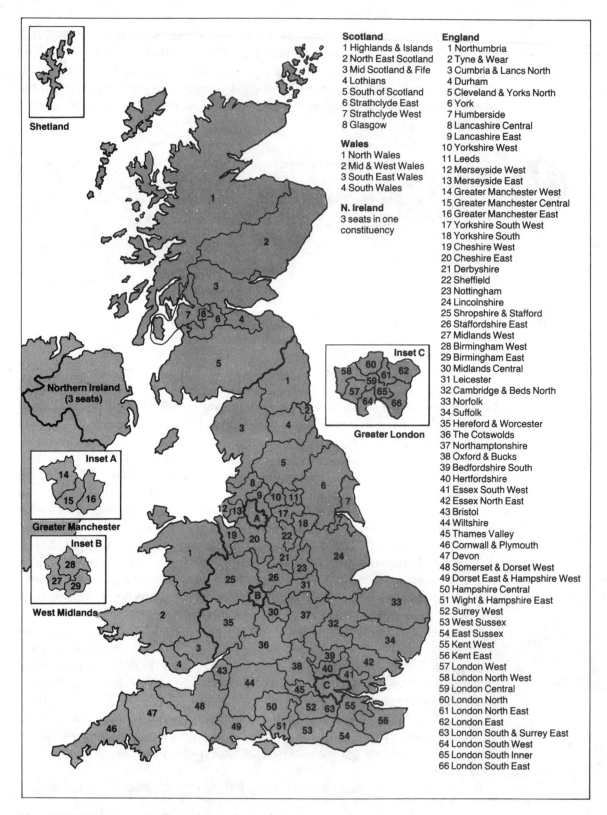

Scotland
1 Highlands & Islands
2 North East Scotland
3 Mid Scotland & Fife
4 Lothians
5 South of Scotland
6 Strathclyde East
7 Strathclyde West
8 Glasgow

Wales
1 North Wales
2 Mid & West Wales
3 South East Wales
4 South Wales

N. Ireland
3 seats in one
constituency

England
1 Northumbria
2 Tyne & Wear
3 Cumbria & Lancs North
4 Durham
5 Cleveland & Yorks North
6 York
7 Humberside
8 Lancashire Central
9 Lancashire East
10 Yorkshire West
11 Leeds
12 Merseyside West
13 Merseyside East
14 Greater Manchester West
15 Greater Manchester Central
16 Greater Manchester East
17 Yorkshire South West
18 Yorkshire South
19 Cheshire West
20 Cheshire East
21 Derbyshire
22 Sheffield
23 Nottingham
24 Lincolnshire
25 Shropshire & Stafford
26 Staffordshire East
27 Midlands West
28 Birmingham West
29 Birmingham East
30 Midlands Central
31 Leicester
32 Cambridge & Beds North
33 Norfolk
34 Suffolk
35 Hereford & Worcester
36 The Cotswolds
37 Northamptonshire
38 Oxford & Bucks
39 Bedfordshire South
40 Hertfordshire
41 Essex South West
42 Essex North East
43 Bristol
44 Wiltshire
45 Thames Valley
46 Cornwall & Plymouth
47 Devon
48 Somerset & Dorset West
49 Dorset East & Hampshire West
50 Hampshire Central
51 Wight & Hampshire East
52 Surrey West
53 West Sussex
54 East Sussex
55 Kent West
56 Kent East
57 London West
58 London North West
59 London Central
60 London North
61 London North East
62 London East
63 London South & Surrey East
64 London South West
65 London South Inner
66 London South East

Fig. 1.4 UK European Parliament constituencies

Source: European Parliament UK office

Representation in the European Parliament

It is intended that each country should have a number of MEPs roughly proportional to its population. In the 1989 elections, for example, four countries – France, Germany, Italy and the UK – each had 81 members, while other countries had less. However, the reunification of Germany in 1990 means that Germany was under-represented and will need about 98 MEPs in future elections to have fair representation.

In the UK, England has 66 constituencies, Scotland has 8, and Wales has 4. The UK uses a majority-vote (sometimes called a 'first past the post') system for its European elections, except in Northern Ireland. In Northern Ireland, instead of having three constituencies there is a single three-member constituency in

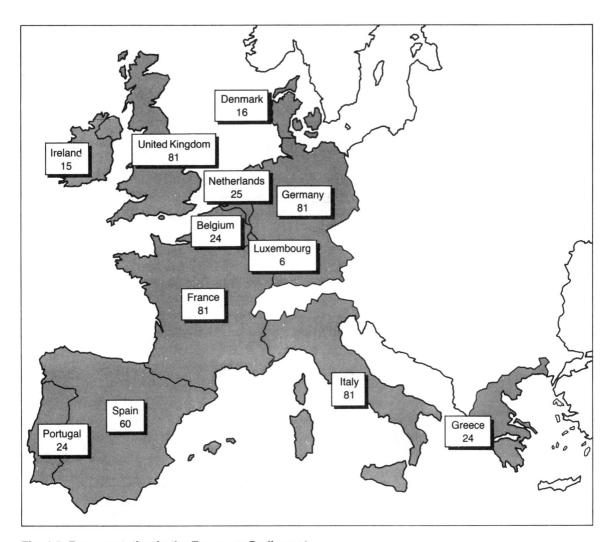

Fig. 1.5 Representation in the European Parliament
Source: European Parliament UK Office

which the MEPs are elected by proportional representation.

Other EU countries use various methods of proportional representation, although Italy is considering a majority-vote system.

Politics – European style

MEPs sit in political groupings within the Parliament rather than by nationality. Thus all Socialists sit together, as do Christian Democrats, and so on. The MEPs in the 1989–94 Parliament represented nearly 80 different national political parties. Most chose to join one of the ten political groups in the Parliament although a few opt to sit as Independents. Most groups contain MEPs from several countries.

So that MEPs can follow and take part in debates in their own languages, proceedings are translated simultaneously into the nine official languages – Danish, Dutch, English, French, German, Greek, Italian, Spanish and Portuguese. These translations are also available in the public gallery. British visitors to the Strasbourg chamber are amazed by its vastness and the orderliness of the debates, which are a contrast to the UK's House of Commons. Would-be hecklers are frustrated because they do not have access to a live microphone and they would not be understood by many of the MEPs, who would need a translation. However, the need for translation detracts from the spontaneity of debate. Sarcasm and emphasis in the voice are usually lost in translation. Laughter comes in the middle of the next sentence if an MEP makes a joke!

Voting is very efficient. Each MEP has buttons on his or her seat and the result of a vote is known within seconds, and is displayed on a number of elec-

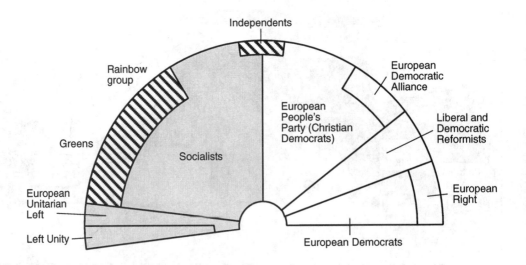

Fig. 1.6 Political groups in the European Parliament
Source: European Parliament UK office

tronic display boards. Precautions are taken to prevent an MEP voting for one who is absent.

The Chamber is colourful since all the documents have to be translated into all nine official languages, and each language is assigned a different colour.

ACTIVITY 1.6

1 What is the name and political party of your Member of the European Parliament?

2 How big (geographically) is the constituency where you live, and how big is the electorate?

3 What were the voting figures in the last European elections?

Parliamentary committees

The European Parliament has 18 major committees. They are concerned with the detailed examination of, and amendment to, the draft laws. Membership of each committee broadly reflects the strengths of the political groups in the Parliament.

Commissioners and Commission officials frequently attend committee meetings to explain the Commission's attitude. Experts and representatives of specialist organisations are often called upon for advice and to give evidence.

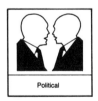
Political

Agriculture, Fisheries, Rural Development

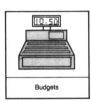
Budgets

Economic, Monetary, Industrial

Energy, Research, Technology

External Economic Relations

Legal Citizens' Rights

Social, Employment Working Environment

Regional Policy and Planning

Transport and Tourism

Environment, Health and Consumer

Youth, Culture, Education, Media, Sport

Development and Co-operation

Institutional Affairs

Budgetary Control

Procedure, Immunities, Credentials

Women's Rights

Petitions

Fig. 1.7 European parliamentary committees
Source: European Parliament UK office

The Council of Ministers

Council meetings are attended by the national ministers responsible for the areas of legislation to be decided on – agriculture, finance, industry, environment, social affairs, and so on. Commission officials also attend and participate in discussions but do not have a vote.

Meetings attended by the national Foreign Ministers have special significance. They co-ordinate the activities undertaken in other meetings of the Council, and also deal with areas of policy which are not specifically covered by the meetings of other ministers – external trade, for example.

Council meetings of heads of state (EU summits) are held twice each year to discuss broad areas of policy. The ordinary decision-making meetings are much more frequent – about 80 to 100 per year.

Council meetings are chaired by the minister of the country holding the Presidency of the Council. This changes every six months, rotating in alphabetical order around the countries. The UK held the Presidency in the last six months of 1992, and will hold it again in the last six months of 1998 (assuming no more countries join).

In some policy areas the Council can adopt legislation on a qualified majority vote. Initially these policy areas were relatively few. However, the Single European Act extended its scope to most policies associated with trade. The Treaty on European Union (the Maastricht Treaty) extended it further to include aspects of social and economic policy. Each country has a number of votes based on the size of its population (*see* Table 1.1). A qualified majority is 54 votes out of a total of 76. This means that a proposal must have significant support before it can be approved. Conversely, one, or even two, states cannot block a proposal that the others approve of.

Table 1.1 Qualified majority voting in the Council of Ministers

France	10
Germany	10
Italy	10
UK	10
Spain	8
Belgium	5
Greece	5
Netherlands	5
Portugal	5
Denmark	3
Ireland	3
Luxembourg	2
Total	76

Note: 54 votes are needed to approve a Commission proposal (to be revised in 1994)

In other policy areas, such as taxation, the free movement of people, and workers' rights, the Council must reach a unanimous decision. This means that even a single small country can block it. This power of veto is considered very important because it protects the sovereign rights of national parliaments on key issues.

ACTIVITY 1.7

On a decision that involves qualified majority voting:

1 What is the minimum number of countries that would have to be in favour of a proposal for it to be accepted?

2 What is the minimum number of countries needed to defeat a proposal?

The European Court of Justice

The European Court of Justice is concerned with the interpretational and application of EU law. Cases can be brought before it by the Commission, by national governments, by companies, and by individuals. The Court also has the power to review the legality of the actions of the Council, the Commission, and the European Parliament in the context of EU treaties.

The 13 judges – at least one from each Union country – are appointed by agreement with the national governments for a renewable term of 6 years.

The Court's judgments are binding on each member country and have primacy over national law.

In 1989 the European Court of Justice dealt with 385 cases, but the number of cases referred to it is rising rapidly as the volume of European Union law grows.

The legislative process

Consultation procedure

A draft proposal is prepared by one of the Commission's DGs. It is then formally approved by the Commission and sent for discussion to the European Parliament, the Economic and Social Committee, national governments, and other bodies. The Commission may take their comments into account and issue a revised proposal.

A final draft is given to the relevant Council of Ministers, who decide whether to adopt a proposal and how it should be implemented (regulation, directive, and so on).

Co-operation procedure

Up to the stage of being considered by the Council of Ministers the procedure is the same. Then the Council, instead of formulating a directive or regulation, agrees a 'common position' which governments of member countries must then implement with legislation in their own countries, normally within one to two years. In the UK the legal foundation for this is the European Communities Act 1972.

The Consumer Protection Act 1989 is an example of legislation that was introduced in response to a 'common position'. 'Common positions' have sometimes been implemented under existing national legislation.

In the UK, EU legislation is examined by Select Committees of the House of Commons and/or the House of Lords, and are sometimes debated by those Chambers.

The democratic deficit

The European Parliament, although it is democratically and directly elected, does not draft Union legislation, nor does it approve proposed legislation. The European Commission drafts the law and the Council of Ministers decides which laws shall be put into effect. Once a Council of Ministers has made a decision neither the European Parliament nor the national parliaments can change it.

It can be argued that decision-making is democratic because the Ministers all represent democratically elected governments. However, their perspective is likely to be national rather than Community-oriented.

The majority of MEPs (from all parties and all member states) think the European Parliament should have more power. Seventy-nine per cent feel it should have some power over the Council of Ministers and 92 per cent want some power over the European Commission. Other suggestions to improve democracy include:

- National parliaments should be given more time to discuss legislation while it is still possible to influence Council decisions.
- There should be a second chamber to the European Parliament, as there is in most national parliaments.
- There should be several representatives of each country at councils of ministers, to represent national *parliaments* rather than national *governments*.

The 1991 UK Government declared that it was opposed to any changes in the legislative powers of the European Parliament, arguing that democratic control over the Ministers is a concern of national parliaments. It did, however, favour tighter control over the European Commission. By contrast, the German Government, supported proposals that would release some of the power from national governments, provided the European legislative process was made more democratic.

The European Parliament is not without power, even though it has only limited power in the law-making process. In 1979 and in 1984 it rejected the Community Budget because it disagreed with the Council's spending priorities. The European Parliament also has the power to dismiss the whole of the Commission by a vote of censure. This would be a very drastic step.

ACTIVITY 1.8

1 Discuss the advantages and disadvantages of increasing the power of the European Parliament.

2 What are the relative merits of the alternatives suggested?

Lobbying

In the UK anyone can arrange to visit the lobby of the House of Commons to 'lobby' his or her MP. This may be in order to give the MP some information that he or she might not otherwise have, or it may be to try to persuade the MP to support a particular view. Many MPs have 'surgeries' in their constituency so that constituents can visit them there to lobby.

MEPs are also available for lobbying in much the same way. The MEP has to travel around Europe extensively to attend committees (in Brussels), and full Parliamentary sessions (in Strasbourg), and to visit his or her constituency. Nevertheless, most UK MEPs are quite readily accessible to constituents.

Unlike the British civil service, the European Commission is also available for lobbying. Because part of the Commission's role is to listen to experts and special-interest groups, it is relatively easy to arrange meetings with officials and even Commissioners. In this way it can be quite responsive.

Lobbying can be two way. It is possible to get information about future proposals from the Commission before they reach the formal stage of submission to the European Parliament. Again this differs from the British civil service, which has much of its activity covered by the Official Secrets Act. Many large organisations have an employee based in Brussels to represent its interests. Smaller businesses can use the services of an agency to fulfil the same role.

ACTIVITY 1.9

What are the relative merits of having a system where the officials can be openly lobbied by experts, businesses and pressure groups (like the European Commission) as compared with the UK civil service?

SUMMARY

1 Milestones in the development of the EU are the Paris and Rome Treaties, the Single European Act, and the Treaty on European Union (the Maastricht Treaty).

2 The major EU institutions are the European Commission, the European Parliament, the Council of Ministers, the European Court of Justice, and the Court of Auditors.

3 EU legislation is implemented principally by regulations, directives and decisions.

4 The European Commission puts forward proposals for the European Parliament's consideration and comment. The Council of Ministers takes decisions on proposals.

5 There are 17 commissioners, based in Brussels. The Commission is split into 23 Directorates General, each responsible for an area of policy.

6 The European Parliament comprises 518 directly elected MEPs, grouped according to politics, not nationality. Its administration is based in Luxembourg, its open meetings are in Strasbourg, and committees meet in Brussels.

7 One person represents each country at a Council of Ministers. The minister of the national government who attends is the one most appropriate to the business of the day. Presidency of the Council passes from country to country, every six months. For some proposals a qualified majority is needed for approval; for others the Council must be unanimous.

8 The European Court of Justice consists of 13 judges. It interprets EU law. Judgments are binding on individuals, organisations and governments. They have primacy over national law.

9 There is an open dialogue between individuals and organisations, and the EU. Many organisations employ personnel to enhance the effectiveness of their lobbying.

Assignment 1

BACKGROUND

Many parts of Europe have toll roads. In France, for example, drivers pay to use most of the motorways. By contrast, in the UK, tolls at present apply on very few roads, and a number of bridges.

As a means of cutting down urban congestion, the UK Government is considering charging motorists who bring their cars into city centres. A number of schemes are being considered, the key operational factors being how various sections of road are priced, whether different types of vehicle and/or user are charged at different rates, and how payments are collected.

There are a number of issues. As well as the environment, road pricing would affect business costs, methods and costs of commuting, and so on.

ACTIVITY

European legislation is proposed to encourage road pricing because of the claimed benefits on the environment:

1 Describe the process that will be followed to arrive at the legislation and the institutions and people involved.

2 Decide who should be consulted in the discussion phase and suggest a timescale. Anticipate the views of the various parties consulted.

3 Take the role of the Commissioner of a relevant Directorate General and formulate a proposal to put before the European Parliament.

4 Adopt roles as MEPs and discuss the proposal, returning it to the Commission for revision, if necessary.

5 Consider the proposed legislation from the point of view of members of the Council of Ministers and decide how the proposal would be implemented if it became EU policy.

2 Policies and their effect on business

OBJECTIVES   1 To identify the source and application of EU budget funds.

2 To describe the aims of the Common Agricultural Policy and the way these aims are achieved.

3 To examine the reasons for regional policies in the EU and the ways of implementing them.

4 To examine the nature of social funding and the debate regarding its future development.

5 To analyse EU policy on research and technology.

6 To trace progress towards European monetary union.

The Union budget

Sources of funds

Redistribution of wealth is an important function of national budgets in all industrialised countries. By this redistribution, resources are transferred to poorer regions and disadvantaged groups, thus bringing about a reduction in the disparities. The funds are generally obtained by taxation, and are distributed by expenditure on specific projects or by grants.

The EU undertakes a similar redistribution of wealth. Although the amounts are large, the redistribution achieved through the EU budget is small by comparison with the effects of the Single European Market, which has made transnational trade so much easier and resulted in significant increases in the flow of goods and funds. However, because the amounts are easily identifiable, the EU budget attracts considerable media attention.

In the early years of the EEC the budget was an accumulation of the expenditure arising from decisions on individual policies. As such it lacked co-ordination. It was funded by contributions from the member states. Each year, national leaders and finance ministers met to agree how much each country should contribute. Every country, of course, would like to be a net recipient of EU funds. Clearly this is impossible, and if any redistribution is to take place some countries must have a net gain while others have a net loss.

The first significant dispute relating to contributions, provoked by General de Gaulle, took place in 1965. In 1973 the UK's efforts to reduce its net national contribution led to a serious political storm. Eventually a system was agreed that encouraged co-operation towards European union rather than simply defending national interests.

EU revenue now consists of VAT contributions, national contributions related to gross national product (GNP), customs duties (on imports from outside the EU), and agricultural levies. In 1992 over half of EU budget revenue was derived from VAT, while customs duties and GNP-based contributions each amounted to less than 25 per cent. VAT revenue comprises 1.4 per cent of the VAT income a country would derive from a 'harmonised base rate'. This apparently complicated system is necessary because each country has different VAT rates, and applies them to different ranges of goods.

Agricultural levies have declined as a source of revenue as the EU has become more self-sufficient in agricultural products. However, variations can occur because imports also depend on the difference between EU and world prices. Similarly, income from customs duties is likely to decline as external tariffs are reduced as a result of GATT negotiations.

The introduction of the GNP-related contribution in 1988 (known as the 'fourth resource') is felt to be more closely related to a state's ability to pay than any other source of EU revenue. Customs duties and agricultural levies relate to a country's level of imports. VAT depends on the country's propensity to consume.

ACTIVITY 2.1

1 Use Table 2.1 to identify the 'winners' and 'losers' in obtaining net receipts from the EU budget.

2 How has the pattern changed during the ten years from 1980 to 1990?

3 Consider each country and suggest reasons for the comparative levels of net receipts and any changes in the ten years.

Table 2.1 Net receipts from EU budget

	1980 ECU(m)	1982 ECU(m)	1984 ECU(m)	1986 ECU(m)	1988 ECU(m)	1990 ECU(m)
Belgium	−273.4	−499.0	−398.2	−283.9	−995.0	−773.9
Denmark	333.9	228.3	487.2	421.1	350.9	422.5
France	380.4	−827.3	−459.8	−561.5	−1,780.9	−1,804.9
Germany	−1,670.0	−3,171.7	−3,033.1	−3,741.1	−6,107.1	−5,550.4
Greece		604.3	1,008.2	1,272.7	1,491.6	2,470.2
Ireland	687.2	671.5	924.1	1,230.3	1,159.3	1,892.5
Italy	681.2	911.4	1,519.0	−130.3	124.2	−416.7
Luxembourg	−5.1	−24.3	−40.1	−59.3	−67.4	−60.0
Netherlands	394.5	86.9	434.8	167.5	1,150.0	38.4
Portugal				219.0	514.9	600.8
Spain				94.9	1,334.3	1,711.3
UK	−1,364.6	−1,193.6	−1,337.0	−1,438.4	−2,070.0	−3,386.9
Admin and external spending	835.9	3,213.5	894.9	2,809.7	4,895.2	4,527.1

Source: Court of Auditors
Note: Negative figures indicate a net contribution to the EU budget.

Application of funds

The two basic characteristics of the EU budget are its very small size compared with national budgets, and the *legal* requirement that revenue must equal expenditure. In 1992 EU expenditure was about 1.15 per cent of the EU total GNP.

The Common Agricultural Policy (CAP) has consistently been the biggest item of EU expenditure. The European Agricultural Guidance and Guarantee Fund (EAGGF) forms the largest part of the expenditure, although other Agricultural and Fisheries expenditure is significant. Agricultural policy will remain, for some years to come, the biggest item of EU expenditure, although it will continue to decline in relative importance. It should fall below 50 per cent of the total budget by 1997.

Current proposals are to substantially increase spending in three areas of EU expenditure – structural policy, industrial policy, and external aid. Structural funds (for the regional and social policies) doubled as a proportion of EU spending in the ten years to 1990. The Commission proposals will result in over half of new spending being directed to these, producing another doubling of expenditure on structural schemes. A key element of structural schemes is that they support investment rather than compensating losers. The aim is to encourage new industries and to assist them in the early stages. Once they become self-sufficient, EU funding is no longer needed. By contrast, subsidies for declining industries and compensation schemes for lost income or jobs, tend to be long term and discourage innovation and competitiveness.

Table 2.2 EU budget expenditure

	1980		1985		1990	
	ECU(m.)	%	ECU(m.)	%	ECU(m.)	%
EAGGF guarantee	11,485.5	70.97	19,955.0	70.18	26,431.0	56.32
Agriculture structures	328.7	2.03	687.7	2.42	2,073.5	4.42
Fisheries	64.1	0.40	111.7	0.39	358.6	0.76
Regional policy	722.7	4.47	1,697.8	5.97	5,209.7	11.10
Social policy	768.8	4.75	1,626.2	5.72	3,667.0	7.81
Research and energy	379.5	2.35	706.8	2.49	1,733.4	3.69
Development co-operation	641.6	3.96	1,043.7	3.67	1,489.6	3.17
Administration	938.8	5.80	1,332.6	4.69	2,381.3	5.07
Miscellaneous	852.8	5.27	1,271.8	4.47	3,584.3	7.64
Total	16,182.5	100.00	28,433.3	100.00	46,928.4	100.00

Source: European Commission

The Common Agricultural Policy (CAP)

Why is a policy needed?

In 1960 agriculture employed 15.2 million people in Union countries. By 1987 the number had dropped to 5.2 million, but the entry of Spain and Portugal increased it to about 10 million.

In many member countries agriculture is changing from a traditional activity to a modern economic sector, having close links with suppliers and the processing and distribution industries. There has been a fall in the number of farms, but an increase in the size and specialisation. Higher yields have been achieved by the use of fertilisers, pesticides, high-quality seeds and feedstuffs. These trends have been most significant in the more prosperous countries. In the less prosperous ones, agriculture is still comparatively unsophisticated. For example, the average size of farms in the UK is 65 hectares while in Greece and Portugal it is less than 5 hectares.

Throughout the world governments find the need to intervene in agriculture, a sector of the economy that is politically sensitive, economically fragile, and difficult to manage.

The Common Agricultural Policy (CAP) therefore aims to:

- ensure security of supply;
- achieve stable prices for farmers and consumers;
- protect the environment;
- make it easier for farmers and farmworkers in the various countries to adjust to new technology and changing patterns of demand; and
- improve links between agriculture and the rest of industry.

Food is essential for survival. In Europe the CAP has ensured that adequate supplies are available without a dangerous dependency on non-EU countries.

Despite technological and biological progress, agriculture is dependent on natural conditions such as soil and weather, which can cause changes in the yield. Demand, on the other hand, remains fairly stable. Without a policy to regulate prices and markets there would be massive swings in prices.

In many areas of the Union modern farming is approaching ecological limits. Pollution of groundwater with nitrates and pesticides is very high, the number of wildlife species is shrinking and the appearance of the countryside is changing for the worse. A policy is needed which prevents farmers using unacceptable methods in their struggle for ever-greater yields. Furthermore in some areas there is no alternative to employment in agriculture. In regions handicapped by poor soil and harsh climate the CAP is essential in preventing depopulation and dereliction.

As well as supporting farming the CAP indirectly supports other industries. Farmers buy machinery, plants, pesticides and fertilisers, and produce raw materials for a wide range of processing industries. They also need to buy clothes, furniture, and services. Thus the whole population of a region is associated with this primary industry.

What is the CAP?

The European Union encompasses a wide variety of agricultural areas, from the north German plains, over the Alps, to the coasts of southern Italy.

The CAP offers prospects of new outlets for farmers but means keener competition. For consumers there is a wider and better choice of food. Specialisation and economies of scale offer relatively cheap prices. The policy also ensures that there is free movement of agricultural products within the Union. It prohibits the charging of customs duties, the granting of subsidies or the setting-up of quotas where these would distort competition.

Moreover 'Union preference' means that priority is given to the sale of EU products, rather than products from the rest of the world. If EU prices are higher than on the world market, the CAP protects the internal market against cheap imports and any excessive fluctuations in world prices.

To achieve the aims of the CAP – the security of supply, stability in prices for farmers and consumers, etc – it is necessary for the EU to intervene in the market for agricultural products, provide subsidies, etc. The costs associated with these actions are shared throughout the Union. However, direct taxation and social security for farmers and farm workers remain national responsibilities.

The aims of CAP are achieved by 'intervention' and 'external protection'.

Intervention

About 70 per cent of products benefit from a support price which provides, under certain conditions, a guarantee of price and disposal. The EU has established intervention agencies for products such as cereals, butter, skimmed-milk products, sugar and beef. When supplies are abundant these agencies buy in the surplus production to stabilise market prices. They are sold again once the market is back in balance internally or by means of exports to non-EU countries.

Originally the intervention agencies bought products at a fixed price (the 'intervention price'). More recently the agencies have issued invitations to tender, and the buying-in price reflects the market situation. On the sugar market the full intervention price is paid for those quantities the Union needs to supply its own market. If farmers produce more, they have to shoulder the burden of disposal themselves. With pork, table wine and some types of fruit and vegetables the agencies may pay for private storage to take a proportion of the product off the market temporarily.

Generally speaking, intervention prices are higher in the Union than on the world market. This ensures that domestic farmers sell to the internal market, protecting supplies. To prevent imports, 'external protection' is needed (see below).

Prices are fixed annually in ECUs. Farmers actually receive money in their own currency, calculated using a special exchange rate. In the UK the 'green £' refers to values calculated using this exchange rate rather than the spot rate.

External protection

About 21 per cent of produce is protected by measures that prevent low-price imports from outside the EU. Products that are not staple foods and can be produced more or less independently of the soil, such as eggs and poultry, quality wines, flowers and many types of fruit and vegetables, are protected by levies or customs duties. However, the General Agreement on Tariffs and Trade (GATT) forces the EU to keep its import duties on a number of products at a constant level. The processing industries for these products – which include rape-seed, sunflower seed, cotton-seed and protein plants like peas and field beans – receive a subsidy if they use EU-grown products. This accounts for about 2.5 per cent of agricultural products.

For about 0.5 per cent of products (specialised products like hemp, flax, hops, silkworms and seeds), the producers receive flat-rate aid according to the hectarage or quantity produced.

Setting prices

The EU population of over 320 million spend about 20 per cent of their incomes on food. Changes in farm prices affect food prices in the shops.

When the CAP was first introduced it was felt to be desirable to protect the income of farmers, most of whom worked on small or medium-sized family farms, because their incomes were less than in other occupations. Direct financial aid could have been given but it was less expensive and less bureaucratic to allow higher prices. However, a guaranteed market and price encouraged producers to take advantage of every opportunity to increase output and thus food mountains came into existence.

Although the EU was slow to respond, eventually support prices were frozen or reduced and 'maximum guaranteed quantities' were established. Direct financial aid was introduced to limit the effect on farmers' incomes.

It would be difficult to revert completely to using world market prices. The quantities traded on the world market are often very small compared with the total production and sometimes reflect short-term surpluses in the main producer countries. They fluctuate wildly and are sometimes below the full cost.

Also, farm-gate prices have risen more slowly than food prices and these in turn have lagged behind the overall cost of living. They have also risen more slowly than disposable income.

Meanwhile, consumers are becoming more conscious of quality. Since high quality is often correlated with lower yields, the introduction of different intervention prices for different qualities has had the effect of curbing total production and achieving better product quality.

Reforming the CAP

The aims of the CAP have not been challenged, but conditions have changed since the policy was first introduced and many of its methods have been and continue to be reassessed.

When the CAP was introduced much of the EU's food requirement was imported. However, per capita consumption has stabilised and population growth has declined. Imports have reduced and the EU is now almost self-sufficient for essential produce.

In the 1980s supply began to exceed demand in sectors such as cereals, milk and beef. Wheat production exceeded consumption by almost 30 per cent, and there were surpluses of butter (34 per cent), skimmed-milk powder (28 per cent) and beef (10 per cent). The world market also had an ample supply of these. Third World countries could only absorb a small part of the surpluses and only if the EU subsidised the prices. In the mid-1980s stocks of feed grain stood at 200 million tonnes, about two and a half times the world trade volume.

World prices dropped to an all-time low in 1987. There was increasing tension between the producing nations as they competed to sell their products, particularly the European Union, USA, New Zealand, Canada and Australia. Export promotion and export refund schemes, like the one introduced by the US government in 1985, resulted in a 'subsidy war'. The chief victims were the developing countries, whose export prospects were destroyed.

By the mid-1980s the original Common Agricultural policies were proving expensive and surpluses were accumulating. To tackle these problems a number of reforms have been introduced. For example, lower intervention prices, close to the world market price, have been implemented. However, this is a threat to some farms and farmworkers.

This threat arises from the fact that there are massive differences in costs between regions. Farms in regions with good soil and climate, large farms, and those with more technology are able to achieve lower unit costs and remain viable at lower intervention prices. However, farms with poor natural conditions, those that are small, and those that use less technology, cease to be viable. Farms like these are concentrated in Greece, Spain and Portugal. These countries have half of the total number of EU farms and over a third of the EU's agricultural workers. In Greece, about 28 per cent of the working population is employed in farming, and in Portugal 22 per cent. Economic support has been needed to avoid economic desolation in some regions.

When deciding what to produce a farmer evaluates the profitability of alternatives. Converting from one product to another often involves considerable investment – for new machines, livestock housing, different production processes, training, and so on. Consequently the changeover may be postponed.

With productivity growing by 1–2 per cent per year there is sometimes a need for stronger incentives than a gradual cut-back in the intervention price. Schemes to provide pressure for change include: quota systems; maximum guaranteed quantities; set-aside schemes; and extensification. For example:

1 A *quota system* was set up in 1983 to control production of milk and milk products. The EU reached self-sufficiency in milk and milk products in 1974. Production continued to rise by about 2.6 per cent annually while demand went up by only 0.6 per cent. In 1984 a quota system was introduced. The total EU production target is apportioned amongst the member countries and quotas are assigned to individual farms and dairies. There are penalties for exceeding the quota.

2 The *maximum guaranteed quantity* encourages farmers to reduce output of specific products, notably cereals, and some fruit and vegetables. When production exceeds the EU-set maximum guaranteed quantity, the price and other support to producers of the product are automatically reduced.

3 A *set-aside scheme* for arable land was introduced in 1988. It encourages farmers to take at least one-fifth of their arable land out of production for five years. The land must be left fallow, or used for non-agricultural purposes, or planted with trees. The farmer is paid to compensate for loss of income, depending on the soil quality and average crop yield.

4 The EU also offers support for farmers to carry-out *'extensification'*. In areas where there is a surplus of at least 20 per cent, farmers qualify for support by reducing their production capacity through using less intensive practices. This involves the reduced use of fertilisers and pesticides. This scheme offers ecological benefits.

All these systems imitate the market mechanism. Any overproduction results in a drop in average returns for all producers. They have the advantage that, unlike a pure market, they can be controlled so that violent changes are avoided.

Transitional aid is offered for farmers to move into new markets. Diversification into flowers and ornamental plants, medicinal plants, aromatic herbs, various kinds of berries and fruits, and plants helpful to the textile or chemical industry are all encouraged. Alternative use of land for leisure, such as riding, also qualifies.

A number of measures have been adopted to safeguard farmers from hardship. But in order that these measures should not artificially ensure the long-term survival of inefficient farms they are transitional, that is, limited to five years. Small farms are totally or partially exempted from levies and quotas, and there is direct income aid, both of which are decided solely on the basis of the income available to farmers and their families and do not depend on production or market prices. There is also an early-retirement scheme.

An essential part of new policies is careful monitoring of agricultural production and Union expenditure so that the problems of the 1980s are not repeated.

The stocks accumulated in the 1970s and 1980s were a problem. At the end of 1986 there was 1.3 million tonnes of unsaleable butter, 850,000 tonnes of skimmed-milk powder and nearly 15 million tonnes of cereal. The cost of disposing of them was estimated at ECU 7 billion, about one-third of the entire agricultural budget. In 1987 a special disposal programme was started. Money was allocated for the programme. One million tonnes of butter was exported over two years, and some was sold off cheaply to consumers in the EU. By 1989 the butter mountain had disappeared. A similar approach has been adopted with the other mountains.

The CAP in the future

Future policies will target the less favoured regions.

The Commission anticipates that the population of rural areas that are close to large conurbations will increase as industries and services move to the periphery of the cities, and into the surrounding countryside. Residential and leisure developments will compete with modern intensive farming for this space. More remote areas will suffer from depopulation, and ageing of the remaining population.

The EU will therefore encourage the development of medium-sized communities, spread throughout the regions, rather than a few compact large developments. The development of businesses which revitalise rural regions – for example, those involving research and science – will be supported in the rural areas. Alternatives to food crops will also be fostered. The growing of timber, for example, has long-term benefits.

The Commission hopes that strict rules will be introduced to govern the application of manure and mineral fertilisers to prevent the leaching of nitrates and phosphates into the groundwater, and the limitation of pesticides. It also intends to introduce regulations that prevent unnecessary suffering in the production methods associated with animals.

There will be a shift in demand for foodstuffs, from staple foods such as bread and potatoes to fresh fruit, green vegetables, and expensive types of meat, The trend towards 'health consciousness' will also be demonstrated by increased demand for 'natural' foods, even where these are more highly priced. The Commission believes that a legal framework is needed to provide the customer with a guarantee that 'natural' products are authentic. Demand for pre-cooked foods and a greater variety of foodstuffs will grow, especially as people begin to eat more food that has its origins in other EU countries.

ACTIVITY 2.3

1 Carry out a survey of agricultural produce in local shops to determine their country or region of origin. What proportion of the products are affected by the CAP?

2 Use a local Yellow Pages or trade directory to estimate the extent of farming- and farm-related business activity in your area.

Fishing

The part of the CAP that focuses on fishing is concerned chiefly with freedom of access to EU waters for member states, conservation and management of resources, and modernisation of the industry.

EU fishery arrangements, which last until 2002, permit access to all EU waters (which extend 200 miles into the Atlantic) for all member states. Fishing zones for fleets operating from coastal ports, and vessels of other member states who traditionally operate in these zones, have been increased to 12 miles.

The resources of the Atlantic and North Sea are protected and managed through the annual fixing of Total Allowable Catches (TACs). Allocation of fishing areas among the member states takes account of traditional fishing activities, the specific needs of regions dependent on fishing and its related industries, and the loss of fishing grounds in waters of non-EU countries. There is legislation covering, for example, the minimum sizes of fish and standards for fishing gear.

The EU defines common standards for quality packaging, and selling procedures. Member states are encouraged to support organisations that improve fishing procedures and fishermen's working conditions. Guide and intervention prices are determined annually, based on the average price over the last three years. The EU defines a withdrawal price, between 70 per cent and 90 per cent of the guide price, based on the quality, freshness, size and weight of the product.

The EU has formed agreements with a number of non-EU countries with the aim of protecting existing fishing grounds and seeking new resources. It is also active in the international organisations responsible for managing and conserving resources in international waters.

Investment funding is provided by the EU for fishing through the Regional Fund, the European Investment Bank, and the Farm Fund (EAGGF). Transitional support is also provided when a permanent reduction in capacity is needed, and the EU may also help to fund experimental projects involved in exploiting species or new areas.

EU activities cover the whole fisheries sector, including fishing and processing and encompass health and safety of working conditions, and health and hygiene during storage, processing and sale.

ACTIVITY 2.4

1 Use the local library's information retrieval systems to locate press coverage of disputes over fishing in the last two years.

2 To what extent are EU and non-EU countries in conflict with UK fishermen?

Regional policy

Everyday politics is largely about the distribution of gains and losses among the population. The perception that there is a reasonably equitable distribution of gains and losses helps provide stability and support integration.

The geography and history of the EU member states has produced large disparities in prosperity and levels of development. To a large extent these differences can be identified more clearly by region rather than by country. Commonly used economic indicators of prosperity include income and levels of employment. In the EU the disparity between the region with the highest income and the one with the lowest is twice as great as in the USA. The disparity between highest and lowest unemployment figures is three times as great.

Some of the disparities can be overcome by creating free market conditions in

Table 2.3 Divergence of GDP per capita

	1970	1975	1980	1985	1990
Belgium	98.9	103.1	104.1	101.6	102.6
Denmark	115.2	110.5	107.8	115.8	108.2
France	110.4	111.8	111.6	110.6	108.6
Germany	113.2	109.9	113.6	114.2	112.8
Greece	51.6	57.3	58.1	56.7	52.6
Ireland	59.5	62.7	64.0	65.2	69.0
Italy	95.4	94.6	102.5	103.1	103.1
Luxembourg	141.4	126.7	118.5	122.4	125.6
Netherlands	115.8	115.5	110.9	107.0	103.1
Portugal	48.9	52.2	55.0	52.0	55.7
Spain	74.7	81.9	74.2	72.5	77.8
UK	108.5	105.9	101.1	104.2	105.1

Source: European Commission
Note: Individual country figures are expressed as a percentage of the GDP per capita of the whole EC for the same year.

Table 2.4 EU unemployment rates[1]

	1970	1975	1980	1985	1990
Belgium	2.3	4.9	9.1	11	8.2
Denmark	1	4.1	7.5	7.9	8.4
France	2.9	4.1	6.7	9	9
Germany	0.8	2.8	5.1	6.7	5.2
Greece	3.8	2.4	4.3	6.7	11.5
Ireland	5.6	7.1	10.5	14.2	16.7
Italy	5.6	6.4	7.9	10	10.4
Luxembourg	0	0.5	1.9	2.5	1.6
Netherlands	1.4	4.1	7.9	9.6	8.3
Portugal	2.5	5.1	7.1	7.1	5
Spain	2.7	4.7	11.7	17.4	15.5
UK	2.3	3.8	7.4	9.2	6.2

Note: [1] Five-year average as percentage of workforce.
Source: OECD

which trade can take place without hindrance. The Single European Act is chiefly concerned with creating conditions for a free market – unhindered movement of labour to areas with lower unemployment, easier access to markets for producers of goods, and so on. A number of investments can also be made, at national and EU levels, to improve the infrastructure so that the market can operate more freely. A good network of roads and railways, good telecommunications, good utilities (e.g. electricity, gas, water and sewage), are features of the infrastructure that are of great importance to businesses. Employees also look for pleasant living conditions, such as shops and housing;

good, easily accessible education and health provision; and convenient recreational facilities.

As well as these 'enabling' investments, national governments and the EU can provide support for new industry, and tackle the problems of declining industries. Unless grants and funding for these purposes are transitionary they become expensive subsidies supporting uncompetitive business activities. However, there is always the danger that a business will transfer its operations from region to region simply to gain the benefits of development grants, and there is considerable evidence of this happening.

Some regions are naturally less favoured because of their geography: those that are remote from big population centres; those with physical geography that hinders communication; those with few minerals or poor soil; and so on. Fortunately many of these regions have been able to benefit from tourism. For some regions the problems are more intractable.

Even the 'favoured' regions can have difficulties. Often they are victims of their own success, being densely populated and in danger of ecological damage.

ACTIVITY 2.5

1 Identify the most prosperous and the poorest countries in 1990, using per capita GDP given in Table 2.3 as an indicator.

2 Analyse the improvement (or deterioration) of each country between 1970 and 1990, again using the per capita GDP as the indicator.

3 Determine whether unemployment figures (given in Table 2.4) are consistent with the GDP as indicators of improvement or deterioration in wealth.

Three Community funds exist to deal with regional disparities:

1 The European Regional Development Fund set up to reduce regional imbalances.
2 The European Social Fund which supports vocational training, retraining of workers, and recruitment of young people.
3 The Guidance Section of the European Agricultural Guidance and Guarantee Fund (EAGGF) which supports schemes to improve conditions for agricultural production and marketing.

These funds have five objectives or targets:

1 Regions lagging behind in development.
2 Regions in industrial decline.
3 Long-term unemployment and vocational integration of young people.

4 Adaptation of agricultural structures.
5 Development of rural areas.

They specifically target problems such as:

- Inadequate infrastructures such as transport, sewerage, water and power supplies, and telecommunications.
- Weak or outdated production methods; products that do not suit the current market.
- Agriculture with the wrong products or poor technology.
- Urban decay and rural depopulation (which cause social and environmental as well as economic problems).
- Unemployment which causes particular problems for young first-time job seekers and for workers with few or inappropriate qualifications who tend to face longer periods of unemployment.

Schemes supported by EU funds invariably take the form of a partnership between the EU, and national, regional or local organisations. They arise from local initiatives so that there is sufficient motivation and activities are matched to local problems. Decisions on funding are taken at EU level because only there is it possible to gain an overall picture of the pattern of need. If, for example, funding decisions were taken at a national level, then it would not be possible to recognise that a 'deprived' region of a prosperous country was actually better off than a 'favoured' area in a poorer country.

Regions identified for receipt of aid under Objective 1 are chiefly located in Greece, Portugal, Spain, southern Italy, Sicily, Corsica and Sardinia, Ireland, and Northern Ireland. Objective 2 regions are scattered throughout the EU but the biggest concentrations are in the UK (Wales, Midlands, north and southern Scotland) and northern France. Those targeted for help under Objective 5 (b) are mainly in France and northern Spain, together with northern Scotland, Cumbria, Wales and the south-west of England. There is no clear concentration of regions that obtain aid under Objectives 3, 4 and 5(a).

The implications for businesses of EU regional policy are discussed in some detail in Chapter 16.

ACTIVITY 2.6

Determine which EU region you are located in, and its 'objective' status for regional aid.

Social policy

The principles of the EU social policy were set out in the Treaty of Rome. They aim to improve the working and living conditions of citizens of EU countries.

In 1974 a council of ministers adopted a social action programme aimed at achieving full employment, better living and working conditions, and increased participation of employees in company decision-making. The Single European Act (1986), while chiefly concerned with establishing the Single European Market, includes a considerable amount of legislation affecting the relationship between employers and employees.

At the meeting of heads of government in Madrid (June 1989) it was agreed that: 'in the context of the establishment of the Single European Market, the same importance must be attached to the social aspects as to the economic aspects and therefore they must be developed in a balanced manner.'

The Commission drew up a 45-point 'action programme', where legislation was deemed to be essential. This led to a Community Charter of Fundamental Social Rights for Workers (the 'Social Charter'), which was adopted at the Strasbourg heads of government meeting in December 1989 by 11 votes to 1 (the UK). The decision of the UK not to sign the Charter meant that progress towards implementing the legislative programme has been slower than the Commission had hoped.

The Social Charter comprises 12 chapters:

1 *Freedom of movement*   Workers should be able to move freely within the EU with the right to carry out a trade or occupation on the same terms as nationals of the host country.
2 *Employment and remuneration*   Rules are set out for establishing a 'fair' wage.
3 *Improvement of living and working conditions*   Employees must have a rest period weekly, and paid annual holiday. The provisions of the charter cover seasonal, part-time and temporary employees. Procedures are defined covering redundancy and bankruptcy.
4 *Social protection*   Employees must have adequate social benefits and the unemployed must receive adequate financial assistance.
5 *Freedom of association and collective bargaining*   This includes the right to belong to, or not to belong to, a trade union; to conclude collective bargaining agreements; and to strike. Procedures for conciliation, mediation and arbitration are recommended. The employment conditions of the police, armed forces, and other state employees have special status.
6 *Vocational training*   Employees should have vocational training throughout their working lives, and there should be opportunities for vocational retraining.
7 *Equal treatment for men and women*   This must be assured in respect of access to employment, remuneration, social protection, education and vocational training, and career development. There should be facilities to reconcile occupational and family commitments (e.g. crèche facilities).
8 *Information, consultation and participation of workers*   Changes that affect the workforce – especially mergers, restructuring, technology, work practices and collective redundancy – should be decided in consultation with employees.

9 *Health protection and safety at the workplace* This includes the creation of a European Health and Safety agency.

10 *Protection of children and adolescents* Excessive working hours are banned and persons under 18 should not undertake night work. There must be equitable remuneration and appropriate training.

11 *Elderly persons* Resources should be made available at the age of retirement to guarantee a decent standard of living, and adequate medical and social assistance.

12 *Disabled persons* Additional facilities should be provided so that the social and professional integration of disabled people are improved. These include housing, mobility, training, transport, access, and ergonomics at home and at work.

The social aspect of the Treaty on European Union (the Maastricht Treaty) goes further, and, amongst other things, introduces the concept of an 'EU citizen' (as distinct from a citizen of a member state) with rights that cross national borders. At the insistence of the UK the social aspects were removed from the main Treaty and they now form a separate protocol. This is discussed in more detail in Chapter 17.

The Social Fund was established under the Treaty of Rome aimed at improving employment opportunities in the EU and thereby raising the standard of living. As indicated in the section on Regional Policy, it is a structural fund. This means that it is available in regions of the EU that are identified as 'less favoured' and the funding is targeted at specific 'objectives'. Its priority tasks are Objectives 3 and 4, that is, long-term unemployed (aged over 25 and unemployed for more than 12 months) and occupational integration of young people (under 25 who have completed full-time education). The business implications of the Social Fund are discussed more fully in Chapter 16.

ACTIVITY 2.7

Some people argue that introducing the provisions of the Social Charter would increase business costs significantly. Others assert that 'good' businesses are already carrying out its proposals.

1 Consider the features of the 12 chapters briefly set out above.

2 Decide what would be the nature of costs to implement the proposals if they were not already in operation. To what extent do you think implementing them would be a good investment, and to what extent are they 'an expensive luxury'?

3 It might be useful to distinguish between a large business and a small to medium-sized enterprise (an SME).

Research and technology

Research and technology play an increasingly important and central role in modern society. Three million articles are published each year in specialised journals.

To get the best value for money in the development and use of technology, the EU is aiming for technical standardisation and the opening-up of public procurement. Public sector departments account for 10 per cent of EU spending, and a further 10 per cent is spent by public sector industries. Before the introduction of open procurement policies only 2 per cent of public spending took place outside the purchaser's own country, to other member states.

The EU's 'Framework programme' is a policy designed to target research into eight areas: quality of life; information technology and telecommunications; modernisation of industry; biological resources; energy; development aid – agriculture and medicine in the Third World; exploiting the sea bed and marine resources; and improvements in scientific and technological co-operation.

Quality of life

To improve the quality of life, funds have been channelled into medical research (particularly cancer and AIDS), age-related health problems (e.g. senile dementia, cataracts), early detection programmes and medical technology. Because natural radiation accounts for 70 per cent of the radiation to which the population is exposed (half arising from the radioactive gas radon which occurs naturally in rock), radiation protection is also being investigated.

The quality of the environment has a direct effect upon people's lives. Soil protection and pollution pathways are being researched and measures are being developed to improve the quality of surface water (in rivers, lakes and the sea), processing of toxic and dangerous waste, dieback of forests (acid rain is now thought to be less significant in this), and the impact of human activities on climate systems.

Information technology and telecommunications

Esprit was the first EU programme for research and development in information technology (IT), beginning in the early 1980s. It has supported development of office systems, computer-integrated manufacture (e.g. robots, computer-aided design), and advanced information-processing methods (e.g. voice recognition and synthesis).

The *RACE* programme is concerned with ensuring that telecommunication systems and services developed in Europe remain consistent. *DELTA* is a programme concerned with the development of computer-aided education; *AIM* is funding development of biocomputing and medical computing; *DRIVE* is developing aids to road-traffic flow (e.g. route guidance, navigation systems, vehicle-to-vehicle communications) and vehicle safety.

New industrial technology

The *Brite* programme is concerned with new technologies, particularly in the motor industry, chemicals, textiles, aircraft, shipbuilding, machine tools, civil engineering, and so forth. These traditional industries are still of great economic importance. *Euram* helps in the development of sophisticated materials (e.g. metals, ceramics) that currently have to be imported under American or Japanese licence. There are also developments to make measurement and analytical results more uniform throughout the Union.

Biological resources

Biotechnology is not a separate discipline but a group of technologies (e.g. genetics, microbiology, biophysics, bio-informatics) with applications in agriculture, the food industry, pharmaceuticals, medicine and environmental protection. Europe had suffered from fragmented research, with duplication and teams working in isolation.

Energy

The 12 member states, along with Sweden and Switzerland, are carrying out research into nuclear fusion energy. This has the advantage that no radioactive waste is generated. Non-nuclear types of energy are also being investigated, (e.g. solar energy, wind power, geothermal power, energy from biomass), as well as energy conservation and new sources of solid fuels.

ACTIVITY 2.8

Choose a local business and investigate what activities it undertakes that might come within the scope of the EU research and technology policy.

Economic and Monetary Union (EMU)

Economic and Monetary Union (EMU) has come to be seen as the post-1992 stage of economic integration. It has long been one of the goals of European integration, and there has been intense debate over exactly what it should involve and how to achieve it.

In 1969 a package deal agreed at the Hague summit included the first concrete steps towards EMU. The Werner report (1970) suggested that complete EMU could be achieved over ten years, in three stages. The final objective was fixed exchange rates and the free circulation of goods, services, persons and capital. It was suggested that achieving this would require the transfer of a wide range of decision-making powers from national to EU level. All principal decisions on monetary policy, ranging from questions of internal liquidity and interest rates to exchange rates and the management of reserves would have to be centralised. Quantitative medium-term objectives would have to be jointly agreed.

Transfer of decision-making powers has so far proved to be politically unacceptable. In particular, national governments have retained the power to change interest rates as a means of economic control.

However, several attempts have been made to stabilise exchange rates. The first attempt, in 1971–2 has been christened 'the snake'. and was short-lived. The punt, the £ and the krone (temporarily) were withdrawn. By 1974 the scheme had, in effect, become little more than a Deutschmark zone, with only the small and open economies of Belgium, Netherlands and Denmark able to sustain it because of their close links with the German economy. However a number of other non-EU countries participated, namely Austria, Norway and Sweden.

However, the benefits of exchange rate stability were too great to be ignored, and the European Monetary System (EMS), established in 1979, incorporated two features aimed at achieving this, the European Currency Unit (ECU) and the Exchange Rate Mechanism (ERM).

The European Currency Unit (ECU)

The ECU is the sole unit of account in the EU. Its value is revised periodically to reflect the relative economic strength of each member state. For this reason it offers users stability in terms of interest rates and exchange rates. The ECU is used: for fixing the central rates in the Exchange Rate Mechanism; as the basis for the divergence indicator of individual currencies; for measuring the creditor and debtor imbalance of the individual nations; and as a means of settlement between the EMS's central banks.

The commercial banks were the first main users of the ECU outside the EU institutions. It is estimated that about 10 billion ECU is dealt with every day in foreign exchange dealings between banks in member states. ECUs are increasingly being used as the unit for short- and long-term loans.

The ECU is used extensively by EU and many non-EU countries, including most large industrialised countries for business transactions. This means that firms can invoice in ECUs rather than a national currency. Italy, France and Belgium led the way in the range and proportion of transactions in ECUs. Transactions in ECUs offer simplified cash management and lower costs for multinational businesses, and fewer exchange risks (due to the ECU's predictability) in pricing, invoicing, payments and financing.

As yet no ECU notes or coins exist. If they did their use would be of benefit to those who travel frequently and for short periods between EU countries.

Using the ECU would avoid the inconvenience of carrying numerous currencies and would eliminate exchange costs. ECUs are rarely used by individuals, although ECU bank cards and traveller's cheques are accepted by all EU banks and some hotels. In France and Italy there are advantageous ECU life assurance policies.

The Exchange Rate Mechanism (ERM)

The ERM is designed to link EU currencies together. Each currency has a central rate against the others set by the Central Bank, governors and finance ministers. Eight of the currencies fluctuate within a band of 2.25 per cent of their central value and the others, which are more volatile, within a band of 6 per cent. Currencies are kept within their bands by bank intervention. For example, if the franc falls to its lowest permitted value against the Deutschmark, the French and German central banks buy francs and sell Deutschmarks to increase the value of the franc. Other European central banks may be asked to participate in the intervention. Central banks have access to unlimited short-term credit to finance such intervention.

Instead of intervention a country may use domestic monetary policy to keep its currency within the limits. For example, raising interest rates will strengthen the currency.

If intervention and monetary policy fail to keep the currency within its limits the government may agree to a realignment (i.e. revaluation or devaluation). This is a last resort and, until 1992, had been used only 12 times since 1979. Indeed the ERM appeared to be a successful system for 13 years.

The UK joined the ERM in 1990, 11 years after it began operating. It was the tenth nation to join – Portugal (which joined in April 1992) and Greece (which stayed outside the system) being the other two. However, the UK and Italy were forced to withdraw, as a result of fierce currency speculation, in September 1992. The £ and the lira were allowed to 'float', effectively being devalued. The peseta was also floated, although Spain remained in the ERM.

In July 1993 speculation against the franc called into question the future of the ERM. Furthermore the reluctance of Germany to reduce its interest rates to defend the system cast doubt about its commitment to the ERM. A reduction in its key interest rates would weaken the Deutschmark and effectively take the pressure off the other EU currencies. Germany's hesitation may be attributed to the economic difficulties it experienced as a result of reunification. Lower interest rates are likely to cause inflationary pressure in its economy.

Yet, despite all the difficulties, there is a reluctance to abandon the ERM, because exchange rate stability means that businesses can plan and invest with less uncertainty and hence greater confidence. It is also designed to combat inflation. The Deutschmark is renowned as a low inflation currency and the economic discipline of keeping other countries' currency within 6 per cent (or 2.25 per cent) of the Deutschmark is believed to be a help in the control of prices.

How far can economic and monetary union go?

Supporters of a single currency for the whole of the EU look to the USA as their model. The USA is a nation of over 240 million people, divided into 50 states. There are no barriers to trade between the states and they share just one currency. However, individual states have some tax-raising powers and a great deal of political independence.

In Europe, the ERM keeps most EU currencies tied to the other currencies within fixed rates. As part of the Delors plan for European monetary union there would be a single European currency under the control of a European System of Central Banks (ESCB), operating across Europe, rather like the Bank of England operates in the UK. Since the ESCB would determine a single interest rate for the whole of Europe as well as controlling the currency, its structure and accountability are of critical importance and would be the subject of very strong debate.

In 1990 the UK proposed an alternative to a single currency – the 'hard ECU'. Essentially this is a 13th currency for which there would be notes and coins so that it could be used as an alternative to the national currencies, without immediately replacing them.

ACTIVITY 2.9

Use your local library's information systems to investigate how EU exchange rates, particularly those not linked to the ERM, have fluctuated month by month in the last year. Compare the changes with those of the US dollar and Japanese yen.

SUMMARY

1 The EU budget is small by comparison with national budgets.

2 EU funds are obtained primarily from VAT, customs duty, and GNP-related contributions.

3 The CAP continues to be the biggest area of expenditure, but is reducing as a proportion of the total budget. Structural funding – supporting regional and social policy – is being increased significantly.

4 The CAP aims to provide stability of supply, a reasonable income for farmers, and reasonable prices for consumers. These are achieved by intervention and external protection.

5 Regional disparities in income and employment levels threaten the coherence of the EU and progress towards integration. They are addressed by investment in infrastructure and transitional compensation for disadvantaged regions, industries and individuals.

6 Social policy is aimed at improving the living and working conditions of the citizens of EU member states. The UK has reservations about the proposals in the Social Charter and the social aspects of the Treaty on European Union (Maastricht Treaty) and these aspects have been transferred to a separate protocol.

7 Regional disparities and social issues are addressed by the European Regional Development Fund (ERDF), the European Social Fund (ESF) and the European Agricultural Guarantee and Guidance Fund (EAGGF). These are structural funds targeted on specific regions and specific objectives.

8 Research and technology policy is directed towards the quality of life, information technology (IT) and telecommunications, modernising industry, development aid, and improving co-operation in science and technology.

9 There continue to be political difficulties in determining the aims of European monetary union and strategies for implementing it. The most successful attempt to stabilise exchange rates has been the Exchange Rate Mechanism (ERM). The European Currency Unit (ECU) is the common unit of accounting in the EU.

Assignment

BACKGROUND

European Monetary Union (EMU) has been a goal of Europhiles for a long time. Consistency in economic policy across the whole of the EU, a single currency and harmonised interest rates undoubtedly would have benefits for businesses trading across Europe. However, achieving the goal has proved very difficult. Some argue that it will never be achieved.

The Exchange Rate Mechanism (ERM) is an important development in the move towards EMU. It was introduced in 1979 and operated with reasonable success until 1992. At that time currency speculations put it under intense pressure and eventually the UK withdrew. In 1993 further currency speculation resulted in the widening of the 'bands'.

ACTIVITY

1 With the help of the financial pages of newspapers, *The Economist* and other journals, trace the history of the ERM from 1992.

2 Summarise the views of those in favour of EMU and those against it.

3 The Single European Market (SEM)

OBJECTIVES 1 **To understand the benefits to be gained by removing the barriers to trade within the European Union.**

2 **To recognise the barriers that had to be removed to achieve a Single European Market, and the role of the Single European Act.**

3 **To trace progress towards the single market and areas where barriers still exist.**

4 **To analyse current EU policies to determine their contribution towards attaining a single market.**

Why have a single market?

The opening lines of the 1957 Treaty of Rome state that :

> The Community shall, by establishing a common market and progressively approximating the economic policies of Member States, promote throughout the Community a harmonious development of economic activities, a continuous and balanced expansion, an increase in stability, an accelerated raising of the standard of living and closer relations between the States belonging to it.

There were many barriers which made it difficult to achieve these goals, and despite the clear aims of the Treaty many continued to exist. They included barriers to the free movement of people, varying national technical specifications, and differences in health and safety standards, environmental regulations, quality controls, taxation, and so on. Moreover the recession of the 1970s tended to make member states focus on protecting their national markets. Even the German market, the largest in Europe, was less than half the size of Japan's and a quarter the size of the US market. Unless Europe could create a single market by bringing together its separate national markets it would lose ground to both Japan and the USA.

Paolo Cecchini carried out a study of the effects of a single market and concluded that the economic gain to the EU, expressed in 1988 prices, would be about 200 billion ECU, or about 5 per cent of the EU's GDP. It would deflate consumer prices by about 6 per cent and boost output, employment and living standards. The direct cost of frontier formalities, he estimated, was equivalent to adding 1.8 per cent to prices, and making arrangements to accommodate the differing national technical regulations added another 2 per cent. There was considerable potential for economies of scale, offering the possibility to reduce costs by between 1 per cent and 7 per cent.

It was recognised that a single market meant free movement of people, goods, services and capital. But what did this mean in practice?

The Single European Market in practice

The free movement of people

European Union nationals and foreign tourists are not subject to checks at the frontiers between member states. There is good co-operation between the member states to control drug trafficking, terrorism and other crime.

Students are free to choose their university and study in more than one state. Their degrees and diplomas are recognised throughout the EU.

Employees and the self-employed – mechanics and accountants, teachers and office workers, doctors and architects, engineers and farm workers – can reside in any member country of their choice for the purpose of employment, and can remain there after termination of employment. There is no discrimination on the grounds of nationality, so employees can seek work and be employed on the same terms, and with the same career chances, as the nationals of that country.

Free movement of goods

Goods can move freely through the EU without being delayed at the internal frontiers, and producers have genuine access to a market of over 330 million consumers. The harmonisation of technical standards, production methods, and consumer protection prevent there being any barriers to trade.

Economies of scale ensure that research and development is cost-effective, and consumers have a wide range of better and cheaper products, while the health and safety of consumers and the public are safeguarded to an equal high level throughout the EU.

Individuals and businesses can choose where to be based without hindrance.

Free movement of services

Companies are able to offer their services throughout the EU and consumers are free to choose the best service at the best price. For example, airlines have the freedom to operate frequently to whatever destinations they choose, producing competition that keeps fares low and improves service, but must maintain high safety standards. Road transport too makes rational use of the vehicles available, at lowest cost and with minimum paperwork.

Co-operation in research and harmonisation of technical standards ensure that telecommunications are widely available and use the latest technology. European television offers the widest range of channels, programmes and services allowing people to demonstrate their tremendous range of cultures and creativity.

Free movement of capital

People can travel throughout the EU using a currency of their choice without restriction, and ultimately, perhaps, there will be a single currency. Individuals and companies can transfer funds freely between member states. Everyone is free to invest or save wherever he or she likes within the EU. There is freedom of choice, from a wide range of services, in the areas of banking, insurance, savings, mortgages, loans and leasing.

The Single European Act (SEA)

It was realised that removing the barriers needed a strong, coherent plan, supported by legislation. The Single European Act (SEA), which came into force on 1 July 1987, provided that plan, and also provided the enabling legislation within which the necessary provisions to remove specific barriers could be fitted.

It was clear when the Single European Act was being formulated that it would take time for the barriers, first, to be identified and analysed, and then to be dismantled by suitable legislation. A timescale was agreed by which all the barriers would be removed by midnight on 31 December 1992. The plan was, therefore, for a Single European Market (SEM) – a free market throughout the EU member states – to be fully implemented by 1 January 1993.

The establishment of a Single European Market made certain regions more attractive than others. Policies were needed to ensure that the less advantaged areas received help. The Single European Act was, therefore, closely linked to the regional and social policies.

It was also appreciated that it would be necessary to protect the integrity of the Single European Market. EU legislation has been introduced to prevent businesses fixing prices, making agreements on market shares, or setting quotas, all of which would interfere with fair competition. Governments are prevented from favouring particular firms in their own country by special grants or tax advantages.

The Single European Act described the internal market as: 'an area without internal frontiers in which the free movement of goods, persons, services and capital is ensured'. Thus, unlike previous attempts to remove barriers, the SEA aimed to be completely comprehensive. It sought to create, step by step, an integrated and coherent framework. It did not tackle just one economic area nor favour any single European State. It concentrated on proposals that would be easily acceptable to all the States. The consequences, as Jacques Delors (President of the European Commission) declared, were that 'in the first six months of 1988 the Community took more decisions than in the ten years from 1974 to 1984'.

The strategy for implementing the Act was based on analysing why each barrier existed, and the consequences of removing it. If some of the reasons for a barrier were sound then alternative methods were sought so that the same results could be achieved with less disruption to free movement. The collection of VAT is a good example. As long as member states have different VAT coverage and rates there is a need to adjust payments when goods cross frontiers. However, there is no need for the transaction to take place physically at the frontier.

The interests of each member state had to be assessed against the interests of the EU as a whole, and each EU directive had to be painstakingly translated into national laws.

A key feature that helped in implementing the Single European Act was qualified majority voting in the Council of Ministers. Unanimous voting was still retained for delicate issues such as indirect taxation (VAT and excise duties), fiscal provisions, the free movement of people, and the rights and interests of employed people.

ACTIVITY 3.1
Despite the Single European Act, movements of people, goods, services and capital are not as free between EU countries as they are within a country.
Identify some of the existing barriers, establish the reason why they exist, and suggest (if possible) how they could be removed.

Harmonisation

In eliminating many of the barriers to a single market, especially the technical barriers, difficulties arose because of different standards between member states in safety, health, environment and consumer protection. Years were spent on trying to reach agreement on technical minutiae. It was realised that the way of overcoming the problems was 'harmonisation'. This involved adjusting national regulations to an agreed EU standard.

The public often see efforts towards harmonisation as bureaucratic interference from Brussels, and the myth has developed that the Commission is trying to create 'Europroducts'. Nothing could be further from the truth. There is a big difference between 'harmonisation' and 'standardisation'. The aim of harmonisation is to ensure that there is a universally high standard of safety, health and hygiene, and descriptions that are understood by all the EU's peoples. Member states must no longer be allowed to keep out another state's competing products simply because they are slightly different from their own.

The Commission is concerned that consumers have the widest possible choice and that products meet acceptable standards in terms of consumer health and safety. On the other hand, it wants producers to have the opportunity to market their products throughout the large European market, achieving economies of scale and reductions in product development costs, without restrictions on competition. In the area of food and drink, for example, it is now possible for the consumer to choose between yoghurts with or without fruit, pasta made from durum or soft wheat, and beer made entirely from natural ingredients or including artificial additives.

In some areas the Commission does aim for standardisation: for example, in telecommunications and other similar high-technology areas where the equipment needs to interlink.

ACTIVITY 3.2

Explain the advantages and disadvantages of harmonisation as compared with standardisation.

Enforcing EC rules

The European Commission has the responsibility of ensuring that the rules of the Treaties and SEA are applied and that member states implement all the EU legislation. Any breaches of the rules brought to its attention are followed up, if necessary, through the European Court of Justice. Action can be against an individual, an organisation, or a national government .

Once directives have been incorporated into national laws, aggrieved parties can take action through the legislative system of the country. If there appears to be a conflict between national and EU legislation, then EU legislation prevails. The European Court of Justice is the final arbiter.

Member states must not apply restrictions on the products of other member states. In particular there must not be discrimination between home-produced and foreign (EU) goods, unnecessarily onerous technical standards or testing procedures, inequity in taxation, over-rigid pricing or profit margin controls, or imposition of import licences or similar procedures. Similar rules apply to the provision of services, and carrying-out a trade or profession.

There are some limited exceptions. Governments can restrict the flow of goods on grounds of public morality, safety, and protection of health and life of humans, animals or plants. However, the exceptions must not be disguised restrictions on trade and the European Court of Justice has generally ruled in favour of free movement of goods, services and employment.

Avoiding bureaucracy

Creating the SEM involved adopting a very large amount of new legislation. However, Directorate-General XXIII of the Commission, and a special unit of the DTI in the UK, are specifically charged with the task of removing unnecessary burdens and cutting red tape. Moreover a compliance cost assessment is prepared for every new UK and EU proposal.

ACTIVITY 3.3

Identify the likely compliance costs associated with new health and safety regulations. Distinguish between the cost of introducing new regulations and the on-going costs to comply with them.

Completing the SEM

From 1985, when the concept of a Single European Market was first discussed seriously, the EU worked towards removing barriers that could be classified as physical, technical or financial. At the Edinburgh summit in December 1992, the 12 EU heads of state 'recognised that the 1985 programme was complete in all essential respects'. Nevertheless, some barriers do remain and the Commission is continuing its efforts to remove them.

Some fiscal consequences of the SEM – a case study

Craftware Limited makes a variety of carved wooden products that are sold in craft shops. As well as selling in the UK – mainly in the Lake District and north

Wales – the company established, some years ago, markets in Spain, Portugal and Greece.

When they first started exporting, documentation was a headache. There was a mass of documentation dealing with transport, insurance, etc and each country had different forms. When the Single Administrative Document (SAD) was introduced in 1988, as part of progress towards the Single European Market, it made life much simpler. When the Single European Market was fully implemented, at the beginning of 1993, Craftware found that goods were reaching customers in EU countries more quickly. This was because there were no delays at frontiers for customs formalities – previously there had been documentation checks and occasional searches. In fact selling goods to other EU countries wasn't like exporting at all! Quite a contrast to Craftware's newest market – the USA.

Craftware finds there is still one aspect of selling to EU countries that differs from selling within the UK – namely VAT. At present goods sold outside the UK are zero-rated for VAT purposes. Because each EU country currently has its own national regulations about the classification of products and VAT rates, boxes sold by Craftware at the same price to customers in Spain and Portugal are resold at different prices in shops just a few miles apart just because of VAT differences between those countries. Craftware's sales manager has always resented these differences. How can there be fair competition while these differences continue?

Fortunately, by the end of 1996, the differences should have virtually disappeared. At that time a new EU-wide VAT system will be introduced based on the 'origin' principle. It will be very much like the one that operates domestically within the UK at present. Each business charges VAT on what it sells and periodically pays the amount collected in this way, less the amount it has paid out on purchases, to Customs and Excise. Thus each business pays tax according to the 'value added' to the goods by that business. Because there may still be differences in national VAT classifications and rates after 1996, it is essential that transnational transactions are identified so that adjustments can be made to each business's liability for VAT. This will be achieved using the VAT registration number of their customers that businesses now enter on sales invoices. This practice started before 1996 so that EU Customs authorities can maintain statistics on the value of trade between EU countries.

Craftware also has to provide Customs and Excise with a quarterly list of sales to each customer. Fortunately, they are able to provide this as a computer file that is transferred directly into the Customs and Excise computer system. By 1996 each country's Customs authority will be able to transfer data electronically to the others so that each company's liability can be accurately computed.

Other fiscal implications of the SEM

The concept of duty-free goods for individuals travelling between EU countries has disappeared with the implementation of the SEM. VAT and any excise duty must be paid in the country of purchase (at the rates applicable in that country). The goods then travel 'tax paid'.

Because of the effect on 'duty-free' outlets, as a transitional measure (until 30 June 1999), airports and shipping lines, for example, may sell goods without the addition of excise duty provided the goods are for the consumption of individuals. Guidelines on the maximum quantities have been devised above which the individual needs to satisfy the authorities that the goods are not for resale. Travellers between EU and non-EU countries will continue to enjoy the benefit of duty-free purchases, with personal allowances governing the amount that can be taken into their home country. They will continue to pay excise duty on goods in excess of the allowances.

When a business transfers goods that are liable to excise duty between EU countries, the formalities do not now take place at the frontier. Movement takes place between bonded warehouses. Duty is payable on release of goods from the warehouse. A system of 'registered excise dealers and shippers' (REDS) allows registered operators to pay on receipt of goods without them having to be deposited in a bonded warehouse. The effect is to speed up goods transfer.

ACTIVITY 3.4

Find out what goods are liable to excise duty in the UK, and what rates are applied to them. Repeat the exercise for another EU country.

Transport

Transport represents more than 7 per cent of the EU's GDP. Prior to the SEA it was a highly regulated market with restrictions on competition in every sector – road, rail, sea, inland waterways and air. For example, there were quotas restricting the number of cross-frontier journeys that hauliers could make, and safety checks were often made on lorries at the frontiers. The removal of quotas, and the harmonisation of safety standard differences so that frontier checks were no longer needed, helped to achieve a more open transport network.

The EU has progressively introduced regulations concerned with the safety of road transport (the so-called construction and use regulations), covering not only the vehicles themselves, but also the training of drivers, working hours, and so on. Major agreements have in fact been reached on the liberalisation of many aspects of transport operations. These are described in Chapter 14.

Public purchasing

Purchasing by government and public agencies accounts for up to 15 per cent of the EU's GDP. EU directives are aimed at ensuring that all companies in the EU have a fair chance of gaining contracts from central and local government, and other public bodies. The directives have only limited application to nationalised industries.

The original directives had the following aims:

- To establish open tendering procedures (any supplier can bid) or restricted tendering (invited suppliers can bid).
- To require publication of invitations to tender, with adequate time limits for responses.
- To prohibit technical specifications which name proprietary goods, or discrimination in favour of certain suppliers.

However, barriers remained, the most significant being as follows:

- A tendency to buy from a supplier based in the authority's own country.
- A lack of information about contracts.
- Discriminatory procedures.
- Complex tendering procedures.

Further legislation was enacted to tackle these barriers, as follows:

1 The *Supplies Directive* (January 1989), which applies to central government, local government and NHS purchasing contracts.

2 The *Services Directive* (July 1993) relates to the provision of services, and to design competitions.

3 The *Compliance Directive* (December 1991) and *Remedies Directive* (January 1993) are intended to ensure that suppliers and contractors can pursue complaints about discrimination and that action can be taken against offending purchasers.

4 The *Utilities Directive* (January 1993) applies to previously excluded organisations such as water, energy, transport and telecommunications.

EC external trade policy

The EU has a common commercial policy covering all non-EU countries. There is, for example, a common tariff applied in all EU countries for goods imported from non-EU countries. The Commission conducts trade negotiations and makes trade agreements on behalf of the EU as a whole, in consultation with member states with the exception of bilateral agreements with non-EU countries, which are negotiated by individual member states. Export promotion work also remains a matter for individual states.

Most trade in goods is governed by the General Agreement on Tariffs and Trade (GATT). GATT is intended to provide an orderly framework for international trade and a progressive move towards opening of world markets. There is an agreement, for example, not to discriminate against trade with other members of GATT and not to increase trade barriers without giving matching concessions in return. The GATT negotiations, known as 'rounds', tackle an agreed agenda of changes. In the recently concluded the 'Uruguay round', it proved difficult to overcome disputes between the EU and the USA.

EU member states are also bound by the obligations of the Organisation for Economic Co-operation and Development (OECD). These include codes of practice for the liberalisation of capital movements, investment and services, and there are rules against discrimination between OECD members.

As part of the development of the SEM, the EU has tried to develop common practices in a number of business sectors. Progress has been achieved in service sectors such as telecommunications and insurance. The second banking co-ordination directive enables banks incorporated in one member state to operate throughout the EU. A similar approach has been incorporated into a directive on non-life insurance and on investment services.

The EU has played a leading role in responding to events in central and eastern Europe. A number of assistance and co-operation programmes have been developed. The EU has signed association agreements with the Czech Republic, Slovakia, Hungary, Poland, Bulgaria and Romania. Negotiations are taking place with Russia. (See Chapter 17)

Consumer protection

The Commission had already begun to raise standards of consumer protection prior to the SEA. The approach is to establish common standards across the EU. Different national standards and legislation present barriers to trade and discourage consumers from buying freely across frontiers. Lower standards can give operators an unfair price advantage over competitors who have to adhere to higher standards.

Consumer protection directives already implemented include:

1 *Misleading Advertising* (effective from May 1988).
2 *Product Liability* (June 1985) makes manufacturers and importers liable for injuries caused by defective products.
3 *Doorstep Selling* (December 1985) introduced a seven-day cooling-off period for certain contracts concluded in the consumer's home or place of work.
4 *Consumer Credit* (effective from February 1990) protects consumers entering into credit agreements and provides a common method of calculating the annual percentage rate (APR) of charges for credit.
5 *Toy Safety* (effective January 1990).
6 *Price Indication* (effective September 1991) requires that selling prices and unit prices be displayed.
7 *Units of Measure* (November 1989) extends the use of metric units throughout the EU for economic, public health, public safety, and administrative purposes. It requires the authorised use of imperial measures for these purposes to cease by the end of 1994. However, it allows the continued use of

the mile, yard, foot and inch for road traffic signs and related distance and speed measurement; pints for dispensing draught beer and cider and milk in returnable containers; the acre for land registration; and the troy ounce for transactions in precious metals.

8 *Dangerous Imitations* (June 1987) deals with imitation food products that might fool consumers into thinking they were food and which could consequently cause injury.

9 *Low Voltage* (implemented in the UK in 1989) harmonises electrical safety standards for all products in the range 75 to 1500 volts DC and 50 to 1000 volts AC.

10 *Euratom* (1993–4) covers approval schemes for household products containing radioactive substances.

11 *Gas Appliance* (June 1990) sets out minimum safety standards for domestic appliances.

12 *Package Travel* (June 1990, implemented in the UK in 1992) sets minimum standards for package holidays, tours and travel.

13 *Dangerous Preparations* (December 1989) requires child-resistant packaging and tactile danger warnings for hazardous household chemicals.

14 *Commercial Agents* (December 1986) regulates the relationships between commercial agents and their clients.

15 *General Product Safety* (effective from June 1994) introduces general obligations on producers, importers and distributors.

Further directives under consideration at the time of writing include marketing of creosote, carcinogens, chlorinated solvents and nickel; rules on cosmetic safety; the liability of suppliers of services; unfair terms in consumer contracts; new selling techniques such as television selling; time-share contracts; footwear labelling; and comparative advertising.

ACTIVITY 3.6

Choose a business and investigate the impact of EU consumer protection legislation on its operations.

The environment

The EU's environment policy has the following objectives:

1 To preserve, protect and improve the quality of the environment.
2 To contribute to protecting human health.
3 To ensure prudent and rational utilisation of natural resources.

The underlying principles are that preventative action should be taken, environmental damage should be rectified at source, and that the polluter should pay.

Environmental protection has to be a component of every EU policy. In defining action relating to the environment, the EU takes account of:

- available scientific and technical data;
- environmental conditions in the different parts of the EU;
- the potential benefits, and costs, of action or lack of action; and
- the economic and social development of the EU as a whole and the balanced development of its regions.

A series of action programmes are used to plan and carry out environmental policy.

By December 1992, 358 directives, regulations and decisions had come into force. They cover specific topics such as water pollution, air pollution, waste, dangerous chemicals, storage of hazardous substances and nature protection. They also cover general measures such as environmental impact assessments and public access to environmental information.

The fifth environmental programme runs from January 1993 to December 2000. It covers activities to combat pollution and protect the environment, and incorporates eco-labelling and eco-auditing.

Particularly relevant to the SEM are directives that set common emission standards for specific industrial sectors, and controls over-production processes. These include cars and lorries, detergents, paint, petrol, dangerous chemicals, pesticides, genetically modified organisms, chemicals that affect the ozone layer, and products derived from endangered species. There are also standards for noise from aircraft, motorcycles, and so on.

Measures currently being formulated include standards for landfill with waste, further controls on the sale and use of dangerous substances, control over the emission of 'greenhouse' gases, and promotion of energy efficiency.

ACTIVITY 3.7

The reprocessing of radioactive, toxic and dangerous waste is a growth industry. It has an important role to play in protecting the environment. However, the public is suspicious about the safety of companies in this sector and there is a strong NIMBY (not in my back yard) reaction whenever a recycling or processing company applies to build a plant.

Identify a recent case involving such a situation. Look up press reports on the case and establish to what extent EU legislation features in them.

Intellectual property rights

Each member state has its own patent system. Under the European patent convention, an inventor may gain patent protection in some or all of the member states by making a single application. The EU Patents Convention introduces the concept of an EU patent.

There are ten separate systems for protecting trade marks in the EU (Belgium, the Netherlands and Luxembourg have a common system). There are proposals for setting up an EU trade mark registration system. Protection of designs is covered by systems and legislation in much the same way as trade marks.

All member states belong to the Berne Copyright Convention so that there is a basic level of copyright protection in all EU countries. Computer programs are protected under a 1991 directive and rental and lending rights are covered by a 1992 directive. Work is being carried out on the formulation of directives for the legal protection of databases, for satellite broadcasting and cable retransmission, and for home copying.

This topic is discussed further in Chapter 11.

Telecommunications and broadcasting

Telecommunications

In most EU countries telecommunications remain dominated by state-owned monopoly postal and telecommunications authorities (PTTs). In Denmark, Germany, the Netherlands and the UK, competition has been introduced. This is strongest in value-added services.

An EU action programme (June 1988) proposed the following:

1 Full liberalisation of the market for terminal equipment.
2 Accelerated work on common standards, which led to a directive on mutual recognition of terminal equipment in April 1991.
3 Separation of the operations and regulation of PTT functions.
4 Full liberalisation of the telecommunications services market, which led to a directive in July 1990 requiring member states to abolish monopolies.
5 Legislation that prevented PTTs abusing their dominant positions.
6 Greater emphasis on Europe-wide services, such as 'cellular digital mobile communications' (cell phones) and a transnational paging service.
7 A liberalised environment for the reception of satellite signals.
8 'Open network provision' (OPN), giving improved access to the network infrastructure for third parties, which has been implemented in three areas – leased lines, packet-switched data services (PSDS) and integrated services digital networks (ISDN).

Broadcasting

Television broadcasting is an important economic activity. With the development of technologies, especially those involving satellites, it has effectively become an international medium. Consequently the EU has been forced to consider the need for international regulation of services.

Two basic principles underlie the regulations:

1 Individual countries should remove restrictions on the reception of foreign programmes, offering consumers a greater choice.
2 All programmes should meet basic standards on matters such as taste and decency.

Twenty countries have so far signed a convention which should lead to harmonisation of laws on advertising and sponsorship and establish standards on decency, the portrayal of violence and the protection of children as viewers.

In 1989 ministers from 26 European countries agreed to the launch of an audio-visual project concerned with broadcasting technology and programme-making. In May 1992 the EU proposed an action plan that will lead to the adoption of D2-MAC as the standard for wide-screen TV broadcast via satellite.

Data protection

In 1990 the Commission noted that 5 out of the EC countries had not ratified the Convention on Data Processing and that the other 7 had implemented it in different ways.

Six new measures were proposed to ensure common data protection standards. These are based on the concepts of a right to privacy and to information self-determination. They require that the data subject's consent is needed before his or her data is processed or communicated. There should be a supervisory body to oversee communication of data between organisations.

In the UK, the 1984 Data Protection Act covers computerised personal data. The new measures extend to structured collections of manual data, not covered by the UK's Data Protection Act. At the time of writing, the UK Government 'does not consider that the provisions of the directive, which go beyond the Convention, are necessary or justified'.

Information technology (IT)

Although the situation is improving, IT equipment and systems still lack compatibility. Different hardware, protocols, operating systems, and application standards make communication difficult. Open systems, based on open systems interconnection (OSI) standards are intended to overcome these problems. They are based on seven levels at which compatibility should be developed.

In 1986 the Commission launched an initiative to establish harmonised testing and certification procedures. Also, as part of the SEM's health and safety provision, new legislation was introduced in January 1993 covering the design and use of computer visual display units.

Company-wide quality management systems have been established through the EN29000 (BS5750) standard. To provide a sector-specific scheme the TickIT was introduced. The company's IT quality management system is certified after a third-party audit.

New media and systems that interchange business and administrative data are becoming common. EU work in this area includes:

- The Trade Electronic Data Interchange Systems programme (TEDIS) to promote computer-based electronic data interchange, which was started in July 1991.
- The Information Market Policy Actions programme (IMPACT) to promote the market for electronic information services, which commenced in December 1991.

Increased dependence on IT for the storage of data – as well as the proliferation of computer viruses – means that new measures are needed to protect the programs and data. In the UK, the Computer Misuse Act deals with this issue. As yet there is no equivalent EU legislation.

ACTIVITY 3.10

Investigate the extent to which local companies use computers to carry out electronic data interchange (EDI), passing information between branches, to customers, and to suppliers. You are likely to find that large businesses and those in the service sector, such as banks and travel agencies, are the main users.

Food law

The original approach to food law was to ensure that the name of a product fairly reflected its content. However, this led to many disputes. For example, British chocolate couldn't be sold as 'chocolate' in some member states because of differences in definition. German law prohibited the sale on its territory of beers brewed in other member states because additives in them contravened the German national purity laws. In Britain we would insist that a Frankfurter sausage included the word 'Frankfurter' in its name to distinguish it from our familiar 'British sausage'. Other disputes were based on the inclusion of the origin in the product's name. for example, must 'Cheddar' cheese be made only in Cheddar, 'Bakewell' tart only in Bakewell, 'Champagne' only in the Champagne region?

The current approach is that EU food law should not be based on the recipes, which have proved so difficult to agree, but instead should deal with food safety, food hygiene, and consumer information. Special attention has been given to quick-frozen foodstuffs, irradiated foodstuffs, food intended specifically for infants and young children, and food produced by novel processes.

A basic principle is that goods that can be legally sold in one member state should be permitted in the other states. Any new national legislation must take this principle into account.

Directives dealing with food additives, flavourings, food labelling (including statements of ingredients and ingredient quantities), packaging materials, sampling and testing, food for specific nutritional uses, and official control of foodstuffs have been adopted. There are some directives dealing with the composition of products. These include cocoa and chocolate, honey, sugar, fruit juices and similar products, jams and similar products, preserved milk, milk proteins, coffee and chicory extracts, natural mineral waters, bottled drinking water.

Producers may apply for EU registration of products which have specific characteristics that differentiate their products from similar food. This provides for protection of products whose quality and/or characteristics are related to a particular place.

Animal, plant and fish health and meat hygiene

In the SEM the veterinary authorities of a country in which a disease has occurred are primarily responsible for ensuring that disease does not spread to non-affected areas.

Trade in animals and animal products is subject to harmonised EU health rules. In some cases the consignment must be accompanies by health certificates signed by the veterinary authority in the exporting country. The checks are particularly intense where goods are entering the EU from a non-EU country.

All meat and meat products must be produced to common health standards. These include, for example, regulations covering hormone growth promoters, levels of chemical residues and standards for breeding stock. The standards adopted are those which cover organisations involved in trade between member states. A single standard of hygiene and supervision applies to all abattoirs and meat-processing plants, except those that are very small. These provisions apply to red meat, game and rabbit meat, wild game, poultry and processed meat.

Regulations cover the production and marketing of raw milk, heat-treated milk and milk-based products from cows, ewes, goats and even buffaloes!

At the time of writing, movement of some plants across EU internal frontiers requires a certificate to state that they are free of pests and diseases. In future all (except very small) producers will need to register, and member states will be responsible for supervising these producers. Plants and plant products will be issued with a 'plant passport' allowing them to circulate freely within the EU, except where restrictions apply to material entering a protected zone. Random checks will be carried out at every stage of the marketing chain.

Regulations covering fish health and fish hygiene were introduced in January 1993. They apply both to wet fish and shellfish.

ACTIVITY 3.11

Investigate the level of knowledge of health and hygiene legislation at a local food store, and at a food-processing company. Establish the extent to which regulations have changed in the last two years and discover if these changes have arisen from EU legislation.

Pharmaceuticals and medicinal products

The principle of controlling access to the market for medicinal products was introduced in the UK in 1968, after the thalidomide tragedy. Beginning in 1965, the EU began to develop a framework of legislation to control medicines in the EU, a key element of which is a set of criteria by which applications for licences are judged. The criteria cover safety, efficacy and quality. The legislation was extended in 1989 to include immunological medicines, radio-pharmaceuticals, and medicines derived from human blood. Directives on the wholesale distribution, legal status, labelling and advertising of medicines were adopted in May 1992, to be implemented by 1993.

Rapid technological developments, including increasing use for biotechnology, has led the EU to introduce legislation that protects innovative companies against unauthorised use of their research work and associated data.

Harmonisation measures have so far not proved sufficient to achieve a single market in medicinal products. The Commission presented new proposals in November 1990 for so-called 'future systems' for the free movement of these products. These include a central licensing procedure for high-tech products, while for others there will be a decentralised system based on mutual recognition of national licensing.

The Commission's view is that disparities in national systems for medicine pricing and reimbursement are a barrier to the single market. In December 1988 the 'Transparency directive' required national authorities to adopt an acceptable set of criteria for fixing prices. The UK's pharmaceutical price regulation scheme meets the requirements of this directive.

Future harmonisation is likely to focus on product substitution (generic or otherwise), product identification and pack size.

ACTIVITY 3.12

Very many products are sold to alleviate the symptoms of common complaints (e.g. coughs, colds, headaches).

1 Compare the prices, contents, and claims of a range of products for one of these complaints.

2 Ask a pharmacist whether there is a 'generic' product available with similar effect and content. How does its price compare with the proprietary products?

3 Find out, via friends or contacts, or next time you travel abroad, to what extent the same products are available elsewhere in Europe.

Working in the EU

Nationals of member states have the right to go to another member state to look for, and take up, work, provided they comply with that state's laws and regulations on employment, and have a valid passport or identity card. They are entitled to the same treatment as nationals of that country in matters of pay, working conditions, training, income tax, social security, and trade union rights. Their immediate family may join them and enjoy the same rights.

However, there are restrictions on work in public service, and the right to work may be limited on grounds of public security, or public health, and in specific individual cases. Also, there are still barriers to the free movement of people in the areas of vocational qualifications, housing availability and the transfer of pension rights.

Finding work

In the UK, Employment Offices and Job Centres are able to supply information on the method of applying for work in other EU countries, including details of the documents needed, rights to benefits, and hints on questions to ask employers before accepting job offers. They are also able to bring details of UK job seekers to the attention of employers in other member states via the Overseas Placing Unit.

Information is also available on immigration and registration in the destination country, health and social security obligations and benefits, taxation, accommodation, and cultural and legal matters.

Education, training and qualifications

Agreement has been reached for the qualifications of some professions to be recognised throughout the EU. Where the qualification is substantially the same, no further training is necessary. Where the qualification has not covered some of the topics contained within the host country's equivalent qualification, up to three years' of additional training or supervised practice is needed to 'top up'.

Specific directives cover doctors, nurses, dental practitioners, veterinary surgeons, midwifes, architects, and pharmacists.

The First General Directive (effective from January 1991) covers any profession regulated in some way by the state and for which at least three years of full-time education, at university or equivalent, are needed. This directive also covers professions covered by chartered bodies. Included within the provisions of the First Directive are lawyers, accountants, teachers, engineers, physiotherapists, and other professionals.

The Second General Directive (effective from June 1994) extends the principle to some state-regulated occupations that require less full-time education.

The European Centre for the Development of Vocational Training (CEDEFOP) is undertaking work on comparability of qualifications at skilled worker level. Sectors covered so far include the hotel and restaurant trade, car maintenance and repair, the construction industry, electrical and electronics work, agriculture, the chemicals industry, food, tourism, textiles, metal-working, sales, and administrative work.

Language and job-specific skills

Training employees to cope with the new challenges of the SEM could significantly improve competitiveness. There is clear evidence of a direct link between export success and language skills.

Technical changes arising from harmonising of standards may result in the need to retrain designers, marketing and technical managers, and quality management staff. Training and Enterprise Councils (TECs) and universities (via the PICKUP scheme) have programmes to assist local businesses. The Management Charter Initiative (MCI) offers a new type of management qualification, based on practical competence.

These, and other schemes, are described more thoroughly in later chapters.

The social dimension

The Community Charter of Fundamental Social Rights was adopted by 11 member states (not the UK) in December 1989. An action programme, containing about 50 proposals, about half of which will lead to legislation, is proposed to implement the provisions of the Charter (see pp. 35–37).

The UK Government supports a social dimension focused on creating and sustaining employment, but argues that each proposal must be assessed against the following criteria:

1 Will it help or hinder job creation?
2 Is action proposed at the lowest possible level, in accordance with the principle of 'subsidiarity'?
3 Are member states' different traditions being respected?

A protocol of the Treaty on European Union (the Maastricht Treaty) notes that the other 11 member states wish to continue with the action plan arising from the Social Charter. The UK will not take part in discussions on this protocol and any decisions will not be applicable to the UK. The UK did, however, ratify the main Treaty (2 August 1993).

There is further discussion of the social aspects of EU integration in later chapters.

Health and safety

The SEA makes specific mention of health and safety. There are two reasons for its prominence:

1 Progress towards technical harmonisation and standards provides an ideal framework for implementing agreed levels of health and safety.
2 Member states are in agreement that health and safety directives are an acceptable and attainable way of improving working conditions.

In the UK, the Health and Safety Commission gives advice to government on EU proposals. Industry has opportunities to express its views through the CBI representative on the Commission, and directly to the Commission through UNICE.

The EU adopted a directive for health and safety in June 1989 analogous to the UK's Health and Safety at Work Act 1974. It sets out the basic responsibilities of employers and employees and related organisational requirements. It covers:

- assessment of risk;
- introduction of preventative measures;
- use of competent health and safety advice;
- information and training on health and safety matters; and
- consultation with workers' representatives.

Subsequent directives have covered:

1 Workplace requirements (June 1989) including structural safety, electrical installations, fire safety, ventilation, lighting, windows and doors.
2 Work equipment (November 1989) including existing equipment, and the selection of new equipment.
3 Personal protective equipment (November 1989) when risks cannot be avoided by other means.
4 Manual handling of heavy loads (May 1990).
5 Visual display units (May 1990) covering the design, selection and use of workstations, training and eye examinations.
6 Carcinogens (June 1990), biological agents (November 1990) and asbestos (June 1991), including risk assessment, exposure prevention, emergency procedures, health surveillance and record keeping, information and training.
7 Genetically modified organisms (April 1990), including the responsibilities of organisations involved in this activity, and the endorsement by a competent authority for the deliberate release of organisms for research and development.
8 Safety signs (June 1992) should be harmonised.
9 Temporary workers (June 1991), for whom special arrangements are often needed because of possible lower levels of experience and training.
10 Temporary and mobile construction sites (June 1992).
11 Extractive industries (November 1992 and December 1992) aimed at reducing the incidence of accidents and ill health among those who work in the oil and gas extractive industries (onshore and offshore) and underground (for mining and other purposes).
12 Special arrangements for pregnant women, women who have recently given birth, and women who are breast feeding (October 1992).

Legislation implemented after December 1992 includes fishing vessel safety; activities in the transport sector; physical agents; information to workers; and working times.

ACTIVITY 3.13

Choose one workplace (e.g. a building site) and establish what changes in health and safety regulations have been introduced in the last two years. Try to find out whether these are the result of EU legislation.

Capital movements

The UK abolished exchange controls in 1979. Greece was the last to announce the end of controls (scheduled for June 1994).

Member states with balance of payment difficulties have access to loans of up to 16 billion ECU, normally financed by market borrowing.

The European Monetary System (EMS) has two main components:

1 The Exchange Rate Mechanism (ERM), intended to provide exchange rate stability, which it achieved from 1979 to August 1993, when the bands were increased to 15 per cent except for the Deutschmark and guilder (2.25 per cent) after intense currency speculation.
2 The European Currency Unit (ECU), used for administrative and other purposes throughout the EU and made up of a fixed quantity of EU currencies which were last changed in September 1989 to comprise:

Belgian franc	3.301000	Italian lira	151.800000
Danish krone	0.197600	Luxembourg franc	0.130000
French franc	1.332000	Dutch guilder	0.219800
German mark	0.624200	Portuguese escudo	1.393000
Greek drachma	1.440000	Spanish peseta	6.885000
Irish punt	0.008552	UK pound	0.087840

ACTIVITY 3.14

Undertaking a business trip to France, Spain, Portugal, Italy and Greece would require you to have currency for each country, even though the main bills could be paid by credit card.

1 Assuming you decide to obtain £100 worth of each currency, calculate the amount of each currency you would get, taking into account the exchange rate for buying the currencies and commission charges.

2 If you only spent half of each currency and had, therefore, to change the remainder back into £, how much would you finally have, using the exchange rate for buying £ and commission charges?

3 What would be the total exchange cost of the trip?

Financial services and insurance

The first phase in moving towards a single market allowed firms based in one member state to compete on equal terms with domestic firms in other member states, provided they set up local offices and conformed to national rules and regulations. They had to obtain authorisation in each member state where they wished to operate.

The second phase is to allow them to operate on the basis of a single authorisation in their home state. This development is particularly important because of the opportunities arising from the advent of electronic fund transfer.

To ensure stability and integrity a number of directives have been adopted covering solvency ratios, risk exposure, and capital adequacy, to be implemented between 1992 and 1996. Discussions are being held that should lead to a harmonised compensation scheme to protect depositors from losses resulting from the failure of an EU-authorised credit institution.

As well as traditional banking activities, legislation covers investment schemes, unit trusts (and their equivalents in other EU countries), stock exchange listing and prospectuses, insider dealing and pension funds.

Progress has been slow towards a single market in insurance. The Non-life Insurance Services directive (adopted 1988, effective from 1990) introduced the facility for an insurer to cover a policy-holder in any member state. The Motor Services directive (November 1992) and Life Services directive (May 1993) take the process of liberalisation further. The directives provide for:

- Branches and agencies of an EU insurer to be authorised and supervised by the home state rather than the host state.
- Home state supervision of the assets to cover insurer's liabilities in all member states.
- The abolition of prior approval (and generally prior notification) of policy conditions and premium rates.

ACTIVITY 3.15

Contact a local insurance company and ascertain how easy it would be for you to insure with them a holiday home in, for example, France.

Company law and taxation

The EU's policy is to minimise difficulties for businesses operating in more than one member state and to harmonise the standards of investor protection. The priority areas for harmonisation have been company accounts and the qualification of auditors. Special arrangements are made for small companies. All companies now have the option to publish accounts in ECUs as well as the currency in which they were drawn up.

Since July 1989 there has been a new type of business association intended for two or more businesses, located in two or more member states, and who wish to operate across the internal frontiers. Discussion on the legal framework for this, and the level of mandatory worker participation, is continuing. The 'Socieras Europeae' (SE) will be the European equivalent of a plc.

From 1995 a subsidiary is prohibited from acquiring shares in its parent (already prohibited in the UK). Changes in share disclosure laws have required only small amendments to UK law.

Proposals for minimum standards of conduct in takeovers of public-listed companies, similar to the *City Code on Takeovers*, published in the UK by the Takeover Panel, have failed to achieve a 'common position' between member states.

The Ruding Committee published its recommendations on corporate taxation in the EU in March 1992. The emphasis is on subsidiarity.

Three proposals on company taxation were adopted in July 1990:

1 *Merger Directive* allows deferment of tax charges on capital gains arising from cross-border company reorganisations.
2 *Parent/Subsidiary Directive* eliminates double taxation, and has special provisions for Germany, Portugal and Spain.
3 *Arbitration Convention* deals with transfer pricing disputes between the tax authorities of member states.

ACTIVITY 3.16

Obtain, from Companies House, details of how to establish a 'Socieras Europeae' (SE).

Competition policy and state subsidies

The EU is concerned that trade between member states is based on free and fair competition, and that new barriers do not arise as old ones are removed. Powers for the EU to enforce rules on competition were established in 1962, except in the area of transport.

Provisions of the Treaty of Rome

- Article 85(1) of the Treaty of Rome prohibits actions by firms that would restrict or distort competition. Transgressors are subject to substantial fines.

Third parties injured by anti-competitive behaviour may seek redress through national courts. In general it is considered that businesses with a turnover of less than 200 million ECU and less than 5 per cent of the market are not covered by this Article.

- Exemptions may be granted from the prohibition by the Commission under Article 85(3) for agreements that improve production or distribution of goods, or enhance technical or economic progress, provided that consumers attain a fair share of the resulting benefit. Block exemptions under this Article are allowed in the areas of exclusive distribution, exclusive purchasing, franchising, patent licensing, know-how licensing, co-operative research and development, insurance, motor vehicle distribution, cargo-liner conferences, co-operation between small road or inland waterway transport firms, and intra-EU air services.
- Article 86 of the Treaty prohibits the abuse of a dominant position in a market. Establishing or maintaining a dominant position is permitted. Such abuse includes predatory pricing; limiting production, or markets or technical development; refusal to supply; discriminatory trading conditions. There are no exemptions.
- Article 90 extends the disciplines of Articles 85 and 86 to member states.

Merger control was introduced in September 1990. The key features are:

- Coverage of mergers where worldwide turnover exceeds 5 billion ECU or rather less if a major part of the turnover is in one member state.
- Mergers leading to or strengthening a dominant position and inhibiting competition are prohibited.
- Intervention by a member state is limited. Only public security, prudent controls and media diversity are acknowledged as legitimate national interests permitting intervention.
- The EU must be notified and mergers suspended for at least three weeks.
- The Commission will examine the consequences and give a decision within four weeks as to whether proceedings are necessary. If they are, then the final decision on the merger will be made within four months.

Organisations are free to charge different prices in different parts of the EU or to different categories of customer, provided it is not contrary to Article 85 or 86 (see above).

Exclusive distribution and sole agency agreements restrict the territories in which the parties may operate. They are prohibited under Article 85(1) unless covered by the exemption. Even if covered by the exemption there must be no refusal to supply in response to an unsolicited order from a customer, nor must there be any attempt to stop transshipment from one territory to another.

Aid granted by member states is incompatible with the aims of the Treaty if it distorts competition. A state wishing to grant aid to a company or industry sector must notify the Commission, which will consider whether the benefits outweigh the potential cost of distorting competition and issue a decision. The

Commission is highly sensitive to this issue. State aid is generally only acceptable within the EU's framework of regional and social structural policy.

ACTIVITY 3.17

Discuss the case for and against exemptions from monopoly and fair competition legislation.

Collaborative research and development

The development of new technology, particularly in the areas of aerospace, computing and telecommunications, is very expensive. Agreements have in the past been arrived at between companies and between governments. The Commission is concerned to make these more widespread so that technology will advance at a rate that at least equals Japan and the USA. Schemes involving business organisations, universities, and government research laboratories may receive up to 50 per cent of costs of collaborative projects.

The third generation of European Community Research and Development funding, from April 1990, was assigned to 15 research programmes in the following sectors:

	ECU bn.
Information and communication technologies	2,321
Industrial and materials technologies	888
Environment	518
Life sciences and technologies	741
Energy	814
Human capital and mobility	518
Total	5,800

EUREKA is an organisation of 20 members. They comprise the 12 EU countries, Austria, Finland, Hungary, Iceland, Norway, Sweden, Switzerland, and Turkey. The organisation encourages industry-led collaborative projects in a wide range of high-technology areas. It is distinct from, but complementary to, EU Research and Development projects. Between 1985 and 1993 it generated 623 projects (value ECU 12 billion), including 174 projects (value ECU 4.4 billion) that included a UK partner, and 56 that were UK-led. In all, 472 UK organisations have been associated with projects, including over 70 small to medium-sized enterprises (SMEs).

SUMMARY

1 The Single European Act's goal was to create a Single European Market by eliminating barriers to the movement of people, goods, services and finance by 31 December 1992.

2 A key feature of EU policy is 'harmonisation', which allows for the retention of national and regional differences while establishing EU-wide high standards of quality and safety, and promoting fair competition. 'Standardisation' is an approach used only as a last resort to eliminate technical barriers.

3 Progress towards a single European market has resulted in very large amounts of new legislation. Compliance costs are always computed and every effort is made to minimise bureaucracy.

4 Current EU policies are designed to continue progress towards a truly single market. In this chapter we have studied legislation and policies in the following areas: removing physical and fiscal barriers; public procurement; consumer protection; the environment; telecommunications and broadcasting; information technology and data protection; food law and meat hygiene; animal and plant health; pharmaceuticals and medicine; financial services and insurance; company law and taxation; and competition and mergers.

5 This chapter has also introduced topics relating to the single market that are discussed in more detail in later chapters, including transport and distribution; capital movements; external trade; intellectual property rights; health and safety; employment; and the social dimension.

Assignment 3

BACKGROUND

During the period between 1987 and 1992 a massive amount of legislation was introduced with the intention of creating a single European market and removing barriers to trade.

Current EU policies continue to promote the concept of fair competition and a single market. Consequently, almost every business in the UK has been affected.

Unfortunately, in many cases, the legislation has been portrayed as 'bureaucracy imposed by Brussels' despite the fact that decisions on legislation are made by the Council of Ministers at which the UK is always represented by a government minister. Adverse publicity also overlooks the fact that there is a positive effort to minimise bureaucracy and assess the cost of compliance when proposals are formulated.

ACTIVITY

Choose a business sector (e.g. retail, wholesale, manufacture, finance, insurance) and investigate the changes that have resulted from progress towards a single market. To keep the investigation to manageable proportions, deal with three of the areas given below:

- removing physical and fiscal barriers;
- public procurement;
- consumer protection;
- the environment;
- telecommunications and broadcasting;
- information technology and data protection;
- food law and meat hygiene;
- animal and plant health;
- pharmaceuticals and medicine;
- financial services and insurance;
- company law and taxation;
- competition and mergers.

Part Two
THE EUROPEAN BUSINESS ENVIRONMENT

4 Geography and communications

1 **To describe the geography and natural resources of the EU countries.**

2 **To identify the various methods of transport available to European businesses. Explain the strengths and weaknesses of each, and recognise the problems of congestion.**

3 **To recognise the fast-improving opportunities to communicate without the need to travel that arise from EU-supported telecommunications.**

EU geography

Over a period of nearly 30 years the European Union grew to include 12 countries. These countries decided to build their futures together. However, they have a tremendous range of economic and social differences. Some of these differences arise from the geography and history of the countries, others from the ease (or difficulty) of communications. Although technology is now available to overcome many of the natural barriers that separate regions and countries, the availability of natural resources, and the histories of the peoples will continue to influence their approach to life and work, and their attitudes towards the EU.

Examine the map of France in Figure 4.1. It shows the major physical geographic features of France. Note how the Pyrenees form a natural barrier that coincides with the frontier with Spain. Communication between France and Spain is difficult except at the seaward ends. By contrast the frontiers with Belgium and Germany have no similar natural barriers. People and goods flow freely between the countries.

The Massif Central and the Alps leave a corridor which funnels transport and communication along the Saône–Rhône valley. This is the main north-to-south route for roads, rail and inland waterways. The development of population centres and industry reflects this structure.

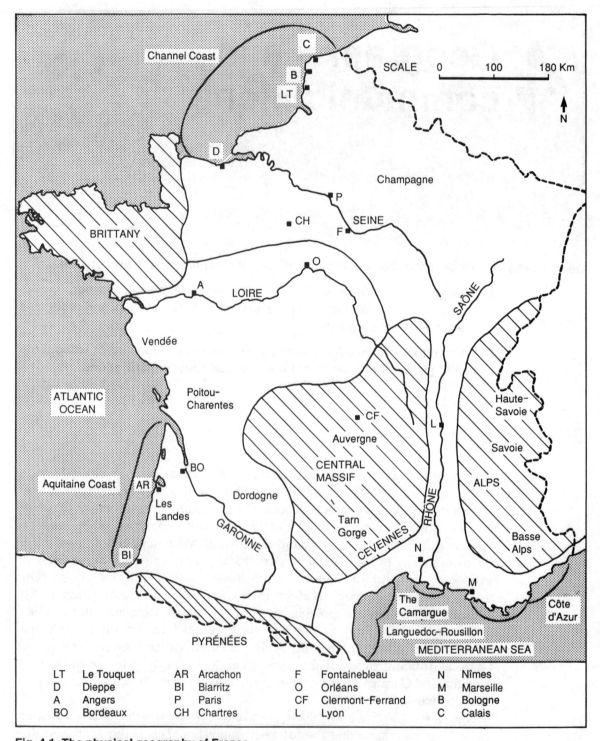

Fig. 4.1 The physical geography of France

LT	Le Touquet	AR	Arcachon	F	Fontainebleau	N	Nîmes
D	Dieppe	BI	Biarritz	O	Orléans	M	Marseille
A	Angers	P	Paris	CF	Clermont-Ferrand	B	Bologne
BO	Bordeaux	CH	Chartres	L	Lyon	C	Calais

ACTIVITY 4.1

As you read through the following sections on other EU countries carry out similar analyses so that you become familiar with the natural features that characterise the countries.

Table 4.1 EC population, 1991

Country	Population (m.)
Belgium	9.9
Denmark	5.2
France	55.9
Germany	78.5
Greece	10.0
Ireland	3.5
Italy	57.5
Luxembourg	0.4
Netherlands	14.8
Portugal	10.4
Spain	39.1
UK	57.1

Source: Eurostat

A study of the population figures (*see* Table 4.1) shows that there are great variations in the populations of the EU countries. There are also significant differences in population density, but it must be remembered that national average figures can be misleading if there are large conurbations (in which population density often exceeds 360 per square kilometre). The main area of population is in the north-west of mainland Europe (southern Netherlands, northern Belgium, the Rhine–Ruhr area of Germany) and the south-east of England. There are also dense areas of population in northern Italy, and around Paris, Naples, Madrid and Barcelona.

ACTIVITY 4.2

While reading through the following sections on individual countries plot the large population centres on a map of Europe.

Geography – country by country

Belgium

Belgium extends 230 km from north to south, and 290 km from east to west and has a 66 km North Sea coastline. Inland from the coast are lowlands – fertile polders (reclaimed land), the sandy Flanders plain, the heaths and woodlands of the Kempen. In the south are the wooded Ardennes and Belgian Lorraine, an area that extends into France and Germany. Between the coast and southern areas lie an alluvial, fertile plateau. The country's highest point is the Signal de Botrange (694 m) in the Haute Fagnes.

The river Scheldt originates in northern France and flows through Ghent and Antwerp into the Netherlands. The Meuse also flows into the Netherlands, rising in the French Vosges mountains and passing through Namur and Liege in eastern Belgium. Some coal is mined in the Meuse–Sambre and Campine fields.

Belgium's capital Brussels is also a key city in the EU, and is the main conurbation in the country, with a population of almost 1.3 million. Over 9 per cent of the people living in Belgium are foreigners. Of these nearly 35 per cent are from Italy and another 30 per cent from other EU countries. It is predominantly a Roman Catholic country.

Belgium is a nation of two languages. About 5.5 million of the population live in the northern part of the country, Flanders, and speak Flemish, which is similar to Dutch. In the southern, Walloon, area, the language is French. Most Walloons cannot speak Flemish and most Flemings will not speak French. Nowhere else in the EU are there such distinct ethnic and linguistic communities. However, the different Belgian groups do not see themselves as separate like the Welsh and Scots in Britain or the Basques in Spain.

Denmark

Denmark consists of the Jutland peninsula, 100 inhabited islands, and 383 islands which are not inhabited. At the southern end of the peninsula is a 67 km border with Germany. Its coast is 7300 km long, bordering the North Sea, Skagerrak, Kattegat and Baltic Sea. It is a flat country, its highest point is only 173 m above sea level. The longest river is the Gudena, which flows from central Jutland to the Randers Fjord.

The country has extensive natural resources in the form of oil, fish and agricultural land, and it is a fertile country, famous for its dairy products and bacon.

Copenhagen, the capital, is the largest city in Scandinavia, with a population of just under 1.4 million. It lies on the islands of Sjaelland and Amager.

Danish is the principal language. There is a German-speaking minority in South Jutland. Almost all Danes (98 per cent) belong to the Evangelical-Lutheran church.

France

France has a 3120 km coastline bordering the Channel, the Atlantic, and the Mediterranean, while its 2170 km land frontiers are almost all mountainous barriers – the Pyrenees in the south-west, the western Alps in the south-east, the Jura and the Vosges in the east. A wide variety of landscapes range from flat farmland north of Paris to the volcanic remains in the Massif Central. There are four principal rivers, the Seine, which flows through Paris into the Channel, the Loire (famous for its châteaux) and Garonne, both of which flow into the Atlantic, and the Rhône which flows into the Mediterranean.

Wheat, maize and oats are grown extensively, but the traveller through the farming areas is more likely to notice the sunflowers. Fruit and vegetables are grown, particularly in the south, but France is best known for its vines, especially in Languedoc and Burgundy, and around Bordeaux. There are iron ore deposits in Lorraine, coal in the north-east, natural gas in the south-west, potash in Alsace, and bauxite, which derives its name from Les Baux, a town in Provence. Industry is concentrated in the north around the coal and iron deposits close to the river Rhine.

Paris is not only the capital, it is the focal point of France, with roads and railway lines converging on it from all directions. The French have a strong attachment to their own region, but Paris has a special status not shared by any other city. Paris has a population of around 8.7 million. The other great conurbations are Lyon (1.2 million), Marseille (1.1 million) and Lille (0.9 million).

There is a distinct difference between the north of France, where the Germanic influence is strong, and the Mediterranean south. There are also significant differences between the west, on which the Atlantic has a strong influence, and the east, which is continental. The official language is French, but other languages are spoken in some of the provinces, including Breton, Alsatian, Basque, Corsican and Catalan.

Traditionally the French are very nationalistic, and over 90 per cent of French people are Roman Catholics. About 8 per cent of the population comes from other countries, with some 3 per cent from other EU countries, half from Portugal.

Germany

To the north, Germany is bounded by the North Sea and the Baltic, to the south by the Alps, Lake Constance and the Rhine. It is made up of mountain areas, uplands (1500 m) and plains. The highest mountain is the Zugspitze (2963 m) in the Alps. The main rivers are the Rhine, which forms the country's south-west boundary, the Danube, the Elbe, the Weser and the Moselle.

Mineral resources include lignite, coal, iron and copper ores, and potash.

The capital is currently Bonn, a relatively small city. However, a decision has been taken to move the capital back to Berlin, now that the German Democratic

Republic (East Germany) and the Federal Republic (West Germany) have been reunited. There are 16 states (or *Länder*) in the reunited Germany, each of which have their own administration, policing, culture, education and judiciary – all the functions that are not specifically allocated to central government. The largest conurbation is the Rhine/Ruhr area, famous for its heavy industry, with a population the order of 9 million. Berlin has a population of about 2.5 million. Other large cities are Munich (1.9 million) and Hamburg (1.6 million).

Although they speak the same language (German), the peoples from what used to be the Federal Republic and those from the Democratic Republic are still two different communities. West Germany (FDR) was one of the richest countries in the EU while East Germany (GDR) was a centrally controlled communist country with all that implied in scarce, poor-quality, consumer products, low prices and low wages. It will be years before the two 'cultures' are reconciled. Of the total population, 43 per cent are Protestants and 43.3 per cent are Roman Catholics.

Over 7 per cent (4.4 million) of the population of the FDR were foreign residents. Of this number, almost 1.4 million were from other EU countries, including 565,000 from Italy and 292,000 from Greece.

Greece

Greece's 2000 islands stretch from Kastellorizo in the east, as far south as Crete, and as far west as Corfu, and account for about 20 per cent of the total land area. Only 134 of them are inhabited. Greece has a coastline of 15,021 km. Agion Oros on the Athos peninsular is a self-governing part of the Greek state. The northern frontier which separates the country from Bulgaria, Turkey, Yugoslavia and Albania is 1212 km long. The country is mainly mountainous, its tallest peak being Mount Olympus (2917 m). There are no major rivers.

Greece is very much a farming country, producing fruit and vegetables, raisins, tobacco and olive oil for export. It has deposits of lignite, bauxite and iron ore. Oil has been discovered in the northern Aegean.

The capital is Athens (population 3 million), famous for its links with ancient civilisation, symbolised by the Acropolis. The Greek Orthodox church is the official state religion, and 96 per cent of Greeks belong to it.

Ireland

The Republic of Ireland is 486 km from its northernmost to its southernmost tip, and is 275 km from east to west at its widest point. The country is divided into four provinces, Connacht, Leinster, Munster and Ulster. There are central lowlands with a fringe of hills and mountains, the highest of which is Carrauntuohill (1040 m). The Shannon (370 m) is the longest river and there are many lakes.

Ireland manufactures many base metals. It uses its plentiful supply of water, peat and natural gas to produce energy.

The capital, Dublin (population 920,000), is located on the east coast at the mouth of the river Liffey. Over three-quarters of the 90,000 foreign residents in Ireland come from other EU countries. The official languages are Gaelic and English, and 95 per cent of the population is Roman Catholic.

Italy

Two independent states, the Republic of San Marino and the Vatican City State are surrounded by Italian territory. The familiar "boot" shape extends from the fringe of the Alps in the north, which rapidly gives way to the plain of the river Po, to the southern 'toe', off which lies Sicily, containing Europe's biggest volcano Mount Etna (3326 m). To the west lies Sardinia and the west coast is dotted with smaller islands like Elba, Ponza, Capri and Ischia, mostly mountainous. To the east is the Adriatic Sea. Down the 1000 km peninsula runs the 130 to 250 km-wide Apennine range of mountains. The highest peak is Gran Sasso (2914 m). Italy has other volcanoes, Vesuvius near Naples and Stromboli on the Lipari islands. The longest river is the Po (652 m) running from the Cottian Alps through a delta to the Adriatic. The Arno, which passes through Florence, and the Tiber, on whose banks Rome is built, both rise in the Apennines.

Italy has few minerals; the only significant ones are sulphur, bauxite, lead ore and marble.

Rome, the capital, has a population of 2.8 million. The other large cities are Milan (2.8 million), Naples (2.5 million), Turin (1.5 million) and Genoa (800,000). The national language is Italian. Other languages are spoken in some of the regions: French in the Aosta Valley, German and Ladin in areas of the Alto Adige, and Slovene in Trieste and Gorizia. Almost all Italians are Roman Catholic.

Luxembourg

Luxembourg is a tiny, inland country, bounded by France, Germany and Belgium. It is hilly and rich in woodland. The Oesling, a 450 m-high plateau is part of the Ardennes. The main rivers are the Our, the Sure and the Moselle. The Moselle valley is famous for its wines – Rieslings, Auxerrois and Sylvaners.

There are deposits of haematite in the south which have resulted in a large-scale iron and steel industry.

Over 25 per cent of residents in Luxembourg are foreigners. Although Letzeburgesch is the national language, French and German are the administrative languages. About 95 per cent of Luxembourgers are Roman Catholic.

Historically Luxembourg had closer ties with Germany than its other neighbours, but today it is more and more associated with France. Its location in the heart of Europe makes it ideal as an administrative centre despite its tiny size. It has an excellent network of motorways linking it with France, Germany and Belgium and has always been the 'crossroads of Europe'.

Netherlands

The Netherlands extend roughly 300 km from north to south and 200 km from east to west. Behind the North Sea coast are polders, as in Belgium. The islands of Zeeland and South Holland are linked by dikes to prevent the recurrence of flooding caused by storms. Over half the country is below sea level and the land is criss-crossed by lakes, rivers and canals. Only in the south-east is there higher land.

Minerals such as coal, oil and natural gas are found in Netherlands.

The capital is Amsterdam (population 940,000) although the centre of government is the Hague. Rotterdam (population 1.03 million) is the world's largest port. Canals, windmills and the typical Dutch gabled houses make Netherlands visually distinctive.

Dutch is the official language. There is a small Frisian community in the north-east of the country, speaking its own language. However, nearly 32 per cent of Dutch people speak two languages, and over 10 per cent speak three. Of the total Dutch population, 36 per cent are Roman Catholic and 32 per cent are Protestant (mainly Dutch Reformed Church).

Portugal

Portugal is longer north to south (560 km) than east to west (220 km). Its only land frontier is with Spain (1215 km); its Atlantic coastline is 837 km. The nine islands that make up the Azores are in mid-Atlantic, 1500 km from the coast of Portugal. The two islands of the Madeira group are off the African coast, 1000 km south of Lisbon. The river Tagus separates the mountainous north from the plains and plateaux of the south. The coast has alternate sandy beaches and rocky headlands. The country has three important trading ports, Lisbon, Oporto and Setubal, which stand at the mouth of the rivers Tagus, Douro and Sado respectively.

As well as being rich in woodland oak, eucalyptus and pine, Portugal has several minerals – tungsten, iron pyrites, tin and uranium.

Lisbon, the capital, has a population of 1.3 million. It is located on the banks of the Tagus, and has been a trading city for centuries. Over the last 20 years over 2 million Portuguese have emigrated, about half a million of them to other EU countries. The official language is Portuguese, and most of the population are Roman Catholic.

Spain

Spain has a total of 3904 km of coastline, with the Atlantic and Mediterranean, and a land frontier of 5849 km with France and Portugal. It is the second most mountainous country in Europe (after Switzerland). Mountain ranges alternate with river valleys. The centre of Spain is a plateau, the Meseta, which is arid but pierced by the Douro and Tagus rivers which flow east to west into Portugal. The Guadiana and Guadalquivir cross Andalusia, where sub-tropical areas alternate with permanently snow-capped peaks. It is here that Mulhacen, the highest mountain on the Spanish mainland (3481 m) is located. However the Peak of Tenerife in the Canaries (3718 m) is the highest point in Spanish territory.

The rivers Ebro, Turia, Jucar and Sequa flow east into the Mediterranean, where there are many fine beaches. The Navia, Nalon, Nervion and Bidassoa are short rivers rising in the Cantabrian mountains; they irrigate the green coastal strip which extends west from the Pyrenees and forms one part of the north of the Iberian peninsula. The other part, Galicia, north of Portugal, has humid weather and green countryside, through which the Mino flows. Its climate is more typical of countries further north.

Madrid, the capital has a population of 4.2 million. It is a city of museums and art galleries, notably the Prado. The other large cities are Barcelona (population 2.7 million) and Valencia (population 850,000). In 1984 there were 227,000 foreign residents, more than half (134,000) from EU countries – mostly from the UK (28,537), Portugal (23,000) and Germany (23,609).

The official language is Spanish (Castilian), although Catalan, Basque and Galician are officially recognised in their respective autonomous communities. Many cultures, including those of the Romans, Visigoths and Muslims, have influenced Spain. The predominant religion is Roman Catholic.

Spain has the most pronounced regional dissimilarities of any of the EU countries.

United Kingdom

The Channel, which separates Great Britain from mainland Europe, has great significance and contributes a great deal to its feeling of independence from the rest of Europe. The United Kingdom consists of Great Britain – comprising the ancient kingdoms of England to the south and Scotland to the north, and the principality of Wales in the west – and Northern Ireland, which opted to remain within the UK when the Republic of Ireland gained independence in 1922.

The Pennine Range running from the Cheviot Hills on the Scottish border to the Midlands has been a significant boundary between west and east. Scafell Pike (977 m), in the Lake District in north-western England, is the highest mountain in England. In north Wales, Snowdon is higher (1085 m), but the highest peak in the UK is Ben Nevis in the Grampians (1342 m). There is now little dense woodland in Britain but there are large areas of heaths and moorland. The most significant river is the Thames, on the banks of which lies London. However, large ports are situated at the mouths of other important rivers, such as Bristol on the Avon, Liverpool on the Mersey, and Glasgow on the Clyde.

The UK has four capitals: London is the capital of England and the seat of UK government, Cardiff the capital of Wales, Edinburgh the capital of Scotland and Belfast the capital of Northern Ireland. London, as well as being the largest city in the UK, is situated in the area of highest population density. Other main population centres are around Birmingham (West Midlands), Manchester, Liverpool (Merseyside), Leeds (West Yorkshire), Newcastle (Tyneside) and Glasgow (Clydeside). Of the UK population 80 per cent are English, 9 per cent Scottish, 5 per cent Welsh, and 3 per cent Northern Irish. There are approximately 2.3 immigrants from the Commonwealth, of whom almost a third live in the London area. There are almost 400,000 migrant workers from the EU, over 66 per cent from Ireland.

The official language is English but there are sizeable communities in Wales who speak Welsh, and in western Scotland and the Hebrides Gaelic is still spoken. There are large ethnic communities in many of the larger cities, notably from the Indian and Asian continents.

The Protestant (Anglican) church is the official religion in the UK with the Queen as its head. In Scotland the Presbyterian Church of Scotland is the established church, governed by the Moderator of the General Assembly. There are strong Roman Catholic and Nonconformist traditions in Great Britain. In Northern Ireland there is a sharp division between the Protestant majority and Roman Catholic minority.

Table 4.2 Knowledge of foreign languages[1]

	English	French	German	Italian	Spanish
Belgium	26	71	22	4	3
Denmark	51	5	48	1	1
France	26	–	11	8	13
Germany	43	18	–	3	1
Ireland	99	12	2	1	1
Italy	13	27	6	–	5
Netherlands	68	31	67	2	4
Spain	13	15	3	4	–
UK	–	15	6	1	2

[1] Percentage of population speaking the language.

Source: Gallup 1989

ACTIVITY 4.3

1 Identify the nine official EU languages and calculate the number of people who speak each as their 'first' language.
2 Use Table 4.2 to calculate the total number of EU citizens who speak each official language.

ACTIVITY 4.4

The EC gives a high priority to preserving regional culture, a part of which is the language. Languages spoken in specific regions are designated 'minority languages'. Identify five or more minority languages.

Communications

Road

The northern countries of western Europe all have excellent motorway systems and there are good routes in some other areas too. It is possible to drive from Dover to the south of Italy by motorway, except for about 20 miles, the only blackspots being the Alpine tunnels. The Mont Blanc Tunnel, for example, has an excellent approach from the French side but only a two-lane road on the Italian side, which can easily be blocked by traffic.

Many large cities have orbital motorways but some, such as Zurich, Lyon and Munich have yet to be by-passed by motorways. However, you are not guaranteed a fast journey even when there is a by-pass. The M25 round London is notorious, and the Périphérique around Paris is just as bad on Friday afternoons. Organisations such as Germany's ADAC and the UK's AA and RAC issue regular bulletins on European road conditions.

Computer packages are available to assist in the selection of a route. It is possible to choose a route that uses motorways or ordinary roads, include or avoid intermediate towns, and take account of the average speed that you normally achieve on various types of road. Lap-top computers that will operate in a vehicle, together with mobile phones, allow the driver to obtain up-to-date information and communicate with the office.

Route planning should consider the time of day the journey will take place. Commuter areas should be avoided in 'rush hours' if possible. Germany has long periods of heavy traffic – from 6 am to 10 am and from 4 pm to 8 pm. Greece has four periods to be avoided: morning, evening and either side of

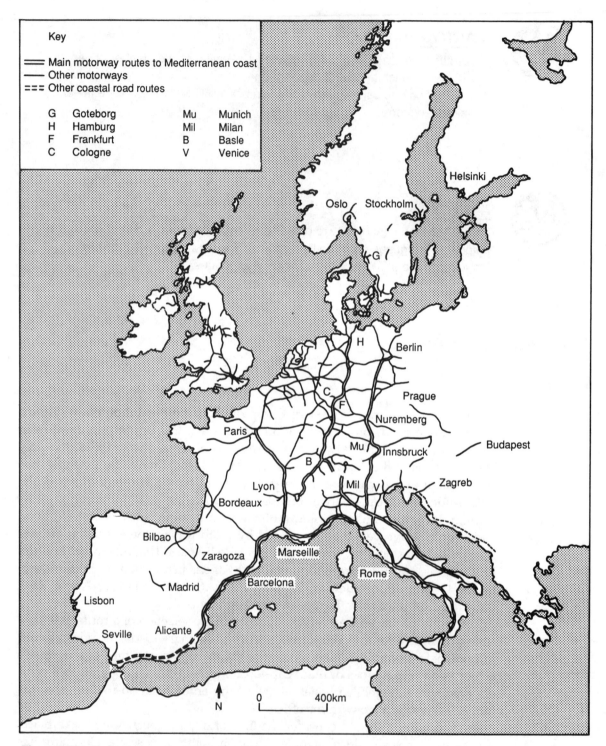

Key

═══ Main motorway routes to Mediterranean coast
─── Other motorways
=== Other coastal road routes

G	Goteborg	Mu	Munich
H	Hamburg	Mil	Milan
F	Frankfurt	B	Basle
C	Cologne	V	Venice

Helsinki

Oslo   Stockholm

G

H   Berlin

C   Prague

F   Nuremberg

Paris   Mu   Innsbruck   Budapest

B

Lyon   Mil   V   Zagreb

Bordeaux

Bilbao

Zaragoza   Marseille

Madrid   Barcelona   Rome

Lisbon

Seville   Alicante

0   400km

N

Fig. 4.2 The European motorway network

lunch time. However, French, Spanish and Italian roads are quiet from 12 noon to 2 pm. During public holidays roads are busier than usual. In almost all of Europe there is a national holiday on 15 August (Assumption Day). In the UK our late summer bank holiday is later than this.

Traffic varies with the season, too. In France, cities empty during August for *les grandes vacances*. The Autoroute du Soleil from Paris to the Mediterranean is packed with traffic on the day of *le grand départ* and it is common for traffic to come to a standstill for up to 10 hours on this motorway. In most countries the peak holiday time coincides with the school summer holidays. In Italy this is from mid-June until late-September. Spanish school holidays begin early in June, and in Portugal they begin in early July.

Improvements to the road systems are often made in advance of special events. In Italy, for example, major road building took place for the World Cup, and similar development took place in Spain for the 1992 Olympics and Expo '92.

In France, Italy and Spain over 90 per cent of motorways are toll roads involving pay-as-you-drive. There are also stretches of road in Austria, Greece and Portugal which are toll roads. In 1991 the UK gave consideration to introducing its first private toll road, on a 30-mile stretch north of Birmingham. Environmentalists have, for a long time, called for road-pricing as a means of 'traffic calming' on congested roads. Motorists do not automatically shun roads that have tolls. In France, for example, the ordinary roads in the north are relatively traffic free, despite being straight and in good condition, and the *péage* (toll) is extensively used.

Accident records vary. Particular roads, like the N620, the main route across Spain between the Portuguese and French frontiers has a bad reputation and the N340 into Madrid is nicknamed the 'highway of death'. Greek drivers have the worst driving record. In 1990 road deaths in Greece averaged six per day; caused by flouting of speed limits, ignoring stop signs, illegally not wearing seat belts, and so on. The wearing of seat belts is compulsory in all European countries except Gibraltar, and the majority of EU countries, including the UK, now insist on the wearing of rear seat belts.

Rail

It is amazing that trains, a technology developed in the nineteenth century, and developed separately in the various countries of Europe, should be sufficiently standardised to be able to cross Europe without hindrance. However, the UK traveller will notice some differences. For example, platforms in Europe are usually lower, so that there are several steps up to carriages.

The conditions under which the trains operate varies around Europe. The services in southern Europe, for example, have to cope with much higher temperatures, and air conditioning is a must on long-distance journeys and highly desirable on shorter routes. In the Alpine areas, tunnels and bridges have taxed

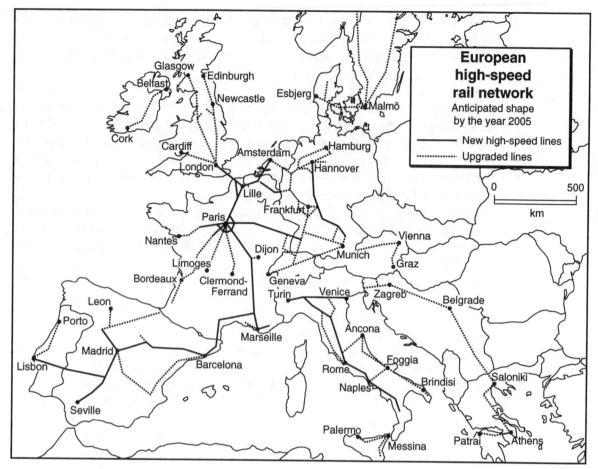

Fig. 4.3 The European high-speed rail network

the engineers' skill to the utmost, and it is still the case that gradients in these areas are more severe than anywhere in the UK.

In general, except for commuter services, trains in continental Europe travel further between stops than in the UK. There has been a greater incentive, therefore, for the development of high-speed trains.

When goods have to be transported over long distances the railway has a distinct advantage over road transport, and is environmentally preferable. On shorter journeys, such as those found in the UK, the cost and problems of assembling wagons to go to the same destination, and of distribution from the railhead, means that road transport is more convenient.

France's railway network is one of the most comprehensive in Europe and the TGV (*train à grande vitesse*), capable of speeds of up to 380 kmph, provides high-speed links from Paris to other big cities – Paris–Lyon (2 hours), Paris–Strasbourg (4 hours), Paris–Brussels (2.5 hours), Paris–Geneva (3.5 hours).

Fig. 4.4 The route of the Rhine–Danube canal

Sea and inland waterway

In the ten years from 1980 to 1990 the EU countries' share of world shipping tonnage dropped from 30 per cent to 14 per cent. Leading companies like Royal Dutch Shell and British Petroleum had already changed to 'flags of convenience' when P & O considered making the same move with its 200-strong fleet in 1991. In 1980 there were 1500 ships flying the flags of EU countries – by 1990 there were just 300. Ships which are registered in countries like Liberia and Panama – the main 'flag of convenience' countries – are able to undercut the competition because they are subject to fewer restrictions and are able to employ cheap Third-World crews. For example, the crew costs for a 30,000-tonne bulk carrier can be cut by almost 60 per cent. Norway and Denmark have protected their national fleets by offering incentives to shipping operators.

Canals and inland waterways were once important transportation routes for goods within the UK. The development of railways and roads has meant that these waterways now carry only a tiny proportion of total goods. However, the situation is quite different in continental Europe. A number of major navigable rivers and canals, together with the long distances, make this method of transport viable for bulk cargoes.

EU proposals for liberalisation of shipping are discussed in Chapter 12.

Bus, Tram and Underground

The different types of bus transport are clearly differentiated in the UK. On the one hand there are the long-distance coaches, the equivalent of the inter-city trains. Although they cannot compete with rail in speed they are very competitive on price, and offer comforts like television. Some people argue that they are safer for an unaccompanied traveller. Other bus services cater for commuters in both rural and urban areas.

The pattern is similar elsewhere in Europe. However, differences arise as to whether governments choose to maintain state or local government control or to deregulate services as happened in the UK. If it is accepted that buses are a public service, rather than a purely profit-making venture, then some element of control has to be retained. Some routes are profitable (e.g. urban, rush-hour) while others (e.g. rural) cannot be financially viable. The licence to operate is usually granted on a 'mix' of routes so that the bus company cross-subsidises.

Many cities in Europe have trams as an alternative to, or as well as, buses. Although the routes are less flexible, and there is a capital cost of laying track, they are better environmentally than buses.

Underground systems of transport operate in many of the larger cities of Europe. The London Underground is well known, as is the Métro in Paris. However, other cities such as Barcelona have similar systems.

By air

There is a trend towards air travel around Europe. The European Commission initially gained the agreement of the member countries for a removal of price-fixing on EU routes, making it easier for new operators to get routes. The third stage, to be implemented by 1996, is to remove the right of national airlines to dominate routes in their 'own' airspace.

Critics of the scheme fear that European routes will be dominated by a few large carriers as happened when deregulation in the USA resulted in a free-for-all that ousted the smaller airlines from major routes. In Europe, however, small operators using aircraft with fewer than 80 seats will have protection against big competitors.

Traffic Commissioner Karel Van Miert said in 1991 that: 'The proposals should lead to lower tariffs on at least some routes, where fares are too high.' The Secretary General of the Association of European Airlines argued that: 'The story of cheap air fares is the biggest lie I have ever heard. Not a single piece of EU legislation has helped airlines to reduce costs.' Sir Michael Bishop, chairman of British Midland, the independent British airline disagreed:

Fig. 4.5 British Airways destinations in Europe

Business travellers are paying falsely inflated fares to Europe because of lack of competition. Twelve of the 15 busiest air routes out of Heathrow are only operated by the two respective national carriers, providing similar frequencies and identical fares. . . . Since we have entered service on the Heathrow to Paris route, Europe's busiest with 2.3 million passengers per year, previously operated only by British Airways and Air France, business travellers have been able to save over £100 per trip.

British Midland claim that businesses are paying up to 30 per cent too much for flights to Europe. It claims that £236 million per year could be saved on the top 15 routes out of Heathrow when the legislation comes into force in 1996.

The key issue is the level of profit. If operators are forced by competition to reduce profit, but can still achieve acceptable returns, then it will be good for consumers. However, increase in services will need better air traffic control in some countries, such as Greece, so that there is the capacity to handle more aircraft. Ultimately the only solution seems to be to have a centralised air traffic control system. This is unlikely before the year 2000.

ACTIVITY 4.5

Plan a business trip with visits to Barcelona, Milan, Hamburg, and Lyon, travelling: (a) by road; (b) by rail; and (c) by air.

Telecommunications

Increasingly, communication between business people does not need them to physically travel. Telephone and fax make it possible to converse or pass messages at very high speed. European postal services and courier services are generally good too, with special delivery services that provide a 'next day' service for letters and small packages to most of the main business centres.

European telephone networks are of a very high quality. Digital exchanges have been installed in all large cities and industrial regions. Communication satellites and fibre-optic cables provide very high capacities, which means that 'lines busy' messages are now very rare and the quality of transmission is excellent. Digital systems make it possible to have audio-conferencing and even video-conferencing, so that a meeting can be held at which participants can hear and see each other even though they are in their offices hundred of miles apart. Although mobile phones and paging systems are at present nationally based, the EU is supporting development that will soon make them Europe-wide.

The speed, reliability and security of telephone systems, especially those dedicated to specific users, and where necessary with security enhanced by automatic encryption of data, are resulting in more and more businesses sending data directly from their computers to customers, suppliers, and business partners using a technique known as 'electronic data interchange' (EDI). Also electronic funds transfer (EFT) is used by most financial institutions, and many larger businesses, to settle debts and transfer funds.

Television has so far remained primarily a nationally based medium. However, the EU is supporting development of satellite-based and cable systems that will be Europe-wide, which should make this method of advertising more cost-effective.

ACTIVITY 4.6

Investigate the availability of mobile phones in Europe. To what extent can they be used across frontiers?

SUMMARY

1 The EU countries are diverse in terms of physical geography and natural resources.

2 Europe has a good road and rail network. Most large EU cities suffer from severe road congestion.

3 EU-registered shipping declined significantly between 1980 and 1990.

4 Air travel is a fast-growing method of transport. There are plans to further deregulate air travel.

5 Telecommunication systems provide a fast, secure and reliable means of holding conversations, and passing financial and other data.

Assignment 4

BACKGROUND

This chapter has briefly outlined the characteristics of the countries in the European Union.

If you are going to do business in an area you will need to know more about it. For example, it would be useful to know which are the principal cities and towns in that area and something about them; what the climate is like; what industries and agriculture there is; whether it has its own airport, and so forth.

ACTIVITY

1 Choose three areas for investigation. Negotiate with your fellow students so that you are each studying different places.

2 Collect information on the area.

3 Prepare a summary of the facts that you have gathered. Write notes on what makes it attractive as a place to do business in/with.

5 EU economies and markets

OBJECTIVES
1 To describe briefly the attempts to achieve European economic integration.

2 To identify some of the indicators that can be used to assess the economic strength of a country.

3 To describe the key features of the economies of the EU member states.

4 To identify the principal trading partners of the EU countries.

An overview of EU economies

Before examining the economies of the EU and its member states it is useful to consider briefly the overall framework of European economic integration.

European economic integration began soon after the end of the Second World War. Three stages in this integration can be identified in the period up to the end of 1992:

1 The first period, one of high growth in the 1950s and 1960s, resulted in the creation of a number of European institutions and the beginning of a legal framework to liberalise trade within Europe. The emphasis was on the removal of border controls and the elimination of quotas and tariffs. Active intervention in the economy by European institutions was limited to agriculture because of its special nature and considerable significance in national economies.

2 The long period of economic growth came to an end at the time of the 'oil crisis' of 1973, which caused massive increases in European energy costs. Much effort was needed to maintain the level of integration that had been achieved, and the only significant further move forward was the creation of the European Monetary System (EMS).

3 The third phase, beginning in the mid-1980s, was characterised by an broadening of the European agenda. Within industry there was much restructuring, and investment in new technology was beginning to bear fruit. Both of these tended to cross national boundaries. At the same time social and regional issues were seen as having a crucial role to play in the economic development of Europe.

The ratification of the Treaty on European Union (Maastricht Treaty) may in the future be seen as start of the fourth stage. Progress through the rest of the 1990s depends on Europe's ability to retain, through a period of recession, the level of integration already achieved.

Many economists felt that the Exchange Rate Mechanism (ERM), after providing 13 years of exchange rate stability, could be one of the foundations on which further monetary union should be built. Currency speculation in September 1992, which caused the withdrawal of the UK, and again in August 1993, when the bands were increased to 15 per cent, threw doubt on the soundness of the mechanisms, and the commitment of member states. Germany, increasingly the 'hub' of economic activity, was criticised by many for its failure to intervene strongly to protect the ERM.

A feature of the early 1990s was a reduction of intervention in industry at national level, and there was no compensating intervention at European level. The chief industrial policies of the EU have been to encourage deregulation and competition and these seem likely to continue throughout the 1990s. There has also been support for research and development, especially where there is cross-border co-operation.

There is still intervention in agriculture but the basis is shifting and there appears to be a recognition that the systems need to be adaptive to adjust to changing circumstances. The only other significant intervention has been in the steel industry, where European control seems to have been the only alternative to damaging national protectionist policies.

Freedom of movement of goods and services has been much improved, and capital mobility too has grown rapidly, although this is more of an international phenomenon than a European one. On the other hand, Labour mobility has remained low – most migrants are from outside the EU. There are clear dangers arising from labour mobility when different regions have basic economic differences. The reunification of Germany demonstrates how delicate the situation can be, and how carefully it needs to be handled. The EU has, quite rightly, been very careful about allowing the entry of countries with weak economies into the Union – the most recent ones were Greece, Spain and Portugal.

Progress towards harmonisation of taxation and company law has been slow.

The EU is attempting to tackle the problem of regional disparities. Dealing with this by social policies is proving controversial.

The EU is developing stronger relationships with other trading groups, notably EFTA. It is cautious in its approach to the eastern European countries, in many of which instability is all too clear.

ACTIVITY 5.1

Discuss the social and economic implications of admitting to membership of the EC a state that is economically weak.

The economy of the EU

The EU is one of the three largest economic blocs in the world. In 1991 the EU's GDP was greater than that of the USA and more than twice the GDP of Japan, its two main competitors.

The EU also has the largest population, 330 million. The USA's population is 251 million, and Japan's 124. However, the average US citizen is by far the richest in the world, with the Japanese second and Europeans third, although the latter two are catching up. Japan's strong economy is also demonstrated in its low unemployment rate and inflation figures. It can be seen from the statistics that although several EU countries have significant levels of imports from Japan, there is very little success in exporting to Japan.

A fundamental difference between the EU and its two main competitors is the fact that it remains 12 separate states, each with distinct economies and economic policies. 'Sovereignty' is jealously guarded, overtly as in the case of the UK, less obviously in the case of Germany as demonstrated in the ERM crisis. The principle of 'subsidiarity' is intended to protect sovereignty, keeping decision-making at national level wherever possible.

ACTIVITY 5.2

In the UK, important economic decisions are made by central government, and local government works within the economic framework set by central government. In the USA and Germany far more of the big decisions are made regionally (in States and *Länders* respectively).

In some sense, however, Europe is a state in which the countries are regions.

To what extent do you think economic planning and decision-making should be centralised?

National economies

Geographical size, climate, topology, natural resources and population are significant to the economics of a region or country, and these have been studied in Chapter 4. Other key factors for a business wishing to do business with EU countries are consumer purchasing power and buying patterns, these are considered in Chapter 10. In this section we will investigate the nature of trade in each member country, its gross domestic product (GDP), its imports and

Table 5.1 EU economic statistics, 1991

		Belgium	Denmark	France	Germany[1]	Greece	Ireland	Italy	Luxembourg	Netherlands	Portugal	Spain	UK
Area	sq km x 1000	33	43	547	249	132	69	294	3	37	92	505	244
Population	million	9.9	5.2	55.9	61.2	10.0	3.5	57.5	0.4	14.8	10.4	39.1	57.1
Density	people/sq km	300	119	102	246	76	51	196	145	400	113	77	234
GDP	ECU x billion	132	92	746	1050	40	27	711	6	198	34	300	627
GDP per capita	ECU x 1000	13.00	17.60	13.34	17.17	3.96	7.71	12.36	16.00	13.37	3.22	7.68	10.98
GDP by sector													
Agriculture	%	2	5	4	2	13	12	4	0	4	9	5	2
Manufacturing	%	22	20	22	33	19	37	23	22	22	30	27	23
Other industry	%	9	9	10	7	11	0	12	0	12	10	10	12
Services	%	67	67	64	59	57	51	61	78	62	51	58	63
Imports	ECU x billion	78	22	149	210	10	13	116	n.a.	85	14	51	166
EU	%	73	51	60	52	62	66	57	n.a.	65	66	57	52
USA	%	4	6	8	7	0	16	6	n.a.	8	0	9	10
Japan	%	3	0	0	0	0	5	0	n.a.	0	0	0	6
Other	%	21	43	32	41	38	13	38	n.a.	27	34	34	32
Exports	ECU x billion	78	23	140	272	5	26	108	n.a.	87	9	34	129
EU	%	73	53	58	51	64	72	54	n.a.	76	68	61	48
USA	%	5	9	7	11	7	9	11	n.a.	5	7	9	14
Japan	%	0	0	0	0	0	0	0	n.a.	0	0	0	0
Other	%	22	38	35	38	29	19	35	n.a.	19	25	30	38

Note:[1] figures for GDP, imports and exports are for West Germany only.

Source: Eurostat

Table 5.2 EU growth, inflation and unemployment, 1990 (%)

	Belgium	Denmark	France	Germany[1]	Greece	Ireland	Italy	Luxembourg	Netherlands	Portugal	Spain	UK
Growth rates	3.0	1.9	3.1	3.8	1.5	4.5	2.9	3.2	3.5	4.0	3.9	1.0
Inflation rates	4.3	2.7	3.8	3.3	22.3	2.7	6.8	4.2	2.9	14.4	7.1	10.2
Unemployment rates	8.2	8.4	9.0	5.2	11.5	16.7	10.4	1.6	8.3	5.0	15.5	6.2

[1] figures for Germany relates to pre-unified West Germany.

Source: Eurostat

exports, and its main trading partners.

GDP gives some indication of a country's 'weight' in economic matters, and hence its influence in European affairs. Some idea of a country's 'wealth' can be derived from the per capita GDP, the balance between exports and imports, and the per capita final consumption.

Five countries are by far the most significant in the EU, in terms of GDP and population: France, Germany, Italy, Spain and the UK. In 1990 they accounted for 87 per cent of the EU GDP, and 84 per cent of its population.

Unless otherwise indicated, figures given for each country are for 1991.

ACTIVITY 5.3

Assess the relative strength of EU countries using the GDP per capita, growth , inflation and unemployment rates given in Table 5.1 and Table 5.2. Differences will be most clearly seen from pie charts.

Belgium

A major problem faced by the Belgians is the large public sector debt. This amounts to 130 per cent of the GDP and is aggravated by continuing budget deficits (5.2 per cent of the GDP in 1992/3). The country's difficulties are enhanced by the fact that there are two very distinct cultures within the country – the culture of the French-speaking Walloons and the culture of the Dutch-speaking Flemings. Traditional industries include steel-making, petrochemicals (Petrofina is Belgium's largest company), materials processing, and food. In the north there is a large, but declining textile industry. In the south the traditional industries of steel and mining are also in decline.

Metal processing is highly developed accounting for 38 per cent of industrial employment. Electronics (14 per cent) and chemicals (13 per cent) are also important areas of employment. The traditional industries are Flemish textiles and Venetian glass.

Chief exports are machinery and vehicles (26 per cent), iron and steel products (13 per cent), textiles and clothing (7 per cent), chemicals (6 per cent). Main destinations for exports are: EU (73 per cent), USA (5 per cent), Switzerland (2 per cent) and Sweden (2 per cent).

Primary sources of imports are: EU (73 per cent), USA (4 per cent) and Japan (3 per cent).

Denmark

Danes enjoy very high living standards by comparison with other EU countries. Strong links with other Scandanavian countries – Norway, Sweden and Finland – may contribute to the perception that they are reluctant Europeans.

Their geographical location between the North Sea and the Baltic Sea has, in the past, been of strategic significance to NATO and in the future may be equally important to supporting the developing independence of Baltic states such as Poland, Lithuania, Latvia and Estonia.

Denmark's main industries are agriculture, tourism, oil and natural gas extraction. Its economy is shifting away from agricultural domination to service and modern, light industries.

Chief exports are foodstuffs (especially meat, dairy products, fish, etc) (27 per cent); furniture, clothing, etc (26 per cent); machinery and transport equipment (25 per cent); chemicals (9 per cent). Main destinations for exports are: EU (53 per cent, including Germany, 18 per cent), USA (9 per cent), Sweden (11 per cent) and Norway (8 per cent).

Primary sources of imports are: EU (51 per cent, including Germany 23 per cent), Sweden (12 per cent) and USA (6 per cent).

ACTIVITY 5.4

Denmark was very quick to recognise the Baltic states when they became independent of the USSR (now the CIS) in 1991. What do you think are the advantages to Denmark of their independence?

France

France suffered from a severe recession in the early 1980s with high unemployment and inflation. A necessary shift in policies took place in 1983, towards free market approaches. This, together with an improvement in world trading conditions, resulted in a recovery by 1987. France still, however, lacks strength in any specific sector of industry.

An expansion of public ownership in 1982 was reversed in 1986 with a policy of privatisation. In 1988 a neutral policy was adopted – an end to privatisation but no renationalisation.

There are very close links between the ministries responsible for the economy, the professional civil servants, and the leaders of the business community (especially banking, insurance, and large business conglomerates). However, relatively few employees in the private sector belong to trade unions, although there are government regulations imposing minimum wages and restricting redundancies.

France tends to be 'inflation-prone'. Since 1986 the competitive environment and stringent public-spending restrictions are highlighted as factors that have kept inflation down. Salary restraint, a relatively high level of unemployment and lower raw material and oil prices have also been contributing factors.

Personal income tax is highly progressive, takes into account family size, and exempts a large proportion of the population by having a high threshold. In

1986 only just over half of the population paid income tax. Social insurance contributions are high. An average production worker would expect to pay 7 per cent of his or her income in tax and 17 per cent in social insurance (1988 figures). Radical changes are needed if its taxation system is to be harmonised with other EU countries. There is a sense of unease about this in France because such a change could destabilise the economy and adversely affect some public services, notably education. There is an underlying sense of nationalism that could come to the surface under pressure, although mainstream political sentiment is very much in favour of progress toward European Union integration.

French banks are amongst the largest in Europe (indeed Credit Agricole is the fourth largest in the world.) As well as the private banks there is a nationalised bank, the Banque de France, which manufactures and distributes bank notes and supervises the banking system, amongst other functions.

Oil price shocks in the early 1970s and a lack of natural energy sources (such as coal) spurred the French to develop nuclear-powered electricity generation plants. France is now the second largest producer in the world, after the USA, supplying over 50 per cent of France's energy needs. France is the EU's largest energy exporter, and the UK is its biggest customer, followed by Switzerland and Italy. France generates electricity at a cost 45 per cent lower than the UK and 54 per cent less than Germany.

France is the largest agricultural country in the EU and the second largest wine producer (after Italy). It also has a large industrial sector, producing steel, motor cars and manufactured goods. Its main industrial areas are around Paris and Lyon.

Chief exports are machinery and vehicles (35 per cent), manufactured goods (28 per cent), foodstuffs (12 per cent), and chemicals (11 per cent). Main destinations for exports are: EU (58 per cent), USA (7 per cent), and Switzerland (5 per cent).

Primary sources of imports are: EU (60 per cent) and USA (8 per cent). France is the UK's third largest customer, accounting for about 10 per cent of UK exports. Originally the main exports were petroleum-related goods but manufactured goods and the service sector have now shown massive growth. The French market for consumer goods is very similar to that in the UK. Demand for gardening and DIY goods is expanding and good-quality British food and drink products are increasingly popular. Gift-ware, china, jewellery and stationery are also growing. Golf is the fastest growing sport in France, but here UK manufacturers face keen competition from Japan and the USA. Amongst capital goods, demand for health care, security and pollution control equipment is significant.

Germany

In Germany there has been less movement towards service industries than in other European countries.

There is extensive German investment in production overseas – Spain and South Korea in particular – to benefit from cheaper labour costs. There is also considerable investment in the federal states (*Länder*) that were East Germany, where the workers are used to lower wages (but also lower prices). However, it is proving difficult to attain the high quality on which German product sales are based.

Germany is by far the largest of the EU countries and is the EU's strongest industrial nation. Even before reunification its GDP was more than 25 per cent higher than France, the second largest. Clearly Germany will continue to be the leading economic force in the EU.

The basic law of the German federal constitution states that *Länder* are responsible for all matters that are not expressly allocated to central government. Central functions include foreign affairs, defence, currency, customs, air transport, and the postal service. Thus Germany is one of the most decentralised countries in Europe. Public sector decision-making is delegated to the lowest possible level and federal involvement takes place only where local authorities are unable to cope. This offers the advantages of autonomy and flexibility but it is difficult to co-ordinate.

There is a large body of legislation protecting consumers and competition and regulations governing such things as transportation, mail, telecommunications and utilities. There is a strong guild tradition in which tradespeople have to undertake special training and gain formal qualifications. Also, the central German bank is largely independent from the government.

Germany's economic growth is close to the EU average but starts from a higher than average base. Its economic success has been attributed to its social market economy, which is intended to achieve a balance between market efficiency and social interests.

Germany has the highest labour costs in the world, but these are partly compensated for by the growth in productivity. German products are renowned for their quality and reliability. The working week is the shortest in the world, 31.2 hours per week on average. However, Germany also has the lowest number of hours lost through strikes and absenteeism.

One of Germany's main strengths is its highly developed transport and communications system, facilitating mobility and distribution. However, traffic congestion is still severe in some areas. Housing is expensive throughout Germany.

Germany's economy is heavily dependent on exports. The biggest export areas are machinery (20 per cent), road vehicles (18 per cent), chemicals (13 per cent), electrical appliances (9 per cent), iron and steel (6 per cent), and food, beverages and tobacco products (4 per cent). Main destinations for exports are: EU (51 per cent), USA (11 per cent), Switzerland (6 per cent), Sweden (3 per cent), and the CIS (previously the USSR) (2 per cent).

Primary sources of imports are: EU (52 per cent), and the USA (7 per cent).

Greece

Until the 1960s most of Greece's businesses were family-owned, reflecting a preference for trade rather than long-term industrial projects. The nature of Greece's industrial base may be judged by the fact that the biggest ten commercial companies include Toyota, Philips, Siemans, Proctor and Gamble, Texaco, and 3M – none of them Greek-owned. Greece's largest industries are agriculture, merchant shipping, and tourism.

Chief exports are industrial products (44 per cent), farm products (including tobacco, raisins, cotton, wine, olive oil, citrus fruits) (29 per cent), ores and metals (6 per cent), textiles and chemicals (3 per cent). Main destinations for exports are: EU (64 per cent, including Germany 25 per cent), USA (7 per cent), Egypt (2 per cent), CIS (1 per cent), states that previously formed Yugoslavia (1 per cent).

Primary sources of imports are other EU countries (62 per cent). In the four years up to 1989, the UK's trade with Greece increased by 300 per cent. Amongst capital goods in demand are iron and steel products, road vehicles, and electrical machinery and appliances.

Despite the lowest per capita GDP in the EU, the Greek market for consumer goods is sophisticated. Price and quality are usually of equal importance, but 'designer' label clothes are very much in demand, irrespective of price. Food, beverages and clothing demand is increasing (especially breakfast cereals, and frozen and pre-cooked foods), but the UK has failed to take a share of this, except in whisky, where there was a 64 per cent increase in 1989–9.

The DTI believes that the major opportunities for exports to Greece are in foodstuffs, agri-business and food processing, telecommunications, aerospace and airports, updating the retail sector, financial services, and consultancy. The retail sector is dominated by small family-run outlets, and multiple branches are rare except in the largest chains of supermarkets and government stores. There are only six genuine supermarket chains, and most of these are concentrated in greater Athens and Salonica. Of the five main department stores, only one has a branch outside Athens.

ACTIVITY 5.5

If a country is identified as a potential export market for certain products it usually means that there is a market there but no domestic suppliers. Which of the markets identified by the DTI do you think that Greece could develop domestically?

Ireland

Irish standards of living are low compared with other EU countries. Reforms to the CAP will have an adverse affect on the Irish economy because of its dependence on agriculture and food products.

The country's high level of unemployment is also a concern. Ireland is geographically on the periphery of the EU, and without the support of EU regional policy would be in danger of suffering from the levels of poverty and depopulation that have been common, on and off, since the great famine of the 1840s.

Since achieving political independence from the UK in 1922, Ireland has sought to demonstrate economic independence. The Irish vote in favour of Maastrict was symbolically important in putting the Treaty back on course for ratification, and in asserting Ireland's commitment to the EU. However, EU social policy and free movement of people threatens Ireland's strict laws on contraception, abortion and divorce.

Ireland has a very high-profile scheme for promoting outside investment in new technology. As well as an important agricultural industry and a great deal of tourism, Ireland is a promising territory for oil and gas extraction.

Chief exports are machinery and transport equipment (30 per cent), food products (especially meat and dairy products) (23 per cent), textiles and other manufactured goods (21 per cent), and organic and other chemicals (13 per cent). Main destinations for exports are: EU (72 per cent, especially the UK, 35 per cent), USA (9 per cent), and Canada (1 per cent).

Primary sources of imports are: EU (66 per cent, including the UK, 42 per cent), USA (16 per cent) and Japan (5 per cent).

ACTIVITY 5.6

1 Industry is sometimes classified as 'sunrise' or 'sunset' according to its future prospects. Which of Ireland's existing industries would you put into each of these categories?

2 Ireland is often regarded as being at a disadvantage, being located 'off shore' from continental Europe and separated from it by the UK. Are there any areas of economic activity for which its location is not a disadvantage, or for which its location is an asset?

Italy

During the late 1960s and early 1970s many Western countries had significant levels of industrial and social unrest. Price increases originating from the cost of oil and raw material hit the Italian economy at a time when conflict was at its height. An agreement was reached to link wages to inflation, thus protecting the workers' real incomes. This, however, only put off the problem because of the rising level of public spending on social security and health care.

In 1983 the link between salaries and inflation was changed by the government, and major employers took a much tougher stance in industrial relations. During the years that followed profits and investment improved, and by the late 1980s a great deal of industrial modernisation had taken place and Italy experienced considerable economic growth. Milan, in particular, boomed. Italy has many small to medium-sized businesses and these formed the basis of that growth. However, recent Italian governments have been forced to tackle problems such as high inflation and an inefficient public sector. When Italy joined the European Monetary System in 1979 it was forced to abandon the practice of devaluing the lira as a way of protecting its economy. Consequently, inflation fell from 16 per cent in 1982 to under 5 per cent by 1988.

Industry is concentrated in the north, while the south is predominantly agricultural. The wealth-gap between the northern and southern regions continues to widen.

Unemployment, especially in the south, is considered to be one of the reasons why organised crime in Camparia, Calabria and Sicily is so high, although its cause and effect relationship is difficult to prove.

There is a great deal of heavy industry in the north, especially around Milan. The area has a population of about 4 million. Steel, heavy engineering, machine tools, plastics, oil-refining, electronics, paper-making, printing, and domestic products (especially shoes, clothes, furniture) are the principal industries. There are some 130,000 factories and the region produces 40 per cent of Italy's manufactured goods. Turin is also another centre of industry with aerospace, robotics and high-technology industries being most common.

Between the northern industrial region and the capital, Rome, is an area which produces much of Italy's clothing (including Bennetton), footwear, ceramics, electronics, and medical equipment. Although there is comparatively little industry in southern Italy, new industry is being encouraged, mainly near Naples, to avoid overdependence on agriculture.

Tourism made a major contribution to the economy in the past but is progressively less important. Increasing affluence in the north has encouraged Italians to take their holidays abroad, and the Italian cost of living has deterred foreign visitors.

Chief exports are machinery and vehicles (34 per cent), textiles and clothing (18 per cent), chemicals (7 per cent) and food products (5 per cent). Main destinations for exports are: EU (54 per cent), USA (11 per cent), Switzerland (5 per cent), and Libya (1 per cent).

Primary sources of imports are: EU (57 per cent) and USA (6 per cent).

Luxembourg

Luxembourg is by far the smallest of the EU countries. Its inhabitants enjoy low levels of unemployment, modest inflation and relatively high economic growth. The country is heavily dependent on trade with other EU countries, and its location in the heart of the EU makes it a natural focal point for political and financial activities.

Luxembourg is, for its size, a major producer of heavy engineering products. Steel and machinery account for 90 per cent of exports. Other exports are chemicals and agricultural products. Major world companies such as Goodyear and Du Pont are based in Luxembourg. However, the main contribution to Luxembourg's GDP arises from commerce and finance (32 per cent).

Netherlands

The development of the 'Europort' in the Netherlands has led to the country being the principal route for trade between the EU and the rest of the world. Foreign trade exceeds 60 per cent of the country's GDP.

The Netherlands has very strong political and economic links with Germany, the powerhouse of Europe.

The Netherlands regards itself as a leader in the process of European integration, and it was appropriate that the Treaty on European Union should have been signed at the Dutch town of Maastricht during the period of Dutch presidency of the EU Council of Ministers.

The Netherlands has a wide manufacturing range, including substantial chemical, electrical engineering and motor industries. Agricultural products are also an important sector, while the oil and gas extraction industry is growing rapidly.

The country also has the head offices of many civil engineering, consultancy, accounting, and financial services organisations.

Chief exports are minerals (24 per cent), textiles and other finished goods (21 per cent), food and beverages (including dairy products, fresh meat, canned and bottled products, fish, cocoa, chocolate) (17 per cent), vehicles and electrical appliances (19 per cent), and chemical products (15 per cent). Main export destinations are: EU (76 per cent, including Germany 26 per cent), USA (5 per cent), Sweden (2 per cent), and Switzerland (2 per cent).

Primary sources of imports are: EU (65 per cent, including Germany 26 per cent), and the USA (8 per cent).

Portugal

Portugal is one of the EU's most underdeveloped economies. It has a weak economy and a persistent balance of trade deficit.

About 25 per cent of the workforce is employed in agriculture but with low productivity. The climate, topology and soil are not favourable to agriculture. Inadequacies in transport and communications add to the country's difficulties.

There are many small firms in traditional industries such as textiles, footwear and food processing. International investment has established pulp and paper manufacture, light engineering, textiles and pharmaceuticals industries, chiefly around Oporto in northern Portugal.

Portugal's principal income-earner is tourism.

Exports include textiles and clothing (30 per cent), electrical machinery and equipment (16 per cent), wood, wood products and paper (14 per cent), and food and drinks (8 per cent). Main export destinations are: EU (68 per cent, including Spain 7 per cent), USA (7 per cent), and Portuguese-speaking countries (4 per cent).

Primary sources of imports are other EU countries (66 per cent).

ACTIVITY 5.7

Identify which countries are Portuguese speaking and explain why so much of Portugal's trade is done with them.

Spain

Two years are of special significance in recent Spanish history. In 1978 a democratic system, suspended since General Franco came to power after the 1936–9 civil war, was re-established; and in 1986 Spain was accepted as a member of the EU.

During General Franco's rule Spain had a closed, protected, regulated and monopolised economy. During the 1980s Spain suffered high unemployment, interest and inflation rates. However, a policy of decentralisation was introduced in 1984, whereby public sector responsibility was passed from state control to the autonomous committees and local authorities. Suceeding governments were then quite successful in preparing Spain for full integration into the EU in 1993.

The economy is now much more competitive and investment is very high, much of it financed by foreign capital. Spanish GDP capita was still the lowest of the five largest EU countries in 1990, but was rapidly catching up.

Despite a sharp increase in its levels of public expenditure, Spanish levels are still low compared with other EU countries. While most European countries built up their welfare state during the period of economic expansion after the Second World War, Spain has had to attempt this task during a recession.

A difficult feature of the transition taking place between joining the EU and full integration is the dismantling of Spain's protectionist policies. It had a complex set of tariffs, quotas, and restrictions aimed at limiting imports. Exports received very favourable tax concessions, effectively providing a hidden subsidy that in some product areas amounted to 'dumping'. As tariff barriers declined in the run-up to full membership, demand for imported consumer goods increased, including clothing, toys and cars. Local businesses in all sectors have suffered from foreign competition, and it has been realised that Spanish management and productivity needs to improve.

The largest industries are agriculture and tourism. Spain attracts over 50 million visitors per year and the country exports wine and food to most of the other EU countries. The future of Spanish agriculture is full of uncertainties. Spain has severe natural deficiencies (e.g. climate, altitude); farms that are often too small in the northern regions and too large in the southern and central regions; and the distribution system is poor. However, the products are distinctive compared with those of northern Europe and competitive, especially in quality, with the other southern European countries.

Furthermore, towards the end of the 1980s Spain suffered a serious crisis in its large and economically vital tourist trade. This crisis appears to have stemmed from a shift in demand from Spain to other Mediterranean countries rather than from an absolute reduction in demand. Provided Spain can overcome the disadvantages that have arisen from unplanned growth and its 'bad press', the tourism trade is still thought to have great potential in the regions where it is concentrated.

Chief exports are motor cars (31 per cent), machinery, and fruit. Main export markets are: EU (61 per cent) and the USA (9 per cent).

Primary sources of imports are: EU (57 per cent) and USA (9 per cent). Many UK firms have formed partnerships with Spanish ones to acquire local marketing knowledge and distribution channels. However, the UK has lost ground to Germany, France and Italy, its share of total exports to Spain declining from 7.7 per cent in 1985 to 6.5 per cent in 1991.

United Kingdom

In the 1960s the UK performed badly compared with the EU average. In the 1970s it had improved but was still below average, and in the 1980s it had crept ahead. A particular strength is the financial sector.

Like Italy, the UK has strong regional differences in its economy and has often suffered high interest rates and inflation. The penalty of reducing these, in 1992–3 for example, has usually been high unemployment.

The UK joined the EU in 1973. The years that followed entry were difficult in terms of inflation, unemployment and adverse balance of payments. Dealing with inflation was the major goal of the government of the 1980s. In the late 1970s and 1980s, governments were able to introduce laws drastically changing the business environment and industrial relations.

The 1980s and early 1990s have been characterised by growth in the service sector, a rise in both the number and proportion of females in the labour market, and the increase of part-time working. In contrast, the number of people employed in manufacturing fell dramatically. Emphasis has been on encouraging the formation and growth of small and medium-sized firms. Older industries such as coal, iron and steel, heavy engineering (such as shipbuilding) have declined. Britain is currently almost self sufficient in oil and gas. New industries such as communications, robotics and computing have been encouraged.

Three areas of weakness could be identified in the UK business environment in the late 1980s:

1 Investment in research and development was only half that of Germany, and much of the UK's spending was on defence-related projects.
2 The UK also had a poor record of investing in education and training. Innovations and new technology cannot be exploited unless management and the workforce have the appropriate skills. In 1990 the UK was placed 22nd out of 23 industrialised countries in the overall quality of its workforce. UK firms committed only 0.15 per cent of turnover to training compared with 1 to 2 per cent in Japan, Germany and France.
3 While an integrated high-speed rail network is taking shape in mainland Europe, the UK is lagging well behind. Increasing congestion on the roads is a reflection of the comparatively low investment in public transport compared with France and Germany.

Industry is undoubtedly 'leaner and fitter' in the 1990s than it was a decade earlier, due partly to the recession of the early 1980s and partly to government policies. Paradoxically this made it more difficult for business to survive in the recession of 1990–2.

Most large firms operating in the UK are multinationals with extensive activities overseas. Among the 100 largest manufacturing firms, 20 are foreign-owned. Fifteen hundred manufacturing firms, about 1 per cent of the total but accounting for 20 per cent of total sales and 14 per cent of employment, were foreign-owned in the mid-1980s. American, Japanese, EFTA and Far Eastern organisations are all concerned to have access to the EU market after 1992.

Chief exports are machinery and transport equipment (34 per cent), manufactured goods (27 per cent), oil and gas (22 per cent), and chemicals (11 per cent). There is also a very large 'invisible exports' sector comprising banking and insurance. Despite the uncertainty of its weather compared with the countries of southern Europe, the UK attracts visitors from many parts of the world, making tourism a major industry. The principal attractions are the UK's heritage and the outstanding scenery, notably in the national parks. Main destinations for exports are: EU (48 per cent), USA (14 per cent), and Commonwealth countries (such as Australia, Canada, New Zealand) (over 5 per cent).

Primary sources of imports are: EU (52 per cent), USA (10 per cent) and Japan (6 per cent).

ACTIVITY 5.8

Use the data given in Table 5.1 to determine which EU country is most dependent on: (a) agriculture; (b) manufacturing and other industry; and (c) the service sector.

SUMMARY

1 Integration of EU economies has passed through several phases. Periods of progress have alternated with periods of consolidation.

2 Although the 12 EU countries each manage their own economies, there is an increasing interdependence that owes much to the level of intra-EU trade.

3 Economic indicators show significant differences between the characteristics and strength of the economies of member states.

4 For almost all EU countries, the majority of transnational trade is with other EU countries. Some still retain traditional trading partners, often established during colonisation.

Assignment 5

BACKGROUND

It has only been possible to include one year's economic statistics in this book. A truer picture of a country's economy is achieved by tracing the changes to the economic indicators over a number of years. Care must be taken, however, that you are comparing 'like with like'. With Germany, for example, it is necessary to distinguish between pre-unification and post-unification, and although data for the FDR (West Germany) are readily available, those for the GDR (East Germany) are less prolific and less reliable.

ACTIVITY

1 Obtain up-to-date data from an organisation such as the European Commission's Eurostat service, and trace the changes in EU member state economies for the last ten years.

2 Identify any countries that have shown significant improvements, as indicated by increases in GDP per capita and growth, and reductions in inflation and unemployment.

3 Identify changes in the nature of the economy, as indicated by the balance between agriculture, industry and services.

4 Identify changes in transnational trading patterns, reflected by volumes of imports and exports of various products, a shift in the balance between imports and exports, and differences in the levels of trade with principal trading partners.

5 Compare the economic progress of individual countries against the EU average.

6 Business culture

OBJECTIVES   **For a selection of major European countries:**

1   **To outline the types of business organisational structures and the nature of industrial relations.**

2   **To identify the factors that influence the chances of promotion and how they differ between countries.**

Introduction

Business culture is a difficult concept to define and assess. Many of the factors we would use to distinguish between business cultures are qualitative and subjective. There may be differences between reputation and actuality. Managers, operatives, customers, suppliers, unions, tax authorities, health and safety officials, and the local community may have quite different perceptions of a business.

The business culture of a particular organisation depends very much on the business sector in which it operates. Retailing, manufacturing, banking, and other business areas all have their own, different, characteristics. Business culture also depends very much on whether the organisation operates entirely in a limited geographical area, or whether it is transnational (operates across frontiers but with a clear 'home' country) or whether it is multinational. The wider the range of contacts, the greater is the exposure to other business cultures and the more likely it is to adapt its own. There are many other factors which influence business culture – for example: the organisation's legal status (e.g. sole trader, partnership, limited company) and the obligations implied by this status; its size and market position; trading conditions (e.g. sales success, levels of unemployment); trading methods and the ways in which the organisation interacts with, for example, suppliers and customers; how the business is structured to facilitate its operations and management control; and on the style of management (e.g. authoritarian, participative); the qualities and attitudes of all those involved with the organisation (e.g. their upbringing, qualifications, training, experience, ambitions); the level of technology within the organisation; language, particularly within a transnational or multinational organisation, and the ease with which its people communicate; and finally, the nature of the society in which the organisation operates (e.g. religion, attitudes towards minorities, equal opportunities).

Business culture can be transmitted from the top; it can also originate at grass-roots level. It involves the roles, behaviour and attitudes of the participants and their values and ideas.

It is dangerous to draw conclusions which generalise about the people or businesses of a whole nation. If you were to generalise about Britain, there would be very many people and organisations which did not conform to the profile. The comments given below on some of the countries of Europe should be read with that caveat clearly in mind. However, there are differences between the people, life-styles and business methods among the various European nations which are worth noting. The characteristics described in this chapter relate mainly to organisational structure. In later chapters there is further discussion, considered in the framework of establishing a business and marketing outside the domestic market

A study of the UK's history shows that regional and local differences were very clear in the early stages of the Industrial Revolution, but as communications have improved these differences have lessened. It will be interesting to see if the same kind of harmonisation occurs in Europe as the various countries work together more and communicate better.

ACTIVITY 6.1

Business success is often measured by indicators such as profitability, return on capital employed, market share, and so on. However, these are not appropriate for describing the organisation's business culture.

From the viewpoint of an employee, identify five characteristics that you would use to distinguish between an organisation that has a 'good' business culture and one that does not.

Repeat the exercise from the viewpoint of a senior manager.

Business environments

Belgium

The distinction between Dutch-speaking Flemish in the north and French-speaking Walloons in the south is very pronounced. However, it is a sensitive issue and every effort has to be made to avoid blunders in conversation.

Belgians generally have a formal attitude towards business activities, in terms of dress and methods of business communication.

There are two common types of company. A corporation, which has SA (Société Anonyme) or NV (Naamloze Venotschap) after the company name (depending on the language), can be listed on the stock exchange and must have at least three directors, appointed at a general meeting of shareholders. There is a legal requirement for the company to prepare an annual inventory, accounts and management reports. A private limited company has the letters SPRL or BVBA after its name and needs only to have one director.

Any company that has more than 100 employees must have a works council which meets at least once per month to discuss company progress and working conditions. Employers and employees are represented in equal numbers on this committee. Participants almost invariably adopt an attitude of co-operation at these meetings.

Denmark

Danes tend to be liberal-minded and tolerant, with a strong sense of social welfare and a co-operative spirit. Independence and enterprise are evident from the tendency of Danes to leave larger firms to start or join small businesses. More than half of industrial jobs are in firms of less than 200 staff.

Business dress is less formal than in most other EU countries. Denmark was one of the first nations to adopt the principle of male–female equality of opportunity, and this is reflected both in the number of women in senior management and the attitude of Danes towards household duties.

The two main types of businesses are the private company denoted by the initials ApS (Anpartsselskab) and the public company denoted by A/S (Aktieselskab).

A public company must have at least three directors. All its managers, and at least half of its directors must either be EU nationals and reside in Denmark or another EU country, or, if they are not EU nationals, reside in Denmark.

In companies that have at least 35 employees the employees are entitled to elect a number of additional directors, that is up to half of the number of directors appointed by the shareholders (rounded up).

Employees may insist that there is a works council, comprising equal numbers of employer and employee representatives, if the company employs more than 30 people. These councils do not have any executive power but are widely used as a channel of communication.

France

France is a large country with a low population density and distinct regions. People have strong regional loyalties and are reluctant to move, except to Paris. Paris is very definitely the 'hub' of France in every way. A Parisian who is transferred to one of the regions feels exiled.

Western France has an *Atlantic* tradition with long navigable rivers and maritime trade. Eastern France is *Continental* in nature with industry based on coal and minerals with the Rhine as a major route for imports and exports. The south is predominantly *Mediterranean* with distinctive culture and agriculture, and a coast dominated by tourism.

Politically France is very centralised. There is no hint of federalism, unlike Germany. The education system demonstrates this very well – the national curriculum and examination system allow for virtually no regional differences. Centralism may be traced back to the *Code Napoléon*, which aimed to cover every eventuality by a framework of rules.

France has a much more homogeneous set of values than many small countries. There is a strong sense of pride in national projects such as Concorde and the Channel Tunnel. The government is directly and indirectly involved in industry and commerce and in some sectors the division between public and private businesses is not clear. There is much protectionism, for example in agriculture.

Although individuals are keen to outwit the government in the area of taxation, and government is often considered to be excessively politically motivated, nevertheless there is a respect for its integrity. Civil servants are well respected and highly paid.

Foreign-owned multinationals represent about 80 per cent of the business machine industry, 70 per cent of oil, and 60 per cent of the agricultural machinery industry. Foreign investment is, however, closely controlled and monitored by the government.

French government and businesses have a good record of long-term planning. Nuclear power and high-speed trains are typical of the investment that has been made over many years and through several changes in government.

There are two types of businesses the SA (*Société Anonyme*) and the SARL (*Société à Responsabilité Limitée*). SARLs are usually small, with a maximum of 50 shareholders to whom the management is accountable. An SA can have one of two forms of management:

1 A board of directors made up of elected shareholders (*le Conseil d'Administration*) headed by *le President* who chairs the board and acts as chief executive. There are normally between 3 and 12 *administrateurs* (directors). This

is the more common structure.

2 A two-tier system with a supervisory board (*le Conseil de Surveillance*) and a management board (*le Directoire*) of two to seven directors appointed by the supervisory board. The management board, headed by the PDG (*Président-Directeur Général*), runs the company.

Any business that employs more than 50 people must have a works committee (*comité d'enterprise*), which is entitled to send two representatives to meetings of the administrative or supervisory boards (but not to management boards). They do not have voting rights.

Business organisations tend to be centralised and, arising from this, they have strongly vertical hierarchies, clear-cut divisions and central planning, and they are elitist and legalistic. There tend to be more layers of middle management than in a Dutch or German company. The formal structure is, therefore, not responsive to the need for change. Informal relationships tend to become established to deal with the realities of everyday business life.

The PDG of a French business usually has a high degree of technical competence and gives more attention to detail than equivalents in other European countries. He or she is usually decisive. Subordinates will often criticise or show scepticism but they usually have a respect for authority based on competence rather than status.

Although performance appraisals are increasingly used in businesses, there is still a tendency to link them with personal criticism, since collective decision-making, and hence collective responsibility, is less common than in some countries. It may be that this arises from the competitive nature of schools and ambition to rise within the hierarchy of business. Relationships in teams formed to undertake a project tend to be formal rather than easy-going and friendly.

It is usual to have a detailed agenda for business meetings. Those attending will usually have prepared carefully and make their contribution at the appropriate time. Thus the meeting is a means of clarifying the situation and making one's position clear. Where a person of authority is present it is the place at which decisions are announced.

Business communications are on two levels, reflecting the nature of the business organisation itself. There is a formal, written level, in which the report is much used, and great importance is attached to clear but concise French, well constructed and correct. There is also the informal level which depends on a network of personal relationships.

Education and qualifications play an important role in careers and promotion. Technical qualifications such as engineering have a high status, as do law and finance. Sales and marketing were, until recently, less esteemed. Women have made considerable progress in the management of retail and service industries, especially law, finance and personnel, but they are less numerous in senior positions in industry, and outside Paris. It is noticeable that many of the senior positions in management are filled by people from 'old money' families.

ACTIVITY 6.2

Paris is the 'hub' of French business and working in Paris is attractive to many French people. To what extent is there a 'hub' in the UK?

Germany

The reunification of Germany in 1990 has produced a confusing scene.

The Federal Republic (West Germany) was probably the richest of the European countries with a strong enterprise economy. By contrast the German Democratic Republic (East Germany) was a communist, centrally controlled economy in which wages and productivity were low, there was considerable overmanning in factories, the infrastructure was in decline, the quality of goods was poor, and most consumer goods were scarce. However, prices were low, especially for essentials like housing, transport, clothes and food and there was virtually no unemployment.

At the time of reunification the people of the East looked forward to more freedom in a democratic state, higher wages, and improvements in their living conditions. What they did not realise was that higher wages would be accompanied by a higher cost of living, that they would no longer be guaranteed a job, and that some of their fellow citizens would be ruthless in exploiting the entrepreneurial opportunities.

The people in West Germany soon realised that the cost of reunification was high. Massive funds were needed to improve the run-down infrastructure of the East and this demanded higher taxes. Industrialists could use the pool of 'cheap labour' from the East for unskilled work, to the detriment of wages and employment levels in the Western sector.

It will be several years before the turmoil arising from the reunification dies down. It is clear, however, that the model of West Germany will be the one that emerges, not that of East Germany.

ACTIVITY 6.3

Assume you are employed by a company with factories in both west and east Germany and have to spend time in each? How do you think the different cultures would be apparent in working practices and attitudes?

It is perhaps fortunate that Germany is a federal country in which the *Länders* (regions) have considerable autonomy. Frankfurt, for example, is the centre of banking and finance; Hamburg is a trading city; Munich is home of the sunrise industries (and of the arts); Dusseldorf, Dortmund and Essen lie in the area famous for heavy industry. Germany has the largest automobile industry in

Europe, with BMW in Munich; DaimlerBenz, Mercedes and Porsche in Stuttgart; Volkswagen in Wolfsburg; Ford and General Motors in Cologne.

Unlike France, where there is a spider's web of road and rail links centred on Paris, Germany has a network of transport and communication links.

The Germans take business seriously. Many countries look to Germany as the producer of good-quality products, and the Germans are conscious of this and take pride in their products, their production methods, and their management methods.

The German government has a shareholding in many key businesses and there is public ownership of many of the services. There are also national and regional schemes to provide subsidies to industry, which result in high taxation. Industry is extensively regulated by legislation and government guidelines. These are viewed as supportive and helpful and, rather than trying to evade them, businesses are more likely to look for ways of enhancing and improving the framework.

Complementing this control over the economy there are organisations to encourage competition and prevent monopolies taking control of any market sector. There is an assumption that a merger will be harmful to competition and companies must prove that this is not the case before the merger is permitted. This tends to reduce the number of takeovers and makes it difficult for a foreign business to acquire a German company as a way into the market.

As in many countries, the banks have a powerful influence on commerce and industry. The Bundesbank is the key bank, with great influence over the financial markets. The biggest three of the others nationally – Deutsche, Dresdner and Commerzbank – offer a wider range of services than would be normal in many countries where there are often separate banks specialising in investment, stock-broker, merchant banking, and so on.

The relatively small number of takeovers and the strength of financial support to businesses by banks and government make it possible to plan strategically and make long-term investments that a less stable and uncertain environment would prevent.

Although Germany is well known for its large conglomerates there are also many family-owned and medium-sized companies. In these, particularly, there is a concern for employee welfare which leads to the provision of facilities that are quite remarkable. Unions in Germany are organised by industry, not by skill, so that a multiplicity of unions representing the workers of one organisation is unheard of. The unions have the highest membership amongst workers in mining, steel-making and engineering.

There is extensive legislation protecting workers' rights and welfare. These are balanced by restrictions on the freedom of unions. This contrasts with the UK where there is relatively little legislation, and employers and unions jealously guard their 'freedom' to act without restriction. In Germany the legislative framework means that strikes are rare, a last resort which follows arbitration and consultation procedures. Even then the strikes are usually short and are used to demonstrate strength of feeling rather than as a weapon to cause serious damage to the employer.

There are two types of limited liability companies. An AG (*Aktiengesellschaft*) is a public limited company while a GmbH (*Gesellschaft mit beschränkter Haftung*) is a private company. Organisations with more than 500 employees have a supervisory board (*Aufsichtsrat*) consisting of up to 20 people which appoints the management board (*Vorstand*). The directors (*Vortstandsmitglieder*) who form the management board have to be reappointed every four years. People who are employed as senior managers, but are not on the management board, have a title which might lead British people to believe they were members of the board of directors – *Directoren*. In smaller companies there is no supervisory board and the directors (*Geschäftsführer*) are appointed directly by shareholders.

Employees in any company with more than five employees have a right to form a works council (*Betriebsrat*). Its elected representatives may consider the company's economic, personnel and social policies and have to be consulted on decisions affecting employment. A company with over 100 employees must set up an economic committee (*Wirtshaftsausschuß*) comprising management and employee representatives to discuss sales, production and financial matters. It has no authority over the management's decision-making powers.

In a company with over 1000 employees, one-third of the supervisory board is elected by employees and two-thirds is elected by shareholders. If there are more than 2000 employees then employees and shareholders elect half each. In the latter case there must be a personnel director (*Arbeitsdirektor*) on the management board.

The Germans respect authority that is derived from status and competence. They tend to be most comfortable when functions have been thoroughly investigated and suitable procedures drawn up. Cutting corners is not popular. The result is that, when the unexpected occurs, people look for a method of dealing with it that is already defined. A business environment which is uncertain or continually changing cannot be accommodated easily with this approach. Improvisation is seen as a failure to plan properly, rather than as a useful skill. Planning and decision-making will usually include consideration of contingency plans. Once plans are made and accepted, subordinates will follow the instructions faithfully; conversely, management is expected to give clear guidance and leadership. When authority is delegated, the subordinate expects to be trusted to get on with the job without excessive supervision.

Despite the presence of worker representatives in company boards, the opportunities for participation in setting targets and feedback on performance are sometimes seen as inadequate, and relationships between superior and subordinate perceived to be too formal.

It is easier for a person to rise from a humble start to a senior position in a German company than it would be in a French one; there are no equivalents to the prestigious *Grandes Écoles*. Engineers have a high status, unlike many countries where marketing or finance have top spot. There is a highly developed apprenticeship system, and higher education is mainly vocational. It is worth noting that, as in most societies, it is as important to 'know the right people' as well as being technically competent.

Promotion tends to come by developing one's own technical knowledge or experience. Job security is highly valued. Many Germans like to stay in their own region. People believe that they should work hard and be rewarded eventually by promotion. Increased salary is not as great an incentive as in many countries. Germany has the smallest difference between the highest and lowest earnings of any European country.

ACTIVITY 6.4

To what extent do you think the UK would benefit from the level of employee participation in decision-making that is usual in Germany?

Greece

Greek industry is traditionally family-run. Those businesses which have grown into large organisations are often closely associated with the banks, particularly the National Bank of Greece. When the socialist party gained power, 30 of the largest companies were nationalised and many of the senior managers were replaced by government appointees. The state now controls 70 per cent of economic activity either directly or by having financial control. Amongst the smaller businesses there was a record number of bankruptcies at the end of the 1980s.

Shipping and tourism are the main industries. Greece is visited by 8 million tourists each year, and foreign businesses have invested heavily in the Greek tourist industry. It is perhaps surprising that a nation which trades with the rest of the world and is host to so many foreign visitors still focuses around the family and village life.

The Ministry of Labour controls the pay structure. Industrial relations lack a formal structure and are confrontational, with a strong political element. Companies use a combination of bonuses and other fringe benefits to motivate and retain their staff. Many Greeks have two jobs, one of which may be their own business.

There are two basic business organisation types in Greece. The AE (*Anonymi Eteria*) is a private company, similar to the French SA, while the EPE (*Eterio Periorismenis Efthinis*) is a public company. An AE board must have at least three directors, elected by the shareholders. The chief executive of an AE is usually designated 'general manager' while in an EPE he or she is the 'managing director', although a business may have both.

An independent and entrepreneurial attitude is common amongst Greeks, and this is seen in their ingenuity in trying to receive money from government bodies rather than paying for something themselves. It is also demonstrated by employees who give the impression that the organisation exists solely for the benefit of the individuals in it. Communication and co-operation between parts of a business are often more a feature of personal relationships than the business organisation structure.

As in many countries, there is a trend towards 'American-style' management with new techniques and attitudes. The banks are keen to promote management discipline, implemented often through tighter financial control. They also favour a longer timescale in business planning, whereas, traditionally, businesses tended to be opportunistic and reactive. Business meetings are usually informal, without agenda or minutes and with participation often in the form of strongly put opinions. Face-to-face meetings are preferred to telephone conversations.

Loyalty and trust are very important, and promotion will often be based on this rather than qualifications, or even expertise. Personal influence, political affiliation, and family associations are important in career development. Women are well represented in the professions, politics and business management, although the 'career woman' is still treated with suspicion.

ACTIVITY 6.5

To what extent do you think 'American-style management' with its associated techniques and attitudes can succeed in a business environment in which traditional values and family ties are important?

Ireland

The Irish have a reputation for friendliness and openness, but this in no way detracts from their business acumen. Like most countries in which there are large rural areas and relatively few large towns, there is strong community spirit and people tend to have a passionate interest in politics, religion and sport.

By law, all companies must have at least two directors and a company secretary. There is no legislation covering employee participation in decision-making or the disclosure of company information to employees.

Italy

The distinction between the north and south of Italy is reflected in business methods. The industrial north tends to be more formal, while businesses in the south operate in a more relaxed manner. However, throughout Italy there is a clear difference from the more precise and punctual approach to business adopted in northern Europe. Government departments are notably slow and bureaucratic so that persistence and patience are essential.

Italians tend to pay particular attention to their personal appearance and the appearance of their office. Family life is especially importance to Italians and the extended family is a means of business introductions and communication, which has much more significance than it would in the UK.

The two principal types of company are the SpA (*Societa per Azioni*) or public company and the Srl (*Societa a responsabilita limitata*) which is a private company. There is no minimum number for the Board of Directors, and directors do not need to be Italian citizens. A company must have a Board of Statutory Auditors, called the Sindaci, numbering three to five people. These people must not be directors, employees or close relatives of directors. The auditors are required to check the financial standing of the company (quarterly), and examine and approve the annual balance sheet and valuation of the company's assets. There is no legal requirement for a company to have works councils or to include employee representatives on the Board of Directors. However, a works committee is usually established and receives information on the company's financial situation, and sales, production and employment data.

Luxembourg

Luxembourg is quite literally at the cross-roads of Europe. As such its business practices have developed in response to the need for international trade. But because of its small size and population (367,000) Luxembourgers are sensitive about, and jealously guard, their separate identity. Three languages are used – Luxembourgish, French and German. Germany has had the strongest influence on its business practice, but the country is culturally and linguistically closer to France. There is also a long-established association with Belgium, derived from a customs-free arrangement made in 1921.

Luxembourg is recognised as a major European centre of banking and investment fund management. Its prominence arises from its 'realistic' approach to taxation of investment. Every new commercial and industrial enterprise must obtain a government licence to trade. This will be granted only if the person responsible produces evidence of good conduct and solvency and has appropriate qualifications or experience.

There are two types of company. The private company, denoted by the letters SARL (*Société à Responsabilité Limitée*), and the public company, denoted by SA (*Société Anonyme*), are both governed by the same legal framework. However, SAs must have a larger capitalisation and permit wider ownership of shares. The Board of Directors must comprise at least three people. Any SA employing more than 15 people must have employee delegates who meet at least six times each year. Three of these meetings must be with management. Employee delegates have special employment protection rights. Any SA employing more than 150 people must, by law, establish a works council composed of an equal number of employer and employee representatives. The works council participates in decision-making on welfare, health and safety, employee selection, appraisal, etc. It has the right to be informed and consulted on working decisions and significant financial matters. Any SA employing more than 1000 people must have one-third of its directors appointed by employees.

Netherlands

Imports and exports account for 60 per cent of the GNP. The Netherlands is the world's largest exporter of poultry, dairy products, house plants and flowers. In turn, they import large quantities of fertiliser and feed-stuffs to support their agriculture industry.

The Dutch own half the trucks that transport goods around Europe. They have a history of shipping, trading and colonisation. The country had no natural resources until natural gas was discovered. As you would expect in a trading nation, the banks have a strong influence on the business world.

The economy is closely linked with Germany's because, being at the mouth of the Rhine, the Netherlands provides the port by which a large amount of Germany's exports leave and imports arrive. From the Netherlands is it possible to reach all of Europe's main economic centres within one day's surface travel.

The best-known Dutch companies are the multinationals Philips, Unilever and Royal Dutch Shell. These three, together with DSM, which mines and processes brown coal, and Akzo, employ 25 per cent of the labour force. However, there are very many small and medium-sized privately owned companies. In the past the state was involved in industry by large holdings in Fokker and DAF but has recently taken a policy of privatisation. Foreign investment in the Netherlands is assisted by government incentives.

The Netherlands has a comprehensive social welfare system, but this places a great strain on the economy because of the high level of public spending it involves. As a result personal and corporate tax levels are high. This results in a high degree of tax avoidance and a black economy, particularly in the building trade. There is a high national minimum wage, increasing entry of women into the labour market, and sluggish investment in industry. Although there is high unemployment, there are many vacancies in the lower-paid jobs sector.

Employers are represented by the Protestant–Catholic NCW and the non-denominational VNO. Employers work closely together. There are three main Union groups, representing about 40 per cent of the total workforce; the Protestant CNV, the Catholic NKV and the Liberal NW. Employers and unions meet at a Joint Industrial Labour Council. Both are also represented on the Social and Economic Council along with government representatives and independent consultants.

There has been a move away from central negotiation of wage rates towards more local deals. Industrial disputes and strikes are more common than a few years ago, but still relatively rare because industrial relations are mainly based on negotiation rather than confrontation. Companies that employ more than 35 people must set up a works council (the *Ondernemingsrad*), which receives financial information from the company and is consulted on investment and personnel matters.

The two most common types of company are: NV (*Naamloze Vennootshapp*), which is a public limited company, and BV (*Beslote Vennootshapp*), which is a private limited company. Both have a management board led by a managing director. A large company – defined by the amount of capital and employees (i.e. over 100 people) – must have a supervisory board of at least three people.

The management board, the works council and the shareholders nominate candidates for the supervisory board (*Commissarissen*). The members of the supervisory board cannot be employed by the company. They approve company policy, appoint the management board and finalise the annual accounts. The supervisory board has many of the powers that shareholders have in British and North American companies. For example, decisions on mergers lie with the supervisory board, not the shareholders.

Dutch companies tend to have clear procedures, which are respected and adhered to. Relationships between all levels is open and tolerant. There is a preference for spoken rather than written communication. Business meetings are held frequently and follow an agenda despite an informality of manner. Everyone is expected to make clear, informed contributions with the aim of achieving a consensus. The importance of making a profit is well understood, even in the lower levels of the organisation. Business plans tend to be cautious, favouring step-by-step development.

The Dutch take a long-term view on matters, including their own careers. Education and qualifications are important factors in promotion. Management tends to be 'home grown' rather than 'bought in'. The sense of company loyalty is reinforced by pension structures. Pay agreements are highly standardised so that there is little financial incentive to move jobs. Individual performance-related pay is against the collective ethos. Most senior executives have been educated at the Universities of Delft (engineering), Rotterdam (economics) or Leiden (law and the humanities). There is an aristocracy, which is seen most clearly in the appointments in banks and the diplomatic service. There are apprenticeship schemes for manual workers similar to the German model, with further on-the-job training.

Even in 1990 there were few women in managerial roles. Women only began to come into the labour market in the 1970s, and now account for about 30 per cent of the workforce. Married women still tend to give up work for good when they have children.

Portugal

Like the Dutch, the Portuguese have a strong trading tradition. There is a historic rivalry between Spain and Portugal; the consequence of which is that Portugal has stronger ties with other European and non-European countries than with its closest neighbour.

Portugal is the poorest of the EU countries. Recent history is dominated by the 1974 revolution. Business has developed rapidly since then, but power is still mainly in the hands of a very small number of families. The Portuguese are well aware of the advantages to be gained from their low labour costs. As in Greece, women have not yet gained the degree of equality they have in northern Europe.

New businesses must be registered with the commercial and tax divisions of the Ministry of Finance. They must make a commitment to comply with health, security and environmental regulations. Major projects must demonstrate that they have considered its ecological implications.

There are two types of company. The private company is denoted by the initials Lda (*Sociedades por Quotas de Responsabilidade Limitada*) and the public company denoted by SA (*Sociedade Anonima de Responsabilidade Limitada*). Long-established companies are usually managed by a board of directors and a board of auditors. More recent companies generally have a directorate comprising three or five people, a general council comprising no more than 15 people, and a statutory auditor who must be a shareholder. The law requires that workers' committees, comprising 3 to 11 members according to the size of the company, must be established. They must receive financial and other information, but do not participate in decision-making.

Spain

Spain underwent two vital changes as it prepared to join the EU. First, it reduced its preoccupation with its old colonies and Africa and focused instead on Europe, resulting in business activities having a higher profile. Second, it threw off its legacy of Francoism and began to take a greater interest in democratic politics. Since the first referendum in 1976 there have been over 40 polls, but there has been a remarkable stability and continuity in government, with the extreme left and extreme right having only a fringe influence. There is still, however, a wide diversity of regional interests – notably the Basques, Catalans and Galicians, with their own languages and a strong pressure for separatism.

The result is a suspicion, even hostility, towards central government and officialdom.

The government in fact has a strong influence on industry, directly and through the state holding company *Instituto Nacional de Industria* (INI). The state airline, Iberia, and three traditional industries – iron and steel, shipbuilding and textiles – are all effectively government-run.

In general, private business is dominated by family-run and foreign-owned organisations. These foreign companies are the principal source of technological, financial and management expertise. The stock exchange's influence is recent; previously the banks were the sole source of finance for the private sector. The accounting profession is in the process of forming a body to define and regulate standards. Company accounts are far less comprehensive and consistent than they would have to be in the UK.

There are two types of company, the SA (*Sociedad Anonima*) and the SRL (*Sociedad de Responsabilidad Limitada*). A minimum of three shareholders is needed to form an SA, and there are no limits on the capitalisation. An SRL cannot have more that 50 shareholders and its capitalisation must not exceed 50 million pesetas. While an SRL may have one or more directors and does not need to have auditors unless it is listed on the stock exchange or is a bank, an SA may have either a single director or a board of at least three directors.

Traditional Spanish companies have a clear chain of command, and are separated into departments to assist in management control, rather than to assist specialisation. Many older companies are bureaucratic and authoritarian in their management. Data collection to assist with decision-making is not highly regarded and systematic procedures are seen as a fall-back rather than something to be regularly used. Improvisation in the face of crisis and emergency is admired.

Very few of the current decision-making generation speak any language other than their own so any sales literature promoting UK products must be in Spanish.

The rapid growth in economic activity has resulted in a serious shortage of skilled managers. A number of business schools are being set up, some of them privately run, and many managers are trained abroad, notably in France. Women have not made significant progress in reaching senior management positions yet. Until the current period of growth in economic activity, job security was an important consideration. People were still reluctant to move to another location for promotion because the family remains an important social aspect of Spanish life, and a secure base. However, there is now a shortage of skills, particularly in cities like Madrid and Barcelona, and this means that moving from job to job is possible, providing a faster promotion route than remaining in one company. Regional accents are still an impediment to progression in some career areas, where background is still the most significant factor.

ACTIVITY 6.7

1 If you were taking up a post as a junior manager with a small to medium-sized company in Spain, what differences would you expect to find from the junior manager's role in the UK?

2 How would you adapt to the situation?

SUMMARY

1 Other European countries have more than one type of business structure, just as in the UK, where there is a private limited company and a plc. Associated with each are rules about such things as capitalisation and composition of the board of directors and management.

2 Countries such as Germany and the Netherlands have legislation that gives employees greater representation in company policy-making than in the UK.

3 Each country has its own customs regarding relationships between managers and subordinates and among colleagues. Differences are lessening, however, as an 'international' business culture develops, particularly among younger managers.

Assignment 6

BACKGROUND

Assume the UK-based organisation for which you work has agreed to work closely with a similar-sized company in another EU country (you may decide which). The aim is to benefit from economies of scale in the development, marketing and production of a new product

You are seconded to the other company for a year to ensure that liaison between the companies is trouble-free.

ACTIVITY

1 List the differences you would expect to find in: (a) management structure and style; b) decision-making; (c) technology and working practices; (d) problem-solving methods; and (e) employee motivation and attitudes.

2 How could these differences affect co-operation between the two businesses?

3 What actions could you take (or recommend) to anticipate and avoid, or overcome, any problems?

7 Who's who in Europe

1 To appreciate the limitations of judging the nature of a country's business activities on the basis of a survey of just its largest companies.

2 To describe current trends, and identify the main organisations, in the retail sector.

3 To outline the characteristics of the financial sector, including banks, insurance companies and finance houses.

4 To investigate the extent to which service industries are changing as a result of the SEM.

5 To analyse EU manufacturing industry, identifying the sectors that are in decline and those that are growing, and considering their regional distribution.

6 To appreciate the importance of small to medium-sized enterprises, as suppliers and support services for large organisations, and for their potential to grow and take on new employees.

Introduction

Just as it was difficult to give a truly representative explanation of a country's business culture because of the tremendous variations, so it is difficult to portray a true picture of a country's industry by describing its largest companies. It is possible, however, to understand the broad differences between the countries of the EU, and to appreciate the nature of the small companies that supply the main organisations and provide complementary and supporting services.

Retail

There is a noticeable convergence of consumer demand throughout the EU. Branding, promotion, and pricing increasingly cross frontiers. The English–American popular culture – coke, jeans, and so forth – is the major influence, and is not confined to Europe.

Another important factor is the quality of distribution and transport networks. Even perishable items such as fresh fruit and vegetables can be available throughout the EU because they can be transported from Spain, for example, and be on sale in shops in northern Europe, ready washed, sorted and packaged, in 48–72 hours.

Throughout Europe there is a decline in the proportion of income spent on food and other 'essentials'. However, the trend is most noticeable in the affluent northern countries of the EU than in 'poorer' regions – Greece, Portugal, southern Italy. There is a limit to the amount that people will spend on essential items and the data indicates saturation in these markets. People's additional disposable income is either saved or spent on items in the 'luxury' category – holidays, leisure, cars, travel – in increased proportion. This means that businesses in the 'essentials' sector must concentrate on increasing their market share.

Co-operatives, supermarkets, and hypermarkets usually buy direct from the manufacturer. Many are so large that they can put pressure on manufacturers to reduce prices. This replaces the traditional purchasing chain of manufacturer–wholesaler–retailer. Cash-and-carry warehouses, such as SHV in the Netherlands, offer a wholesale service to small retailers.

Distribution, discussed in Chapter 12, is a key factor in profitability and convergence of demand. Many of the large distribution organisations have established European warehouses, especially in Belgium, from which there is easy access to the big population centres.

There are now uniform product coding systems and machine-readable marking (bar codes) of individual items and packs for most products. This means that prices are displayed on the shelf rather than on the product. As well as reducing labour costs, this facilitates price changes.

Point-of-sale terminals which read the bar code on each product allow the retailer to give the customer a bill which includes the product description as well as the price. They also allow the collection of data on sales, which includes when as well as what is being sold. The data allows just-in-time techniques of stock replenishment, cutting-down on the amount of stock that needs to be held in individual shops and eliminating the need for stock storage space in these shops, which are often located in areas where rents are high.

Electronic payment systems – credit cards and debit cards – are used extensively throughout Europe. The most common are Visa and Mastercard, but there are a number of others, and many stores have their own account cards (e.g. Marks & Spencer and Debenhams in the UK).

There is a trend towards consumers wanting to do one-stop shopping – buying all that they want in one place. Buying patterns are also changing, with evening and weekend shopping becoming more common. Because an increasing proportion of consumers have their own cars and they do not, therefore, have problems of carrying their purchases, it is feasible for them to shop once per week or even once per month.

Increasing use of cars to get to and from shops has resulted in shopping centres being established on the outskirts of towns. These invariably have large car-parks and easy road access.

Denmark and Luxembourg have the highest proportion of hypermarkets and supermarkets – 57 per cent and 56 per cent of all retail outlets respectively. Italy has most retail outlets (over 1 million), but they are mainly small; in 1990, hypermarkets and supermarkets represented only 10 per cent of these outlets. By contrast, in France, with a similar population, 46 per cent of the 660,000 retail outlets were hypermarkets or supermarkets. The UK and Netherlands have a lower proportion of hypermarkets but more supermarkets, giving a similar overall percentage of about 43 to 45 per cent.

Large supermarket groups include Danske Supermarked in Denmark; Leclerc, Intermarche, Carrefour, Auchan, System-U, Cora, and Euromarche in France; Tengelmann, Aldi, Asko in Germany; Dunnes, Quinnsworth and Superquinn in Ireland; Esselunge in Italy; Groupe Cactus in Luxembourg; Vendex and Ahold in Netherlands; Sonae, Inovação, Pão de Açucar and Pingo Doce in Portugal; Pryca (owned by Carrefour) and Continente (owned by the French Promodes group) in Spain; and J Sainsbury, Tesco, Marks & Spencer, Argyll group, Asda group, and Isosceles in the UK.

Originally hypermarkets and supermarkets sold mainly food, but increasingly they have diversified into non-food products, DIY and motor spares, electrical products, music and video, furniture, and so on. Another trend is towards specialist superstores. Typically a superstore will sell, for example, DIY and garden products, or electrical and electronic goods, or carpets.

Multiples and department stores are most common in Denmark, France, Germany, Ireland and the UK. In many of these stores products are more clearly separated than in supermarkets, and often the store is on several floors. There is also a trend towards 'shops within a shop' in some sectors – specific brands sold from distinct counters, in many cases by staff employed by the product's distributor/manufacturer. In the UK this began with cosmetics but it is spreading to other product types.

Some store groups concentrate in specific product groups – Dorothy Perkins in the UK for example. Others have a wider range but have an image that associates them with a particular sector, W H Smith and Boots for example. Groups like Kingfisher operates several chains of stores each with its own product type. Many stores have their own brand, but sell 'branded' goods as well. By contrast, some stores, such as Marks & Spencer in the UK, sell only products with their own distinctive brand name.

Major multiples and department stores include GIB, Delhaize de Lion, Louis Delhaize, Colruyt and Dutch-owned Vendex in Belgium; Magasin du Nord in Denmark, Monoprix and Au Printemps in France, Karstadt/Neckermann and Metro Kaufhof in Germany, Roches in Ireland; La Rinascente and Standa in Italy; El Corte Ingles in Spain; and Marks & Spencer, Sears and John Lewis in the UK.

Co-operative movements are generally struggling to hold their market share throughout the EU although in some countries they still have considerable influence. In Denmark, for example, FDB is the largest distribution chain and the second largest company, with sales of over 31 billion kroner and employing nearly 13,000 people. Other major co-operatives are Co-op AG in Germany; Co-op Italia (sales of 16,725 billion lire) and Conad in Italy, and GRULA (sales of 14 billion escudos) in Portugal.

Independent retailers continue to survive alongside the large supermarket and store groups, to a large extent by participation in buying groups and joint promotions. Large buying groups are Promodes and Casino in France; Rewe and Edeka in Germany. The German group Spar Handels is classified as a 'voluntary group', as are Vege, Despar and A & O Selex in Italy, Ifa Espaniola and Sogeco in Spain. In the UK Spar and VG are familiar names.

Another feature of retailing, not confined to Europe, is franchise operations. In France there are over 460 franchises with a total of more than 23,000 outlets. The UK and Germany also have a large number of franchise operations.

Mail order selling is holding its own, although the traditional method of selling through agents and weekly payments is on the decline. Telephone ordering, supported by computerised systems, and the widespread use of credit cards is a feature of modern mail order trading. In some highly competitive sectors such as personal computers, and other electronic and photographic equipment, mail order companies with low overheads have made it difficult for other methods of retailing to remain profitable. Among the largest European mail order organisations are Otto Versand and Quelle in Germany.

ACTIVITY 7.2

Conduct a survey in local retail outlets. Establish the proportions of goods that originate in: (a) the UK; (b) the EU; and (c) elsewhere.

Banks, insurance and finance

The banks have a long history of heavy regulation. Banks usually 'borrow short and lend long'. This potentially dangerous situation is protected by customer confidence, and by maintaining adequate liquidity and reserves. Governments usually intervene to impose minimum limits on levels of liquidity and reserves.

Another reason for government intervention is the impact that bank lending can have on industry, and hence on the economy. There is also a fear that excessive concentration of finance into too few financial institutions will give them an unacceptable level of political power.

In France, Italy, Greece and Portugal banks are predominantly publicly owned. Except in the UK, Belgium and Luxembourg there is protection against foreign competition. Important differences can also be seen in the range of activities undertaken by the banks. The traditional role has excluded any direct involvement in the stock exchange in some countries, but such restrictions do not apply in Germany, France, Italy, Netherlands and the UK.

The bulk of retail banking is still confined within national boundaries and controlled by national banks in conditions of very imperfect competition. In the commercial sector, however, there is increasing internationalisation of financial markets, increased capital mobility, and a rapid growth in money, bond and equity markets.

The size of the financial sector in the UK and Luxembourg, expressed as a percentage of the GDP, is twice that of the EU as a whole.

Measured in terms of capitalisation, major EU banks include: Deutsche Bank (Germany), Barclays (UK), Dresdner Bank (Germany), National Westminster (UK), Banco Bilbao Vizcaya (Spain), Lloyds (UK), Mediobanca (Italy), Banco de Santander (Spain), Abbey National (UK) and Banco Central (Spain). The inclusion of the Abbey National in this list of large financial institutions is interesting since it is only comparatively recently that UK building societies have been permitted to undertake the full range of banking activities, rather than having a status that essentially confined them to savings and mortgage lending.

Examination of Belgium's top 20 companies reveals four banks (the largest being Banque General), two insurance companies (Royale Belge and AG Group) and the finance company Almanij. Denmark has two banks, Unidanmark A/S and Danske Banke, among its three largest companies, and two insurance companies, Hafnia A/S and PFA in the top 20. Italy has four insurance companies in its top ten companies, including Generali at number one with a capitalisation some 30 per cent larger than the second largest company, Fiat. Italy's fourth largest company is Mediobanca, a finance house. Banks figure prominently in the list of the biggest Luxembourg companies, and include Banque Internationale, Banque Générale, Caisse d'Epargne de L'État and Kredietbank. In the UK, the two largest banks are Barclays and National Westminster. The Prudential is the largest insurance company.

As mentioned in the discussion of the retail sector, the last ten years has seen a massive growth in the use of debit and credit cards. All the large banks provide these services, either independently or, more usually, through the best known cards, which are Visa and Mastercard.

Progress in electronic methods of processing credit transactions has varied from country to country. France, for example, was three/four years ahead of the UK in the widespread implementation of 'swipe' machines and POS-printed vouchers in petrol stations to replace hand-written vouchers. The automatic checking of credit is now a feature of many retail outlets. Behind this apparently simple process is a sophisticated 'hidden' system of access to the individual's credit data at his or her bank.

ACTIVITY 7.3

Contact an insurance company (not an insurance agent or broker) and establish: (a) the extent of its transnational operations in the EU; and (b) how it is organised to handle transnational trade.

Service sector

This sector has seen considerable growth in turnover and employment in recent years. Part of this growth reflects growing affluence and increase in leisure time. To a large extent it has happened independently of moves towards the Single European Market. Indeed, current trends are towards worldwide holidays, rather than leisure breaks in other EU countries.

The impact on organisations like Grand Metropolitan and Ladbroke has been to provide a volume market which is highly competitive and price sensitive. Hotels and whole holiday complexes have been built in many parts of the EU. While these provide income and employment in many regions that were previously amongst the poorest in the EU, they do pose problems of pollution and other threats to the environment. Also, the EU's major airlines have been faced with the choice of whether or not to supplement scheduled services with holiday flights, to compete with charter companies, many of which are owned by the tour operators.

Tourists offer a massive 'duty free' market, the size of which may be judged by the fact that Duty Free Shops SA is Greece's largest commercial company. So large is this market that the EU has established transitionary arrangements to cushion the effect of VAT and duty changes as part of implementing the SEM.

Travel, tourism and leisure have provided a huge market for manufacturing industry and for other service industries. There is a knock-on effect for new buildings, office equipment and computers, and a massive increase in demand for leisure and sports clothing, equipment, and so on. Marketing and media organisations also benefit from the increase in leisure time.

The SEM has reduced barriers in two areas that are of special relevance to the service sector. First, it has initiated the concept of recognition for qualifications between member states. Initially this recognition applied to certain professions but gradually it is extending to other occupations and trades. Second, it has introduced the right of an individual to take employment, or be self-employed, in another member state. This right of establishment was intended to facilitate labour mobility.

The UK is one of the world's leading nations in the development of computer systems. There are a few large companies, such as Scicon, Logica, and CAP, but the industry is dominated by small companies, many of them employing less than 20 people. The package software industry (e.g. word processors, spreadsheets, data bases, desk-top publishing, computer-aided design) is dominated by US-based companies. There is, however, a large market for training and implementation of these packages.

Other parts of the service sector that are dominated by small companies are management consultancy, accounting and law. Management consultancy is fairly unregulated and there is considerable transnational activity. The larger consultancies, many of them US based, tend to be highly internationalised. In the areas of accountancy and law there is considerable complexity in local legislation and practices, and an apparent reluctance to make changes. A substantial market therefore exists for organisations to provide advice on transnational business activity. However, the practice of 'non-admittance' to courts in the UK, France, Belgium, and the Netherlands maintains a barrier to free movement for the purpose of legal representation. The main areas of activity for accountants are in auditing, taxation, insolvency, and trustee and administration work.

Marketing and public relations organisations were amongst the first to tackle the issue of transnational affiliation. The European Commission, as part of the implementation of the SEM, has gathered and published a considerable amount of data that is useful for marketing and promotion. There are more than 15 European advertising agencies operating in the EU that have turnovers of over 100 million ECU. These include Eurocom, Y & R, Publicis-FCB, Saatchi, and O & M.

Media services, including, for example, writing, photography, graphic design, and film and TV production, are highly fragmented and largely unregulated. Apart from state-owned TV and radio, there are private sector operators throughout the EU. There are several book, magazine and newspaper publishers which operate across the EU, but there is a much larger number of local publishers.

In all the EU countries the post and telecommunications utilities – some state-owned, the rest private – are amongst the largest organisations in those countries.

Industry

General

Between 1980 and 1990 European industry shed over 4 million jobs, about 13 per cent of the workforce. Reductions were greatest in traditional industries such as heavy metals (34 per cent), textiles (28 per cent), chemicals (20 per cent), vehicle manufacture (14 per cent) oil refining (12 per cent), engineering (9 per cent), and electrical engineering (9 per cent). Nevertheless European industry is a world leader in some sectors: the EU produces over 30 per cent of the world's private cars (10 million per year), 20 per cent of world steel, 20 per cent of synthetic textiles and 10 per cent of other textiles, and 15 per cent of cement.

Aerospace

France, Germany and the UK all have major aerospace sectors.

In France, the main companies are Thompson and Aerospatiale (which makes the famous Exocet missile). Matra is also a missile manufacturer, and Dassault makes fighter aircraft.

In Germany the principal company is Fokker and in the UK British Aerospace is the major player.

There is a joint project to build a European fighter aircraft (the EFA). France is undertaking 40 per cent of this project, which includes the development and manufacture of its engines. The other participants are Germany, Spain and the UK. The main competitors to the EFA are produced by US companies – Boeing and McDonnell Douglas.

Agriculture and food

Denmark has extensive natural resources of oil, fish, and land for agriculture. The connection with agriculture is reflected in the activities of some of Denmark's largest companies – Danisco (sugar), MD Foods Amba (dairy products), Carlsberg (drinks), and Korn & Foderstof Kompagniet (animal feeds).

Ireland's industry is dominated by companies in the agriculture and food sectors – An Bord Bainne Co-op (dairy-produce export), Goodman International (meat processing and export), Guinness (brewing), Kerry Group (food processing), Fyffes (fruit and vegetables), Avonmore Foods (dairy products), Waterford Foods (food products), United Food Corporation (meat processing and export), and Dairygold (dairy products).

Netherlands too has major agricultural industries – dairy farming and horticulture. The conglomerate Unilever is based in the Netherlands, and amongst its very wide range of activities are food products and detergents. Other well-known names in the food and beverages sector are Sara-Lee and Heineken.

Brewing and food are strongly represented industries in the UK. Guinness, Bass and Allied-Lyons are the biggest in this sector.

Chemicals and pharmaceuticals

The big French chemical companies – Rhône-Poulenc, Atochem (subsidiary of Elf) and CDF Chimie – are stated-owned. France is a net exporter of chemical products, especially agrichemicals, petrochemicals, and plastics. Biotechnology is a growing industry.

The German chemicals industry has recently undergone a rationalisation process. It is dominated by BASF, Hoechst and Bayer. There are currently some 600,000 people employed in this sector. There is intense research and development into new products, and a strong drive to increase exports.

The UK has a strong phamaceutical industry, headed by Glaxo, Smithkline-Beecham, and Wellcome.

Electricity, water, gas and oil

Some of Belgium's largest companies are involved in electricity and water supply, including Tractebel, Intercom, EBES and Electrafina.

The Netherlands is the base for very extensive North Sea oil and gas operations, and it is the world's fourth largest producer of natural gas. Petrochemical and chemical companies include Shell, AKZO, BP, DSM, Exxon Netherland, DOW Benelux.

Petrochemicals is also a major industry in France with key companies like Elf, Total and Esso.

Among Spain's largest companies are those producing and supplying electricity, including Hidroelectrica Española, Iberduero, Union Electrica Fenosa. Petroleum companies include Repsol Petroleo (Spain's largest company), CEPSA, and Petronor.

Among the other very large UK-based companies operating in the energy sector are BP, Shell Transport and Trading, and British Gas.

Petrochemical companies, such as Shell, Mobil, and BP, have a sizeable presence in Portugal.

Electrical products, electronics and computing

Like the UK, France has a growing computer hardware and software industry. US-owned IBM is the dominant company (as it is in most countries), and there are other major US-owned companies operating in France, including Burroughs, Digital, and Hewlett Packard. Bull is the principal French computer company.

Philips, Netherland's third largest company, is a strong force in the world's electrical industry. It has a wide range of products – industrial equipment, instruments, medical equipment, telecommunications, computers, television, video recorders, domestic appliances, and so on.

The major German electrical companies are Bosch and Siemens. Siemens has entered into a co-operation agreement with Philips of the Netherlands to manufacture semiconductors, and has several partners in the defence industry. German involvement in computer-related technology is mainly in the process control, medical systems and telecommunications sectors.

Italy's largest electronics company, Olivetti, has 21 factories in Italy and abroad, manufacturing office equipment and computers.

Mining, shipbuilding and engineering

Within the EU, quotas govern volumes of basic steel-making, because of over-capacity, and plants are generally working below full production levels.

In France, some traditional industries, such as coal mining, steel, shipbuilding, and textiles have declined. There is now only one shipbuilding yard, in St Nazaire. The two state-owned companies, Usinor and Sacilor, have merged. However, other traditional industries such as heavy engineering, and the manufacture of railway equipment have maintained their market share.

Germany's steel industry, led by Thyssen, is the third largest in the world, behind the USA and Japan. Nevertheless, its workforce was halved between 1975 and 1990 to 150,000 despite a temporary boom in steel demand in the mid-1980s. The strong Deutschmark makes steel imports cheap, and they now account for 40 per cent of the German market. Many German companies have switched to special and coated steels where they can be more competitive. General engineering in Germany suffers from competition with Japan, but diversification, especially among small to medium-sized enterprises (SMEs), investment in automation, and good marketing have enabled Germany to hold its own.

The Dutch coal mining and steel-making are suffering similar problems to these industries elsewhere in the EU.

Telecommunications

France's telecommunications industry has concentrated on digital switching equipment, satellite systems, and fibre optics. The Minitel system, similar to

Prestel, has been highly successful and has very many users; this arises partly from the widespread free issue of Minitel equipment to telephone subscribers in place of telephone directories.

The UK's largest company, in 1990, was BT. It has progressed from being the provider of telephone services within the UK to a significant force in the world's telecommunications industry. Cable and Wireless is another big company operating from the UK in this sector.

Vehicle manufacture

As elsewhere in Europe (and the USA), French car manufacturers are under threat from the Japanese. Peugeot and Citroen/Chrysler have merged. Renault has a stake in American Motors. Peugeot/Citroen and Renault each have 30 per cent of the market. Ford, Fiat, Audi/BMW each have about 10 per cent.

Despite the fact that Germany is famous for 'quality' cars – BMW, Porsche, and Daimler-Benz (of which over 50 per cent are exported) – and has a strong popular car manufacturer (Volkswagon), Germany imports nearly 30 per cent of the vehicles sold in the country, half of them from Japan. Japanese-owned production within Germany (and other EU countries) is increasing, so that technically they are German cars despite having names like Toyota and Honda.

Fiat, Europe's leading and most profitable car-maker, and Italy's second largest company, is based in Turin. As well as cars, Fiat manufactures tractors, civil engineering plant, railway rolling stock, and machine tools and is also involved in civil engineering, energy and other utilities. It has joint ventures with Ford/Iveco to manufacture trucks, with Lucus (UK) and Matra (France) to produce components, with GM (USA) to produce manufacturing systems and with Rolls Royce (UK) and Pratt & Whitney (USA) to develop and manufacture aero engines. It also has a share in Westland Helicopters.

The Netherlands is home to one of the world's largest truck manufacturers – DAF.

Several automotive companies, including Renault, GM and Ford, have established production plants in Portugal.

A number of automotive companies operate in Spain. Some of them are Spanish owned, some are joint ventures, and some are subsidiaries of other EU companies. They include Fasa Renault, SEAT, GM España, Citroen-Hispaña and Peugeot-Talbot España.

Transport and distribution

Belgium is ideally placed as a distribution point for the population centres and industries of northern Europe, with good road and rail communications. Wiggins Teape (south of Brussels) and Ford (Antwerp) are amongst organisations to establish distribution centres in Belgium.

Rotterdam, the Netherlands' largest port, is an important route for imports into Europe and exports out of Europe.

Specialist industries

Denmark is home to a number of specialist industries including Lego (toys), Bang & Olufsen (hi-fi), Grundfos (pumps), Danfoss (control equipment), and Novo (medicines and drugs).

Luxembourg is the base for several specialist processing industries such as Villeroy et Boch (porcelain) and ELTH (thermostats).

State ownership and privatisation

As in the UK, there has been a trend towards privatisation of state-owned organisations in several EU countries. Italy and Spain are the countries with the largest amount of state ownership.

The French government has a big role in industry, but by methods other than ownership. It is involved through planning, taxation, investment, and the interchange of government and industry personnel.

There is a big state-run sector in Italy. The principal state-owned corporation is Instituto per la Ricostruzione Industriale (IRI), which was established by Mussolini in 1933. IRI ranks 14 in the world on turnover and is the third largest organisation outside the USA. It began as a rescue service to ailing companies and eventually grew to encompass 1000 companies, including Europe's largest steel company, Italy's TV network, the state airline, and car maker Alfa Romeo. At its peak it employed over 500,000 people. A process of privatisation and joint state–private ownership was started in 1981 but IRI still owns several large banks, the airline Alitalia, Autostrade (highways), Italtel (switching systems) and big companies in steel-making, engineering, shipbuilding, aerospace and electronics. Alfa Romeo was sold to Fiat. IRI retains a high-tech division which is involved in telecommunications, microelectronics and robotics. IRI's semiconductor company (ERS) is currently co-operating with Thompson (France) on a new computer memory chip.

Other state-run organisations in Italy include ENI – an organisation involved in petroleum fuels with shares in 300 companies and employing 100,000 people – and EFIM, a state-run holding-company involved in light engineering which has shares in 140 companies and employs 60,000 people. Italy's state-owned corporations have extensive overseas interests, including involvement in over 100 businesses.

Spain's state holding company INI has major investments in Iberia (the state airline), Aviaco (the domestic airline), Seat (cars), ENASA (automation), ENDESA (energy), shipping, oil and gas exploration, steel and aluminium production, mineral extraction, fertiliser manufacture, food, and the defence industry.

Another Spanish state-owned company – INH – specialises in oil, gas, petroleum and petro-chemical production.

ACTIVITY 7.5

1 Choose one EU-based multinational company and obtain details of its international operations (e.g. from its annual report).

2 How widespread are its activities in the EU?

3 Is there a significant difference between its level of activity within the EU and its level of activity elsewhere?

Small to medium-sized enterprises (SMEs)

The companies named previously in this chapter are the very largest in the EU. As such they make a major contribution to the economy and employ a large number of people.

However, for every large company there are very many small ones. Small companies, by their nature, are flexible and can adapt to new markets and develop new products more quickly. They tend to have the best potential for growth and hence to take on more staff.

Large companies usually employ specialist staff, and are often organised to concentrate expertise into specific departments. Employees in small companies, by contrast, need to have broad skills, and to undertake whatever task needs to be done.

Small companies may supply the big ones with materials or components, or provide support services. At the same time, there will also be small companies that spot gaps in the market unfilled by the big organisations and establish a profitable niche.

The EU, by its policies, encourages large companies to locate manufacturing or distribution depots in regions of deprivation to provide income and employment. It also actively supports the formation, development and expansion of small to medium-sized enterprises (SMEs) because it recognises that these are the 'seed' material of tomorrow's big industry, and potentially will offer more new jobs as they grow than the relatively static conglomerates.

ACTIVITY 7.6

What features of small businesses make them so flexible, and why are they more likely to grow and take on more staff?

1 There is significant convergence of demand for consumer goods, within the EU and worldwide. Good distribution and transport, computerised sales and stock systems, and electronic fund transfer contribute to the very high levels of efficiency in the retail sector.

2 Large organisations have very great buying power. Independents try to match this by forming buying groups. There is an increasing number of franchises in the EU.

3 Banks and other financial institutions are heavily regulated. In some EU countries large banks are state-owned. There is extensive transnational trading in financial markets, and credit cards like Visa and Mastercard are accepted throughout the EU.

4 The legal and accountancy professions have been very slow to modify practices and liberalise their rules, presenting a barrier to full implementation of the SEM. Marketing, computing and management consultants, by contrast, are operating throughout the EU with little restriction. There are relatively few large organisations and very many small ones in this sector.

5 There has been considerable contraction in traditional industries like mining, steel-making and shipbuilding. The EU has strong electronics, electrical, and aeronautics industries. Vehicle manufacturers are in fierce competition with the Japanese, who have opened a number of manufacturing plants in EU countries.

6 Large EU-based petrochemical, chemical, food and brewing companies are truly multinational, with large organisations in many EU countries and elsewhere.

7 Small to medium-sized enterprises have an important part to play in the EU business scene. Their potential for growth and new employment makes them attractive to the European Commission as a way of overcoming regional deprivation. They supply and support the large companies that are more prominent in industrial surveys.

Assignment 7

BACKGROUND

The construction industry has a relatively small number of very large companies and a very large number of small companies and self-employed individuals. There is a great deal of subcontract work. Large companies often employ small companies or individuals to undertake specific jobs. Traditionally, the industry has a very mobile workforce. People are generally prepared to move to where there is work.

The industry is very sensitive to changes in economic conditions. There is usually a lot of building activity in periods of growth and boom, and very little in times of contraction and recession.

ACTIVITIES

1 Use a directory of European industry to identify the largest construction company in each EU country that is involved in building business premises (factories, offices, etc). For each company, determine its turnover (and convert to ECU for comparison purposes) and the number of employees.

2 Use a copy of Yellow Pages to determine how many construction companies are based in your locality. Obtain the names of five locally-based small construction companies and acquire data on the nature of their activities, their turnover and number of people they employ.

3 Identify the business sectors most likely to consider investing in new retail outlets, warehouses and distribution networks, factories or offices. Distinguish, where appropriate, between the various EU countries/regions.

4 Evaluate the extent to which the SEM has, or could, facilitate transnational construction activities. These might include:

(a) Removal of barriers to trade – e.g. public sector tendering and preferred supplier policies.

(b) Employment issues – e.g. working conditions, qualifications and training.

(c) Financial – public/private sector investment, EU funding.

(d) Technical standards and regulations.

Part Three
GETTING ESTABLISHED IN EUROPE

8 Going transnational

OBJECTIVES
1 To identify the principal types of business activities outside the domestic market.

2 To understand the nature of, and reasons for, exporting.

3 To describe the stages of internationalisation.

4 To list the criteria for identifying 'close' countries and use a formal technique to compare the attractiveness of export markets.

5 To describe the factors to be considered when choosing an export market entry strategy.

6 To analyse the export activities of a small UK business.

Why go abroad?

There are basically four activities that a business may undertake outside the home country:

1 Sale of goods and services.
2 Purchase of goods and services.
3 Recruitment of staff with skills and experience not available in the home country.
4 Manufacture and/or distribution using facilities outside the home country, because labour and materials are cheaper, transport and communications are better, or because of other factors that make it a better location for these activities than the home country.

By far the most common of these activities is the sale of goods or services – that is, exporting.

Exporting

An organisation that wants to sell its products or services in another country faces a more complex task than when it is selling in its own country. Exporting is more complex than domestic trade for three reasons:

1 The distances between the organisation's headquarters, its base in the target country and the customers in the target country are generally much greater than for home trade, so there are logistics problems. It takes more time for goods and documentation to pass between the locations, and the additional distance makes the channels of communication more susceptible to disruption.
2 The business methods of the target country are likely to be different to those of the home country so that there may be problems of mismatches in documentation, methods of payment, procedures for arranging delivery, differences in quality checking and certification, and so on.
3 The language, culture and fashions of the target country are likely be different from those of the home country, which means that market research carried out at home will not be valid for the target country. Therefore products developed for the home market, and pricing and promotion strategies, may need adaptation for an export market.

Reasons for exporting

If exporting is so much more complex than trading on the home market why do so many businesses undertake it?

Product life cycle

Every product or service has a life cycle. This extends from its birth (when it is invented or discovered) through to its death (when it is finally discontinued). This life cycle may be very short (e.g. a hit record) or very long (e.g. a type of sailing boat). It may be that only one of the product is made during the life cycle. On the other hand there may be millions. Before a product can be sold it has to progress from the conceptual stage (where the inventor outlines his or her ideas), through research and development to a prototype, and then to the point where volume manufacture can be started.

In the early stages it may be necessary to spend a lot of money, to pay for the development staff's time, for special equipment to make and test prototypes, to try out different materials, and so on. There is also a high level of risk because it may emerge that the product is not commercially viable. Market research needs

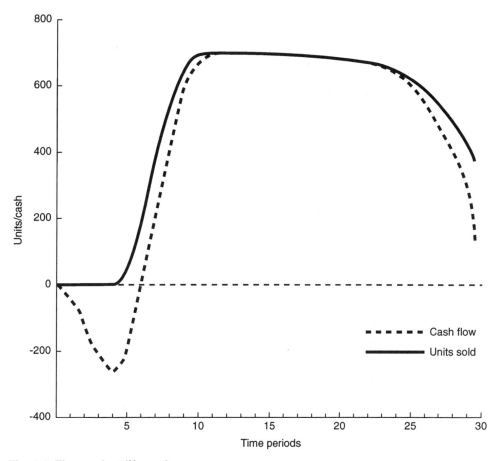

Fig. 8.1 The product life cycle

to be done thoroughly to identify the level of risk and to avoid committing funds to a product that is not likely to sell well. In the later part of the development stage test marketing can be carried out to discover how accurate the market research has been.

At the launch of the product it will probably be necessary to undertake an extensive promotion campaign, with advertising, introductory offers, and so forth. The aim is to establish as big a market as possible in the minimum time. In this initial stage in the product's life there will be no competition, and although it is important to get the price right, the product will not be very price sensitive.

As the product moves towards maturity it will usually be possible to find cheaper ways of manufacturing it. Producing in volume will also offer economies of scale, and thus production costs should fall. However, a successful product will attract competition, and it may be necessary to reduce the price to stay competitive and retain market share.

As the market for the product declines – because fashions or technology have moved on, or because there are alternative or better products – there may still be market opportunities. For example, the main manufacturers may have discontinued the product because they are interested only in high volume production, but a small manufacturer, specialising in 'declining' products, may be able to tap the remaining market, possibly even at a higher price. A market for spare parts may also exist long after the product itself is obsolete.

It is quite likely that a product will be at a different stage in its life cycle in different countries. Launching the product in another country where it is not already available may open up a market that is free of competition, and the development costs will be avoided. It is important to remember, though, that the product may need adaptation for the new market. For example, the product might need a different type of electrical plug, or it might need controls labelled in a different language.

Competition

A successful product attracts competition. However, an expanding market will accommodate additional manufacturers because the newcomers will be able to gain a share of that market while, at the same time, the original companies are able to maintain their sales volume or even continue to increase it. Thus, an expanding overseas market can be attractive to all and encourage a company to export.

In a static or declining market competition can have a very damaging effect on an existing manufacturer. In order to maintain market share it may be necessary to cut the price. In some situations the newcomers will have an advantage. They do not have to make the large investment in research and development, and for them there is not the risk of developing a product and then finding that there is no market for it. Moreover they may also be able to benefit from improvements in technology, producing goods that are cheaper, more reliable, or faster, than those of the original producer. On the other hand, there are situations where the established company has the advantage with a loyal customer base and a well-known brand name.

If competition gets too tough, the choices are to withdraw from the market, or to find new ones. Exporting may thus be a defensive tactic.

Excess capacity utilisation

For a variety of reasons, a company may find that it has the capacity to produce more than it can sell. An overseas market may be an attractive way of utilising the spare capacity, even if the price that can be obtained for the product is less than in the home country, and there are significant distribution costs.

Geographic diversification

A country's economy often experiences periods of boom and periods of recession. Some products are more susceptible to changes in demand as the economic situation changes. For this reason a company may choose to export to one or more countries to spread its risk. It is assuming that the market in one country will remain buoyant when it is depressed in another, and it is certainly true that recession often affects different countries at different times and to a greater or lesser extent.

Potential of population and purchasing power

For some products it is only economic to manufacture in large quantities, for example when the unit value of the product is very small. Or the nature of the production process (e.g. steel, chemicals) may be such that production needs to be undertaken continuously.

In both situations it may be that the home market is not large enough to support the introduction of the product, and a business may look to a wider market to make the investment commercially feasible.

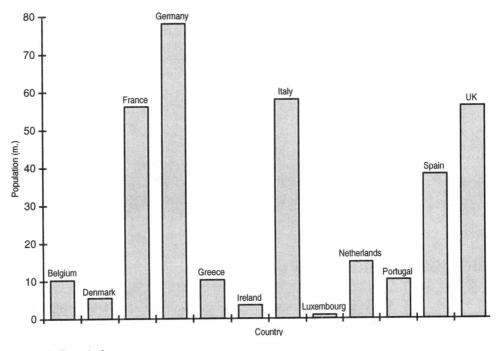

Fig. 8.2 Population
Source: Eurostat, European Commission

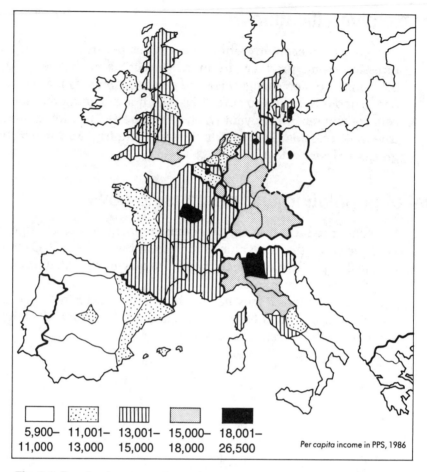

5,900– 11,001– 13,001– 15,000– 18,001–
11,000 13,000 15,000 18,000 26,500

Per capita income in PPS, 1986

Fig. 8.3 Purchasing power by region
Source: Eurostat, European Commission

ACTIVITY 8.1

For each of the following companies, suggest reasons why it might want to be involved in transnational business activities: (a) a wallpaper manufacturer; (b) a courier service; (c) a recruitment agency; and (d) a breeder of show dogs.

Stages in internationalism

Almost all businesses begin on a small scale. At this point they are very familiar with their market and products and need only very basic selling techniques, while distribution is probably straightforward and financial control systems can be quite simple. Most small businesses at the start feel that they are not capable of dealing with the additional risk and complexity of exporting, and will probably refuse an enquiry from a potential customer from overseas.

However, a very attractive enquiry, perhaps coupled with a set-back in their existing market, may prompt them to consider supplying an overseas customer, and subsequently to fulfil unsolicited orders from further customers. This often leads on to the company actively exploring the feasibility of exporting. This is the first stage in exporting for some companies, as they perceive market

> - No interest.
> - Fulfil unsolicited orders.
> - Active exploration – experimental.
> - Active development in 'close' countries.
> - Active development in additional or 'far' countries.
> - Multinational operations.

Fig. 8.4 Stages in internationalisation

market opportunities overseas or react to difficult trading conditions on the home market. However, it is more common, and far easier, for a company with some experience of dealing with export customers to become proactive towards developing a new export market.

The initial step is likely to be an experimental move into the market in a psychologically 'close' country. The chosen market is likely to be geographically close to the home country, but it is equally important that the export territory should have a population with the same tastes and culture, and business methods that are similar to those in the home country.

A cautious approach is to enter only one or two countries and then consolidate and accumulate experience. There will then be the confidence to progress into additional countries which are psychologically more distant. By this time the company may have established sales offices in the export territories, and may even be considering production there.

ACTIVITY 8.2

Which of the following companies are more likely to begin transnational sales as a result of unsolicited enquiries, and which are more likely to begin by active exploration of export markets: (a) a shoe manufacturer; (b) a company that makes hospital supplies; (c) an insurance broker; (d) a snail farmer?

Market infrastructure

Having decided the countries in which you would be comfortable doing business, it is important to establish whether the social and economic environment favours marketing and selling in them. Various nationalities have different attitudes to the acquisition of goods and services. For example, it is very much more difficult to sell household goods in a market where the population tends not to place great importance on the home, and therefore does not have a tradition of buying that type of product.

Even within one country there may be several languages. Selling products in such a country may require two types of packaging and two sets of operating instructions. It may be possible to design packaging that contains two languages but this results in constraints on the designer. When we buy goods we often find operating instructions in several languages. This means that there is no need to decide the destination at the time of manufacture, but to offset this advantage, the instructions will be more bulky (and hence more expensive) and perhaps less easy to follow unless the layout is very good.

Even small mistakes in translation can irritate or amuse the customer. Japanese and Taiwan-made products were particularly susceptible to incorrect spelling and 'strange' grammar when they were first seen in European markets. There are far fewer mistakes now. Furthermore, dealing with language differences is not always a straightforward exercise of translation. Car names are a good illustration of how the words create images. Place names like 'Granada', 'Cortina' and 'Capri' have been the names of very successful models of car in the UK, but would these cars have been so successful if they had been called 'Torquay', 'Bournemouth' and 'Scarborough'? Words which are foreign to the country where the product is sold may appear more exotic than the equivalent domestic word and may therefore give an excitement that helps sales. On the other hand, some products need a homely image so a domestic word is preferable and a name which is exotic or 'macho' would have a negative influence on sales.

There are some words that have rude or unpleasant connotations, or they may be used as slang in the other language. How well would Bums (a Spanish potato crisp) or Pschitt (a French soft drink) sell in the UK? Similarly, different nationalities also have different attitudes towards colours, design, music, and brand names. Dark colours are often less popular in warm, sunny countries where they might appear too drab, but in a colder climate a bright colour would be 'jazzy'.

Education is another social factor to be considered in assessing an export market. Sophisticated products, advertising, and so forth, may appeal to a well-educated target group but a simpler, basic message would be more effective elsewhere.

Within the EU, people's 'mores' – religions and beliefs – are fairly similar to our own, but in export markets like eastern Europe, the Middle or Far East, and Africa there are very significant differences, and ignoring those differences can damage not only an organisation's attempts to sell a particular product, but even its corporate image.

Again, with the high level of awareness of environmental matters in western

Europe, a company which attempts to market products or processes that are 'environmentally unfriendly' is unlikely to be successful – even failing to emphasise a product's user friendliness is a marketing disadvantage.

Clear differences exist between various European countries in what can be termed the 'social organisation'. For instance, there are different attitudes to authority: in some countries government is respected, while in others it is seen as an enemy to be outwitted. And the role of women in society is regarded differently from one country to another. Even in countries where there would appear to be little difference in the social organisation, companies often make subtle changes in their marketing approach. The 'Gold Blend' television advertisements, for example, first appeared in the UK and were highly successful. The 'same' series of advertisements was then introduced onto US television, but although the same actor and actress (both British) were used, in the US version the man developed an American accent while the woman retained her British one. Also, in the US version the man didn't wear a tie – it was felt to be inappropriate for an 'American'.

The countries of western Europe all have free market economies in which a new organisation, offering competition to existing businesses is usually tolerated by the government. Within the EU it is illegal to put barriers in the way of an organisation entering the market, unless it damages competition by its market dominance, or threatens national security. On the other hand, a country outside the EU may be less happy about a foreign competitor.

It may be the country's government that is hostile to foreign suppliers, or it may be the population as a whole. A few years ago the British government supported a 'buy British' campaign which encouraged people to buy products made in the UK and hostility to foreign-produced ones. Some consumers will buy locally-made products even if there is a slight quality or price disadvantage to doing so.

Eastern Europe has a heritage of central control, with a planned economy rather than an enterprise society. Although many of the eastern European countries are moving towards a free market, there are many problems, including a shortage of hard currency, that make it difficult for a foreign company to penetrate the market. Counter-trading, sophisticated forms of barter, was initially thought to be a way of overcoming the currency problem but it has proved difficult to find markets for many of eastern Europe's products. To a large extent this arises from poor quality or poor design. Conversely, design and quality make EU products especially attractive in eastern European countries, but the low prices of their domestic products and low wages make it difficult to establish a market in those countries. Governments are understandably cautious of an outsider that might further damage the already weak economic infrastructure.

In any part of the world, governments may erect barriers to prevent or limit imports into their country.

The barriers may be financial or non-financial, as the following examples show.

- Import duties are the clearest example of a financial barrier. Tariffs like these cause the price of the product to be raised in the destination country, making it less competitive.
- Quotas are another way of controlling imports. By imposing a ceiling on the quantity that can be imported, and assigning portions of the quota to particular countries or companies, governments can exercise direct control over imports.
- Monetary controls, limiting the amount of currency that can leave the country, and exchange rate controls, put a restriction on what can be paid for and hence what can be bought from outside the country.
- Imports can be restricted by having onerous administrative or technical regulations. Health and safety checks are amongst the most common of these. If a sample from every batch of a product that enters the country has to be tested, then this introduces a delay and additional costs (that have to be passed on to the customer or absorbed giving reduced profit).
- By restricting the import channels to a few ports or airports, or by keeping the number of customs staff down, a government can produce a bottleneck that delays the movement of goods, and limits the amount that reaches the market in any given period.
- The government may encourage discrimination against imports. Particularly in a patriotic country, this can be very effective.
- Finally a government may have anti-dumping regulations. Dumping was experienced in the UK when countries with heavily subsidised coal and steel industries attempted to sell some of their surplus production to Britain. Because of the subsidies the price of the coal and steel was artificially low and the UK domestic industries (with lower levels of state support) could not match the prices.

These barriers are illegal within the EU and EFTA (European Free Trade Association) aims to reduce or eliminate them. Almost all of the western European countries that are not members of the EU belong to EFTA. It is currently negotiating a 'package' with the EU that will form the EEA (European Economic Area), which will have many of the features of the SEM. Moreover the GATT (General Agreement on Tariffs and Trade) negotiates agreements between countries world-wide to reduce and remove barriers to trade.

ACTIVITY 8.3

Choose four of the companies mentioned in Activities 8.1 and 8.2 and for each prepare a list of five factors that would be particularly relevant to assessing the suitability of an export market.

A 'close' country will satisfy most of the following criteria:
1. Geographically close.
2. Good logistics (transport, communications and customer density).
3. Same or familiar language.
4. Similar business culture.
5. Existing business contacts.
6. Good knowledge of market.
7. Similar:
    (a) tastes and interests;
    (b) beliefs, customs, etc;
    (c) education (sophistication of wants);
    (d) brands and products;
    (e) working hours and holidays;
    (f) opening hours;
    (g) credit and terms of trading;
    (h) economic development;
    (i) politics;
    (j) legal system.

Fig. 8.5 Criteria for identifying 'close' countries

Identifying international marketing opportunities

It is desirable to undertake a formal assessment of each possible target market before taking a decision. One way of doing this is to prepare a list of criteria which affect the attractiveness (or otherwise) of a market. These criteria are then 'weighted' according to their importance. For each of the criteria a score is awarded for each country. The overall totals for each country are then compared to determine the most attractive market.

Example

Criteria	Weight	Raw scores		Weighted scores	
		Country A	Country B	Country A	Country B
Political stability	1	4	5	4	5
Market opportunity	5	5	3	25	15
Economic development	1	4	4	4	4
Legal barriers	3	4	2	12	6
Geo-cultural barriers	4	3	5	12	20
Language	3	4	5	12	15
Total				69	65

Note: overall, country A (score 69) is more attractive than country B (score 65).

ACTIVITY 8.4

1 For each of the companies selected in Activity 8.3 decide on weighting that reflect the relative importance of the criteria. Be prepared to justify your decisions.

2 For each company, choose two countries and assign scores to the chosen criteria. Be prepared to justify the scores.

3 Calculate the total weighted score for each company/country.

4 Which is the most attractive export market? Which is least attractive?

5 Does the result of this formal procedure concur with your intuitive judgement?

Market-entry strategy decisions

Having selected the target market, a potential exporter needs to decide on the entry strategy. Put extremely, this is a choice between making the export market a central feature of the company's activities and investing heavily in it, or treating exports as a desirable but peripheral addition to the company's existing market base and committing only a modest proportion of the company's resources to it.

The speed of market entry that is required will largely determine the method adopted. It is possible to hire an agent, employ a sales team, franchise the products, enter into a joint venture, establish an office and warehouse for distribution, or even set up a factory to produce in the destination country. Each of these options involve direct costs (e.g. transport) and indirect costs (e.g. administrative staff), but at very different levels. The payback period on investment varies considerably with the different strategies.

Agent

It is relatively easy to appoint an agent. The agent, being already established in the country and having existing customers, can offer a quick entry into the market. This is also a flexible approach because, having no permanent commitment to buildings, plant and staff, it is relatively easy to pull out if the venture is not successful, or to switch to other markets and products.

However, an agent does not necessarily reduce the risk involved in exporting, because an agent will not be as committed to the exporter's products as the exporter's own staff would be. The interests of the exporter and the agent may differ, too. The agent may be concerned simply with maximising profit in the short term, while the exporter is concerned with establishing a reputation and getting brand names well known in the market – a longer term objective.

Although an agent may be able to sell and distribute some of the exporter's products, his or her area of specialism may not coincide exactly with the exporter's product range and it may be necessary to appoint other agents, adding to the complexity of communication and control, and reducing the amount of business each does for the exporter (and hence his or her commission and motivation).

The final decision will depend on the exporter's long-term objectives.

Problems for small exporters

It is particularly difficult for a small company to become established in exporting.

The small company generally has a relatively local market and lack of exposure to other business cultures, which causes difficulty in selecting export markets and identifing customers abroad. It also lacks the ability to commit a large amount of management time and general resources to an export venture.

Even when the market has been identified there is the problem of selecting an agent. Next, motivating the agent at 'arm's length' will not be easy because the company's products will represent only a small proportion of the agent's business. Furthermore, controlling the foreign operation – choosing transport and distribution channels, for example – will require commitment.

A small business may be more exposed financially because of its size. A single bad debt, or loss or damage to goods in transit for just one order, can cause irreparable damage to the finances of a small company. Overseas offices allowing the exporter to 'go it alone' and retain independence are attractive, but need a bigger financial commitment. Different safety and quality standards may involve a small company in expensive modifications.

The paperwork and management of export operations, and the cost of supervising a salesforce, are also proportionally bigger overheads for a small business. If the exporter has a small salesforce then there is a limit to the number of languages in which they can be fluent enough to do business. This will probably lead a small business to target key markets rather than spreading thinly across several. A long-term perspective may therefore be needed when assessing payback. Small companies tend to have shorter planning horizons.

ACTIVITY 8.5

For each of the companies selected in Activity 8.4, evaluate the possible market entry strategies and decide which is best.

Case study – the experiences of a small UK company

Airpower Limited manufactures industrial compressors. It is located on a three-acre site near a city in the north of England. The company began trading in 1902, producing machinery for the textile industry. In 1936 it began manufacturing compressors and over a period of time came to specialise in these.

In 1978 the company was acquired by a large engineering group which provided an opportunity for Airpower to use the group's international network of contacts. Airpower developed an export strategy based on the 'cheap and cheerful' philosophy, undercutting its main world competitor. Overseas markets developed, so that by 1985, 60 to 70 per cent of manufacturing output was exported. However, exports made a significant loss!

During 1985 the sales and marketing effort was redirected, and the company concentrated on developing a strong UK presence. This utilised virtually the whole of the company's sales and marketing resources and exporting was neglected. During the period 1985–9 the company also changed its marketing and product philosophy. Quality became the primary aim, in engineering, design and packaging. Airpower's market position was moved from the lower-priced sector to the medium-priced range, aiming to give value for money. In line with the quality improvement, export prices were increased by between 30 and 40 per cent. Distributors had received little advance warning and were not prepared for the necessary shift in market. It was like trying to sell a family saloon at luxury limousine prices.

In 1989 a rapid downturn in the UK market for compressors started. By 1992 the total market was estimated to be half of that in 1988. Compressors are generally considered as 'low priority' capital expenditure by many businesses and they will postpone a purchase when they are under pressure themselves. Thus Airpower's turnover declined by 30 per cent from a peak in 1988. The company had made a loss in the 1990 and headed for a much bigger loss in 1991. Some redundancies were declared. The company operated at considerably less than its capacity.

The parent group considered Airpower as peripheral to its main activities and contemplated selling or closing the company. The current Airpower managing director who had been with the company for about 12 months believed that, although there was overcapacity in the industry, adversely affecting prices and margins, there was a niche market for Airpower. The energy efficiency of the company's products, and their quiet running and reliability, made them attractive. There was a need for continuous product development to maintain the competitive advantage. In fact, he was sufficiently confident of the company's potential to negotiate a 'management buy-out' from the parent company.

His first step was to effect a drastic, but essential, reduction in the workforce at every level in the organisation. The other three directors left the company and 25 per cent of the company's employees were made redundant. Then the

MD set about building a new management team and raising morale throughout the company. A change in business culture was particularly important because the company was changing from being part of a large organisation to becoming a quite small business, and it was necessary to instil confidence after the fear and uncertainty that had preceded the buy-out.

A management team comprising the MD and five managers was formed. The members of the management team had broad responsibilities and, in addition, had specific roles – sales, accounts, engineering, manufacture, and materials. An open, participative style of management was encouraged.

Trading conditions remained very difficult, and the nature of the market meant that recovery lagged behind a general improvement in the economy. However, Airpower was able to stabilise its situation and move back towards profit. The quality and reliability of its products contributed to this, and the energy efficiency was especially attractive in the difficult economic climate. Morale in the company was transformed. There was a very positive attitude and a feeling that the future was brighter.

Airpower aimed for, and attained, BS5750 and Investors in People status. Accreditation of the managers through the MCI scheme was considered soon after the buy-out, but was postponed. By January 1993, however, the MD felt that the organisation was sufficiently stable for the managers to focus their attention on gaining M1 or M2 qualifications. The local university's Business School was invited to provide an adviser to assist the managers as they assembled their portfolios and undertook the assessment.

The whole of the workforce was well prepared, and confident, that it could meet the challenges that would come when the company began to expand, and this proved to be the case. In particular, the 'second tier' of management was competent to move quickly and easily into positions of greater responsibility.

Airpower's current range of compressors have capacities between 20 standard cubic feet per minute (scfm) and 600 scfm. They vary in price from about £1700 to £21,000 each. A key feature of Airpower compressors is their energy efficiency, which results in up to 85 per cent cost savings in off-load running. This is achieved by new technology, in which sophisticated electronic controls are an important part. Airpower is proud of its product range.

Compressors, servicing, and parts and accessories are sold through a network of distributors. Servicing, and the sale of spare parts and accessories, are an integral part of Airpower's operations. Reliability and good after-sales service – important issues in the compressor market – help to gain customer loyalty. Airpower has a strong team of technical staff, providing training and support to distributors. Airpower is quite prepared to dispense with the services of any distributor that does not meet the required quality standards.

Airpower is a small player in the market for industrial compressors. Three large companies between them hold about 76 per cent of the market. Airpower's market share is approximately 2 per cent. Its current philosophy of manufacturing a high-quality compressor, delivered on time, and supported by an excellent servicing network is more appropriate than the 'cheap and cheerful' approach of the past.

The company was not prepared to sit back and wait for the UK market to improve. It decided to work hard to recapture old export markets and find new ones. Within a year of restructuring, the company had achieved a 300 per cent increase in overseas sales, 77 per cent above the target. The aim now is for export sales to represent about 25 per cent of total revenue.

Considerable success was achieved in:

- Belgium, Netherlands and Denmark, where lost markets were regained.
- Portugal, where the company had never previously been able to achieve sales.
- Russia, where orders were received to replace the compressors in a paper mill.
- Hungary and Czechoslovakia, including a joint venture in Prague.
- Korea, where orders for compressors for the water industry were won on quality rather than price in competition with US, German and Japanese companies.
- Taiwan, where a new agent and three sub-distributors sold 27 compressors from a standing start, many of them to Japanese companies.
- Africa, with growth in Zimbabwe and World Health Organisation sales in Ethiopia.

The company attributes its success to:

1 Planning its approach and responding to market needs.
2 Setting a programme of communication and visits to maintain interest and motivation, as well as keeping agents and distributors up to date with product developments.
3 Learning from past mistakes and assessing every export opportunity against a check-list before going ahead. The check-list includes product specification (e.g. voltage), delivery, price, payment, servicing arrangements, and so on.
4 Establishing a critical path of activities that lead to on-time delivery of a quality product.
5 Building a contingency allowance into the delivery promise. They will reduce it, but will not eliminate it if there is pressure for earlier delivery. They believe it is better to beat the delivery promise than to fail to meet it.
6 Export administration training, undertaken through the international branch of the company's bank.
7 Developing a strong link with the company's export agent and shipper.
8 Using the DTI for advice and support.

Comment on the case study

The case study has a number of features that are commonly found in the following transnational activities of small businesses.

1 Airpower's export business went through unplanned growth in the early 1980s and reached a stage where the company was overdependent on it. Because export markets are sometimes less predictable, a company with a high proportion of export business is exposed to risk. The current management has limited export business to 25 per cent of revenue, containing the risk within acceptable levels.

2 Early attempts at export gave overemphasis to price and sales volume. Price is only one component of the marketing mix. Other factors, such as quality, meeting the delivery promise, and after-sales service are now given the priority they deserve. Sales volume is important, but it is the contribution to company profits that really counts. It is therefore necessary to consider costs as well as price and to ensure that export sales have an adequate margin.

3 Changes during the 1980s were often made without full consideration of impact or timing. A drop in export sales as a result of market repositioning in 1985-9 was predictable, and the company ought to have considered how to redirect the production capacity. The timing was particularly unfortunate with the downturn in the home market.

4 The company now involves all of its management in planning so that all aspects of its activities (e.g. marketing, finance, production) have been considered when decisions are made.

5 The major change is the company's increased investment in its main resource – people. Human resource development and, in particular, management development are now a key part of company policy. The Investors in People status and MCI qualifications are evidence of this commitment (*see* Chapter 15).

The remaining chapters in this part concentrate on strategies for finding and entering export markets. In Part Four the focus is on successfully and profitably maintaining a presence in these markets.

SUMMARY

1 A business may wish to sell, buy or recruit staff, or operate outside the domestic market.

2 Exporting is generally more complex than operating in the domestic market because of the distances involved and resulting risks, and because of differences in business methods, language and market conditions.

3 Businesses export to take advantage of differences in product life cycle, to avoid competition, to utilise surplus production capacity, to achieve geographic diversification, and to gain access to bigger markets and better customer purchasing power.

4 Businesses usually go through several stages of internationalisation, ranging from disinterest to full multinational operation.

5 Choosing between export markets can be facilitated by a technique that involves appraising them using weighted market criteria.

6 The method of export market entry depends upon the speed of entry required, and the level of investment. Small companies have difficult decisions to make because of the level of commitment needed, especially the amount of management time.

7 Exporting needs to be a part of the company's strategic planning for it to be successful and profitable.

Assignment 8

BACKGROUND

Developing skill in the gathering and analysing of key facts about a company is an important part of business training, and it is highly desirable that this is carried out with a real company rather than by means of a case study.

However, it is not always possible to undertake such an investigation yourself, or even in a small group, because many companies are reluctant to disclose what they feel is sensitive information to strangers, and the management of small companies simply doesn't have the time to deal with what seems to them to be a never-ending stream of incompetent interviewers.

If you are employed in an organisation and studying European business part time then it may be possible to undertake a study of your own organisation. You must not disclose any of the data you gather to anyone without specific authorisation by your senior management.

Many colleges have close relationships with local businesses and the data for this assignment may be obtained by your tutor through its industrial liaison group.

Some information about a company in the case study was readily available, from its published annual reports, sales brochures, etc.

ACTIVITY

1 Select a small local company that is involved in transnational trade and agree the choice with your tutor. Decide what information you need and gather that information directly or via your tutor, etc (as discussed above).

2 Analyse the information and prepare a short report discussing the reasons for going transnational, the stages through which the company has progressed towards internationalism, and the current and potential market opportunities as you see them.

3 If possible, present the report to the company's management and obtain their comments.

9 Marketing and selling

OBJECTIVES

OBJECTIVES

1 **To establish what additional factors have to be considered in establishing the marketing mix.**

2 **To distinguish between the selling methods available to exporters.**

3 **To understand the skills needed to successfully negotiate transnationally.**

4 **To identify the reasons for importing and counter-trading.**

5 **To evaluate strategies adopted by businesses involved in transnational trading.**

The marketing mix

In the previous chapter we discussed the reasons for a company becoming involved in transnational trading, and the nature of that trade. The sale of goods and services in another country is the most common transnational business activity and we concentrated on that. Marketing and selling are again the main focus of our studies in this chapter. However, we will spend some time considering the purchase of goods and services, and counter-trading because these are complementary activities, and many organisations are involved in buying from abroad and counter-trading as well as selling.

In an international context, sales to another country are called 'exports', and purchases from another country are called 'imports'. In the context of the EU, and in particular the SEM, these terms are not strictly correct. We should really talk about 'outgoing' and 'incoming' goods and services where the trade is between EU member states. However, in this text, when discussing transnational trade, the terms 'export' and 'import' will be used except when something is specific to EU business activities.

It is clear from our previous studies that success and profitability are most likely if a company incorporates transnational activities into its strategic planning. The past difficulties of Airpower Limited arose largely from a failure to do this. The commitment that is necessary for transnational trading, especially for a small to medium-sized enterprise, is such that the organisation needs to ask 'What market are we in?' and 'What market do we want to be in?'

Deciding what products to sell, and what markets (or more precisely what segments of the markets) to sell in, is usually accompanied by a review of the company's capabilities. A SWOT analysis – strengths, weaknesses, opportunities and threats – is the marketing technique used. A detailed explanation of this technique may be found in a marketing textbook such as *Introduction to Marketing* by John Frain (third edition). The next stage in establishing a marketing plan is to determine the 'marketing mix'. The 'four Ps' – product, price, place, promotion – is the commonly used marketing term. These are discussed below in the context of EU and international marketing.

ACTIVITY 9.1

Investigate what marketing personnel mean by 'market segmentation'.

Product policy

The product offered on the domestic market may need modification for export. Possibly a different modification will be needed for each export market. It may be that the demands of export markets lead to a change in the basic product – from imperial to metric perhaps? Even a change of name might be needed. How well do you think 'Super Piss' (a Finnish product for unfreezing car door locks) would sell in the UK?

It may also be necessary to have a different level of quality for the export market. Introducing a higher quality standard is likely to lead to a higher level of rejects from the production process. Indeed it is not unknown to have two levels of acceptability for products as they come off the production line – the higher standard for export, and the lower one for the domestic market. At least one UK pottery manufacture sells its best-quality products only in export markets, and many fruit and dairy products are completely unavailable in their country of origin.

Sometimes, however, the only way to achieve a price that is attractive in an export market is to have a version of the product that is simpler than the version for sale in the home market. Value analysis is a relatively modern technique that involves the management team examining a product and deciding which features are essential to make it attractive to the customer, and which can be left out. It can be summed up as 'give the customer what he needs, and leave out what he doesn't'. Amstrad are generally credited with being the first highly successful user of the technique, but the Land Rover can be cited as an excellent example of it. Keeping the product simple is a good approach if it has to operate reliably in difficult conditions.

Entering an export market is a good time to think about brand names. Companies often have a variety of products on the domestic market, all well established but without a common brand name that shows the customer that they are from the 'same stable'. A well-chosen, distinctive brand name could establish its image in the market so that, as more products are introduced into that market, they can benefit from the reputation of existing products.

The packaging used for products in the domestic market may need revamping for exports. This may involve: having a different quantity in the pack; stronger packing because it has to travel further and be subjected to robust handling; a different style of packing to be attractive to different consumer tastes; attractive and informative labelling, appropriate to the target market.

Although a company may have patents on its products and may have registered its trade marks and brand names, entering a new market means that these protections need to be reviewed. At its simplest, this may result in the company taking out patents and registering trade marks in the each of the countries to which exporting will take place (an EU-wide scheme is being developed). However, if the broadening of the customer base gives the products a much higher profile and they attract attention and admiration from a wider audience, they may also attract counterfeiters. It might be necessary to be aggressive in suing those who copy the products. It might even be necessary to rely on introducing new models at frequent intervals so that counterfeiters are left with obsolete designs. Computer software, clothes, watches, cut glass, electrical and electronic products, cosmetics, car parts and even coffee are frequently targets of counterfeiting.

Most companies are concerned not just with making a sale but also with establishing a supplier–customer relationship, which results in the customer making repeat purchases and choosing other products from the company's product range. Good quality and good after-sales service are important factors in establishing this relationship. Setting up an after-sales network is particularly difficult and expensive when products are sold across a wide geographical area. It is often an aspect of exporting that is neglected in the initial enthusiasm to begin trading transnationally, with disastrous consequences. How the company approaches after-sales service depends on the nature of the product. A product that is small and technologically complex, for example, is best returned to its origin. However, this approach would not be suitable for a large product unless the customer could dismantle it and return the faulty component. If a local servicing facility is considered desirable, then the choice is between using an established agent or service organisation and establishing the company's own facility. The latter provides a better guarantee of quality, better motivation and direct control, but probably at higher cost.

Pricing

Pricing is perhaps the most critical and difficult strategy to determine for a new export market.

Careful consideration needs to be given to each product and where it lies in its product life cycle in that country. It may help to consider three aspects of the maturity of a product: technical, market, and competitive.

Technical aspect

A newly developed product may have 'bugs' in it and may be relatively unsophisticated in its design. These may manifest themselves in a high failure rate demanding rectification or replacement, and a significant level of modification. Both require a strong after-sales service.

A more mature product will have benefited from many customers' experiences. Adaptations will have been built into new versions of the product, and better production methods may have been found to improve productivity and product reliability.

It may not be financially attractive for a company to replace old machinery to produce a product that is well into 'old age', and the efforts of research and development staff are usually better employed on new products rather than enhancing the old one.

The introduction of a product into an export market could be at any time during its technological maturity. A 'new' product in an export market may well be mature (and hence stable) in terms of its technology.

Market aspect

When considering a new export market it is necessary to ask 'Are the customers ready for it?' Selling and marketing a brand which is already recognised and for which there is an existing demand is a totally different proposition from marketing one that the target population has never heard of.

Competitive aspect

Increasingly wide coverage achieved by European media may mean that potential customers are aware of a product before it is available to them. Thus the product may be 'mature' in the market before it is launched. The danger is that a competitor will enter the market before the originator of the product and become more easily established in the absence of brand loyalty.

The extent to which consumers are sensitive to pricing will depend on the extent to which the product is seen as a 'luxury' or a 'necessity'. This will vary according to market culture and particularly according to the standard of living.

So far we have looked at market-based pricing strategies. It is also necessary to consider costs.

Exporting will involve additional overheads:

- Transport to an export market of a product made in the UK will be more costly than delivery within the UK.
- Distribution will be more expensive if the target market is more widely spread.

However, it is conceivable that the market could be more compact so that once the goods have reached a central warehouse, they can be distributed to retailers or customers more cheaply than in the UK.

It should not be assumed that the cost of a salesforce will be the similar to one in the UK. A large, sparse, sales territory will involve more travel time, and more travel expense, but vehicle and fuel costs are lower in some European countries than in the UK. Sales staff's remuneration needs to reflect local norms.

Product costs for exports need to be calculated completely separately from the domestic costing.

ACTIVITY 9.3

The term 'jeans' can refer to robust work-wear or it can refer to a designer product with a well-known brand name. Consider the implications for pricing of the different types of jeans in a variety of EU export markets.

Place – logistics and channel decisions

How will the product reach the export customers? It depends on what is being sent, where to, how quickly it has to get there, whether there will be regular deliveries, and so on.

The methods may be air, road, rail, sea, inland waterway, or any combination of these. The exporter can use its own transport, include its products with those of other companies, use a carrier who regularly delivers to the customer's location, or ask a carrier to make a special journey and delivery.

For a small package it is practical, fast and economical to use datapost, air-mail, or surface post. For a larger package there is fierce competition between the carriers that operate internationally.

Air freight is generally faster than road or rail over long distances, but is more expensive, especially for heavy products, and there are restrictions on what can be carried – no explosives, toxic chemicals, and so on. However, for perishable goods there may be no feasible alternative to air freight.

The chief argument against rail freight is the delay in assembly at source, and the further delay while the cargo is unloaded at the destination rail terminal. This is minimised by containerisation. The same arguments apply to transporting by ship or barge. In favour of railways, ships and barges are the following: they are capable of carrying large and heavy loads; they are not held up by heavy traffic; there is less risk of accident; they are more likely to arrive on time; and they produce less pollution.

Any delivery that involves more than one method of transport will tend to incur delays because there has to be some allowance in the schedules for the late arrival of the first vehicle.

When exporting, goods generally have to be transported further than in domestic trade. It is therefore often more economic to gather a 'worthwhile' load at a collection point and then transport it to a distribution point where it is broken up into separate customer deliveries. If goods will not all arrive at the collection point at the same time, storage facilities will be needed. Similarly, at the distribution point, warehousing may be necessary until local deliveries can be arranged. Most freight-forwarding companies have sited their main depots at places that have good local road networks and access points to long-haul transport routes (air, sea, rail or motorway).

The introduction of containerisation has simplified the transportation of goods. Individual organisations pack their products into containers which are of internationally standard sizes. The containers are then delivered, usually by road, to freight-forwarding 'nodes' for the long-haul journey in batches – train loads or ship loads – to the distribution node. Standardisation in the size, shape and weight of containers has made it possible for trucks, railway wagons, ships and cargo planes to be designed to accommodate them. You will probably be familiar with the sight of a train full of containers on special flat wagons, or ships stacked high with containers. Handling equipment such as cranes have been developed to lift the container easily from the deck of a ship to the back of a lorry or to a railway wagon. Containers cut down the effort of loading and unloading, and they protect the goods from the weather, from handling damage, and from theft. A container that has been checked and sealed at source is acceptable to Customs and Excise without the need for a check at each frontier.

Promotion

Promoting products in an export market is where the exporter's understanding of customers and consumers is put to the test. If the exporter has got the product and price right, then it is going to be easier to sell the product, but it is still necessary to make the potential customer aware of its presence and persuade him to buy *that* product rather than a competitor's.

If the exporter has chosen to use personal selling, then the sales force has to understand the customer and must be able to communicate. This is most easily achieved by employing nationals of the target country, but recruitment and control will be more difficult unless there is a manager based locally.

The initial promotion of products can often be undertaken at exhibitions and trade fairs. The DTI gives advice and practical help in finding and attending appropriate trade and retail shows.

Advertising is best handled by an advertising agency that specialises in the target country, and has experience of the kind of market that the exporter intends to enter. This form of promotion can, however, be a very expensive waste of money unless the message is carefully thought out and delivered in the right way, at the right place, at the right time. Factors to be considered include media availability and the size and nature of its audience in the target country. It is also necessary to take account of constraints on advertising, as well as the social environment. Advertising in Europe is monitored by national bodies like the UK's Advertising Standards Authority, which has a strong influence but no legislative power over advertisers. There is legislation in each country which protects 'public decency' and vulnerable groups. Individuals who feel they are libelled by items that appear in the media can take individual legal action.

When planning an advertising campaign, the exporter must conform to product restrictions, making sure that it can substantiate advertising claims (e.g. 'probably the best toothpaste' rather than 'the best toothpaste'), and balancing information with emotional appeal. It is generally considered that self-discipline and regulation are preferable to legal action.

Getting advertising right in another country is very difficult unless the exporter really understands the different cultures, and even within a country there can be considerable variation in attitudes. Benetton's 'new baby' advert in the UK in September 1991 produced a storm of protest from people who felt it was 'offensive', although a considerable number felt it was innocuous, if perhaps not very relevant to the company's products.

ACTIVITY 9.5

What methods of promotion would be most appropriate for the different types of jeans in the various EU countries?

Selling methods

There are four ways of operating outside your home country: direct exporting; indirect exporting; carrying out production abroad; and carrying out services abroad.

Direct exporting

An agent will act on your behalf and hold inventory. He or she will sell and carry out administration for you, but although he or she stores your products, you will not receive payment until they are sold to a customer.

By contrast, a distributor purchases stock from you and is then responsible for selling it and collecting payment. You have no further interest in goods once he or she has bought them from you. Many distributors ask for exclusivity, that is, they are the only distributors in the region or even the country.

A freight forwarder will transport the goods to the customer, leaving you with the task of selling and collecting payment.

You may set up a consortium marketing group, in which you and your fellow consortium members jointly own a company in the country that sells your products. One stage further than this is to have your own subsidiary company that sells in the export territory.

Indirect exporting

You may choose to sell through an export house in your own country. The export house represents the buyer and acts on his or her behalf. Although your goods reach the export market you are dealing with a company in your own country and are not, therefore, directly involved in exporting.

'Piggybacking' is a means of exporting in which you make use of the distribution channels of another company in a related (but not directly competitive) field.

Moving production abroad

Licensing your patented manufacturing process (and the know-how) allows you to derive income from your product although it is made and sold by a completely separate organisation. You may, on the other hand, choose to manufacture the components of your product in your own country and ship them as kits to be assembled and sold in the target market area.

Then there are two types of joint venture:

1 One is based on an agreement whereby your partner in the export territory makes and sells the product and you share the profits according to some agreed formula.
2 The other type takes this a step further and you and your joint-venture partner own the company that manufactures and sells the products.

Rather than getting involved in a joint venture you may choose to have a wholly owned subsidiary in the country, manufacturing as well as selling your products.

Providing a service abroad

If you have a service with an internationally known brand name or logo, you may consider franchising it. The franchisee pays you a fee for the privilege of using it. You may also provide management expertise to help the franchisee be successful. Fast-food outlets are the most commonly franchised business operations.

In some ways a licensing agreement is similar to a franchise – the owner of the original confers the right to make and sell to someone else. However, the emphasis in a licensing arrangement is on manufacture rather than the image of the product. The overseas operator may even sell the product under a different name.

If you have particular expertise in a technology or management technique you may enter into a management contract with an overseas operator. Under the terms of the agreement you receive a fee for providing them with training and keeping them up to date so that they can successfully operate in the specialist field.

As with a product, you can provide a service in an export market by operating in a joint venture or with a wholly owned subsidiary.

Negotiating a deal

Whether you are selling or buying, interpersonal skills are important when negotiating, particularly when dealing with someone from another country.

Method	Characteristics
Export house	Represents a buyer abroad.
Agent	Paid commission on sales. Usually has exclusivity of sales territory. Handles more than one company and/or product.
Distributor	Takes title of goods. This lessens risk and improves cash flow but weakens control (i.e. exporter knows less about customer/ consumer and retail price).
'Piggyback'	Uses distribution channel of another company.
Export consortium	Joint representation in foreign markets. Government assistance is intended to encourage SMEs to participate in export.
Freight forwarder	Provides documentation and delivery service to foreign destination.
Direct sales	Own sales team based in target market.
Overseas manufacture	Undertaken by own employees in overseas subsidiary.
Joint venture	*Type 1 – industrial co-operation* Fixed term. Contractual responsibilities of each are defined. *Type 2 – joint equity* On-going. Nature of each's involvement may change over time.
Franchise	Transfers the right to use the exporter's name, logo and all that is identifiable with the company. Exporter usually retains right to control quality and supply of materials. Exporter may retain some control by a management contract.
Licensing	Confers right to manufacture. Exporter may retain control by a management contract. Exporter may insist on own materials and/or components.
Management contract	Know-how and/or company-specific management control systems. Used to retain some control, especially relating to quality, promotion and/or methods of production.

Fig. 9.1 Methods of operating in export markets

Although it may be more difficult and time-consuming to arrange face-to-face communication, it enhances the chances of understanding because it is interactive (which a letter or fax is not) and body language can be observed.

If you are trained in communication skills you will realise that it is often difficult to be sure that your message has been received and understood by the person you are dealing with. Equally, it is difficult to be sure that you have received and understood the message a sender intended to pass to you. These difficulties are magnified when the two of you have different cultures and languages, and the situation may even be made worse by having an interpreter. If you do communicate through an interpreter, make sure you watch the other party to the negotiations, not the interpreter, throughout the conversation, and especially when the interpreter is translating something you have said. Remember, it is the non-verbal communication of the other negotiator, not that of the interpreter, which you are trying to detect.

In everyday life the British do not often bargain for purchases: most of the goods we buy are price-marked and that is the price we expect to pay. In some European countries, however, and commonly elsewhere in the world, bargaining (i.e. negotiating the price and conditions of the sale) is normal for all transactions. Those who habitually bargain are likely to be more competent at it.

It is possible to negotiate until you have the very best deal on a particular transaction, but this is not always the best strategy. If it leaves the other party discontented, and if you feel you have 'screwed them to the floor', these effects may detract from the goodwill and on-going relationship that you want to establish and maintain.

By the same token, negotiating is about presenting your case in the best way possible – and this does not mean telling lies. It is vital that you and whoever you are negotiating with retain their integrity throughout negotiations.

Once a deal is concluded, make sure it is confirmed in writing, and that the wording is clear and unambiguous, in both languages. The version of the document in the customer's language should be taken as the definitive one if there is any doubt about the quality of the translation.

ACTIVITY 9.6

Form groups of four. Two people will take the role of buyers for retail companies. The other two will take the role of salespersons of manufacturing companies.

A particular type of popular shoe costs £5 to make and retails at about £20. It is made in various styles, colours and sizes. Negotiate a deal for a total of 5000 shoes of this type, about two weeks' production for either manufacturer.

To simulate a language difference make use of the services of a fifth person (the interpreter). Out of hearing of the person you are negotiating with tell the interpreter what you want to say. Be present when the interpreter passes the message to the other negotiator.

Importing

To a large extent importing is the mirror image of exporting. From an economic stand-point, exporting tends to be treated as good for a country, whereas importing is bad, because of the effects on the balance of payments. This is simplistic, however, because the key question is whether the imports are to be consumed in the country or whether they are going to contribute to another product which is subsequently exported. Even this, though, does not completely explain the situation.

Thus, nationally, exporting may be good and importing bad, but looking on a European scale the picture changes. Within the EU, each country has its own particular strengths in terms of climate, resources, skills, and so forth. It makes sense to take advantage of these strengths to further the common good. Trade between the countries, whether outgoing or incoming, is therefore to the Community's overall advantage.

What are you likely to buy from another country? You may buy goods to sell to consumers in this country; raw materials or components from which you manufacture your own products; machinery to use in the manufacturing process; or equipment (e.g. computers) to help control the business. Increasingly, too, there is a trade in products (e.g. stationery, packaging, power, oil) that are consumed to keep the business running. Expertise and services are also becoming much more internationalised. Certainly as a buyer of imports you must be concerned to get a product or service of the right quality, at the right price, in the right quantity, and at the right time.

Why should you import rather than buy locally? The answer is 'When you can get a better mix of product, quality, price, quantity, and availability.'

For instance, it may be that the product you want is in short supply from local suppliers – perhaps because of increased demand, or because it is seasonal, or because there are price fluctuations. A good supplier (i.e. one who wants to meet your needs) will find alternative sources so that he or she keeps your business. But if you are only a small customer, or he or she does not have international contacts, you may find it preferable to look further afield for yourself.

So, having identified a source, you then need to assess the cost of buying the goods – taking into account the additional transport costs, paperwork, exchange rates, and so on, and the reliability of that more distant source. Moreover buying from a supplier 'just down the road' may have led you to buy small quantities as and when you require the goods. Longer lines of communication should now cause you to review this policy:

1 A single, larger, periodic delivery may be the best way of minimising transport costs, but you will have to find storage space for the goods and, unless you can negotiate to pay for the goods as you use them, you will have to find a larger amount of money to settle your debt.
2 On the other hand, your supplier may be happy to offer a lower price to offset the cost of many smaller deliveries if you negotiate a long-term contract which involves a steady supply.

Both alternatives mean that you need to anticipate your future needs more accurately, and there is a financial risk if your predictions are wrong.

The following imperatives should be considered in importing.

- The decision to import may arise as a result of an overseas company approaching you, or it may be that you have actively sought sources outside your own country.
- A proactive management is constantly researching for alternative materials and methods so that it can improve quality and reduce costs. It is also concerned to avoid being tied to a single supplier if this adds to the risk of supply failure.
- As a member of the buying team you should also be looking for technical harmonisation so that your products have consistency of performance, and are compatible across a wider market. You will constantly be gathering information on market prices and trends, government policies, and so on.
- It is to be hoped that you have efficient purchasing procedures, and have developed goodwill in the relationships between your company and suppliers. The time when you begin to deal with foreign suppliers is a good time to review the procedures for dealing with enquiries, selecting suppliers, negotiating contracts, preparing documentation, progressing deliveries, and making payments.
- Elsewhere in the organisation there is a need to have good control of incoming goods – checking the quantity and quality.

ACTIVITY 9.7

Investigate the import activities of a wine merchant.

Counter-trading

Counter-trading is kind of barter activity. Instead of receiving payment in cash an exporter may receive part of the payment in the form of other goods. It tends to occur in the following circumstances:

1 The buyer's country has a weak or unstable currency.
2 There are protectionist barriers such as quotas that prevent a simple deal of goods for cash.
3 There is a keen desire and competition to export to a buyer who, in the short term, does not have the funds to pay.
4 There are strong political or humanitarian reasons for exporting to a country.

The key factor, from the exporter's point of view, is whether the goods offered in payment for the exporters' products, are in demand in the home market.

In the 1980s counter-trading was thought to be an good way of trading with the CIS and eastern Europe. However, many of the manufactured goods were of lower quality than consumers in western Europe would accept and fewer deals have been concluded than were originally envisaged. In fact, counter-trading has proved most successful where the export market is able to offer raw materials or crops in return for manufactured products.

An important aspect of counter-trading is the negotiation of 'price'. It is necessary to establish equivalence between quantities of the exchanged products so as to put together a 'fair deal'. Where the products are available from other sources and there is a market price, this may be used as the basis for negotiation. However, the circumstances of the negotiating parties (i.e. how keen they are to do business) is also highly relevant.

To establish parity amongst the goods to be exchanged it is common for consortia to be established in both countries. It is also fairly common for three-way or even four-way arrangements to be agreed with each of the participants in a different country.

Case study – international operations in a large company

ABC Inc. is a large US-based engineering company. It is a successful company but has taken 83 years to get to its current position as a powerful player in its market sector. As a large company it recognises that it lacks the flexibility that only an SME can have.

The company is organised into three product divisions, each of which is quite distinct. World headquarters is in the northern USA. The senior management structure is as follows:

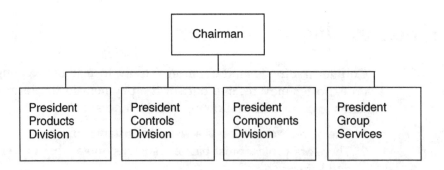

Each division has four vice-presidents, each vice-president being responsible for one of four geographic areas with the following identical management structure.

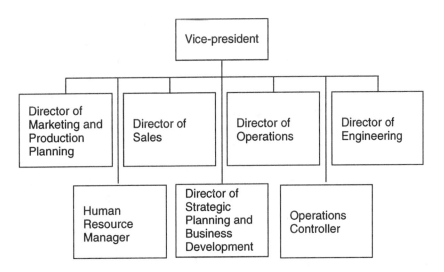

Each division is divided into four geographic areas:

1 America (USA, Canada, South America).
2 Africa (excluding Tunisia, Egypt, South Africa).
3 CIS (all the states that were formerly the USSR).
4 The rest of the world, including Europe, the Middle East, the Far East, Australasia, Tunisia, Egypt and South Africa.

Within the EU the Products Division is located on 11 sites in four countries, the Controls Division on 23 sites in five countries, and the Components Division on ten locations in five countries. There are very few common sites – near London (all three divisions), in northern Germany (Products and Controls), in Spain (Products and Controls), in northern England (Controls and Components), in north-west Germany (Products and Components).

The company has over 30 years' experience in the European market. It employs local nationals as well as expatriates in all the key locations throughout Europe. It claims that it does not have a language problem with any of the official EU languages and that it can handle both commercial and technical communication in most of the central European languages.

ABC Inc. is a market-led company where 'the customer comes first' and 'quality is a goal to be achieved by everybody, including our suppliers'. It gained ISO9000 approval in the UK in 1990. The company expends a lot of time and effort on understanding the market. The classic weakness of a large organisation is recognised to be inflexibility and the company tries to adapt to new situations as quickly as possible.

In the market there are 27 significant customers into which ABC's products can be incorporated. A close relationship has been established with each customer by each division separately. In this way the divisions can tie in their products with each customer's product design. It is important to know the customer.

ABC sells direct to customers – in Germany, Sweden, Netherlands, Morocco, France, Spain, Belgium, Turkey, Algeria, India, Japan and South America – and also to dealers and business end-users in order to get close to buyers of spares and components, but not to individual end-users, thus avoiding a big administrative overhead. The company adopts whichever market-entry strategy is appropriate to a particular situation.

A number of organisations manufacture ABC's products under licence, paying a royalty on the number of items sold. Several joint ventures have also been set up, with a contractual agreement to achieve an agreed aim, usually design and development. Furthermore, a number of acquisitions have taken place in which all or a controlling share of a company is bought, usually to complement products in the existing range.

Comment on the case study

- The organisation has been divisionalised on the basis of geography and product groups.
- There is a high degree of divisional autonomy to minimise bureaucracy and simulate the flexibility of an SME.
- Customers and business partners are carefully chosen to encourage long-lasting relationships and good communications, which are considered especially important in transnational trading.

Case study of an SME

Keepdry Limited manufactures accessories for prams. It was started by its owner 12 years ago. When he left school he worked in his parents' two pram shops. He felt that the bought-in covers were of poor design and decided he could do better himself. He bought some PVC and a sewing machine and after some experimentation produced an all-in-one cover.

Promoting his product at trade shows soon made it possible for him to sell 90 covers per week. At a trade show he received an enquiry from an Australian company for 2000 covers, to be delivered in six weeks. This was not a success. He was not 'geared up' to cope with the volumes, delivery requirements and distances. However, he learned from his mistake – his next overseas venture was closer to home, with carefully worked-out schedules and attainable volumes.

At the end of four years he had three machinists, rented premises, and a self-employed agent to sell to retailers in the UK. Less than two years later he had 26 employees and 12,000 sq. ft of accommodation in a converted mill.

DTI publicity alerted him to the opportunities of '1992' and he exhibited at a trade show in Germany, gaining a useful level of orders. Although sales in

Germany reached a satisfactory level, he did not feel that he was achieving as much as he could and he therefore decided to employ an agent. Unfortunately he made the mistake of granting exclusivity to the agent and had difficulty cancelling the contract when that agent failed to achieve the target level of sales. Two years of potential growth in the most lucrative market were wasted. Again, lessons were learned. Contracts should always have a time-limit and initially these should be short. There should be provision for the contract to be terminated if target sales are not achieved.

Although sales had been achieved in several countries Keepdry's owner was not satisfied. A careful analysis of the reasons why the company was failing to penetrate export markets was undertaken.

His approach had been to send samples and to follow up by telephone and fax. His language skills comprised basic German and French and a smattering of Italian and Spanish. Now he decided it was necessary to *take* the samples, and to explain the benefits of the products to potential customers *face to face* and *in their own language*. Hence he employed a graduate who was fluent in German and French and arranged for her to undertake a marketing course. Germany was made the prime target and much better results were achieved with this new approach.

An action plan was then prepared for the next target country, France, based on a very thorough investigation of the market. It was recognised that each country has different needs in terms of styles, colours and retail selling methods. Part of the investigation was to visit shops in the target country in order to find out what was available and what they wanted. Good-quality literature was produced in three languages – German, French and English – to demonstrate a commitment to international sales. A crucial breakthrough was a small order from a buying group in France which services 200 shops. It took four months of patient discussion to gain the order but good-quality products were delivered on time and regular further orders were received.

An investigation of the Dutch market followed but it was decided that the methods of selling pram accessories did not favour market entry. In Belgium, however, it was possible to establish a trading relationship with a distributor, and this distributor is now the company's fifth largest customer. Market research is now being carried out in Norway.

The company currently employs 120 workers at its 50,000 sq. ft production facility, using 'state-of-the-art machinery'. In 1993 export sales accounted for 9 per cent of turnover and provided valuable income and profit at a time when the UK market was difficult and competition was fierce.

Keepdry's owner offers this advice to companies intending to sell in Europe:

- It takes time and effort to do it properly.
- European paperwork is not difficult.
- You must develop a relationship with the customer.
- Language skills are essential.
- They won't come to you, so go to them.

- If you are in a fashion-conscious market you must stay with the market (in his products the UK is 12 months behind the rest of Europe).
- It's cheaper to sell to a few big customers, than to many small ones.
- Sales and distribution methods differ from country to country and from product to product (buying groups in France, wholesalers in Germany, distributors in Belgium and Norway).
- It's hard for an SME to persuade manufacturers to link your product with theirs because they have very fixed ideas (in contrast with the large company in the previous case study).

Comments on the case study

- The company was persistent in its attempts to enter the markets. Its greatest success came when it employed a person dedicated to investigating the market.
- Language skills and careful choice of customers and business partners (e.g. agents) were the crucial factors in becoming established in a country.

SUMMARY

1 The 'four p's' of marketing still apply to transnational trade but additional factors need to be considered in establishing product, price, place and promotion.

2 It is possible to sell outside the domestic market directly or indirectly. Manufacture can be undertaken outside the home country, or franchising or licensing arrangements can be agreed.

3 Language and culture are key factors in transnational negotiation. When negotiating a transaction, the negotiator's tactics should to be modified if there is a desire to establish a long-term business relationship.

4 Most organisations would benefit from periodically reviewing the effectiveness of their procurement systems. A good time to do this is when considering buying goods from another country.

5 Large companies often retain their sharpness and flexibility by divisionalisation, even though they lose opportunities for economies of scale and risk duplication of effort.

6 SMEs rarely have the resources to enter more than one new market at a time. They must be prepared to commit a significant amount of management time and expenditure – for wages, research costs, transport and accommodation, and so on.

Assignment 9

BACKGROUND

Pinkerton Limited is the small subsidiary of a large UK glass manufacturer. It has a high degree of autonomy. It manufactures and sells optical equipment and its latest product is very sophisticated night vision equipment that can be fitted to a gun, carried like a pair of binoculars, or even worn like a pair of glasses.

Originally, Pinkerton's main market had been the defence industry in the UK. Three years ago, however, it realised that it should widen its customer base and was quite successful in selling to UK security firms, police forces, and so forth.

A strategic decision has now been made to sell its products elsewhere in the EU, and Germany and Greece have been chosen as its first target markets. Germany is of course famous for its optical industry (e.g. cameras, binoculars). However, Pinkerton believes its night vision equipment is better than any of its competitors' products. Greece has been chosen because of its proximity to some of the most volatile and violent regions of Europe.

ACTIVITY

Carry out a market planning exercise on behalf of Pinkerton Limited, to develop a marketing mix for each of the chosen markets.

10 Marketing information

OBJECTIVES

1 To adopt appropriate strategies for acquiring marketing information according to the nature of the export activity (business-to-business trade or selling to the public) and the stage of internationalisation.

2 To identify sources of general and specific information and plan both desk and field research.

3 To specify the marketing data needed to establish a product in a particular EU market.

4 To understand the role of local, national and EU organisations in supplying data on grants and loans, EU law and institutions, and market information.

5 To name the principal databases that can assist with marketing in the EU.

Getting started

Unsolicited orders

The key maxim in business activity is 'know the market', but, in a company new to transnational trading, how would you find out about the market?

If the company's entry into the export market is via *an unsolicited order* it is possible to obtain some information about the market from the customer. Assuming your company has decided that it wants to get into the export market, the sales team, or better still the senior management, should show an interest in the customer, demonstrating that his or her business is valued. This, in any case, is good practice when trying to build up a long-term business relationship with a new customer.

To best satisfy the customer's needs it is necessary to find out what he or she wants and why you have been chosen as a possible supplier. It is unlikely that the customer will hold back information that will help you meet his or her needs. Why has the customer decided to import? Is there a gap in local provision? Does your product meet his or her needs better? Is your quality better? Do you offer better reliability or after-sales service? Is your price better? Can you give a better delivery? How did he or she find out about you?

All the factors that might make you consider importing are the factors that have caused the customer to come to you. They also match closely with the information you need to determine the marketing mix.

ACTIVITY 10.1

Prepare a check-list of actions that would allow a company to provide a customer with a better service, and the information from the customer that would help to achieve this and would assist the company with its marketing efforts.

Active exporting

Another starting point for exporting is the decision *to search actively* for exporting opportunities.

An SME is more likely than a large company to be entering export markets for the first time. It will usually have a relatively small range of products, and its resources are such that it will probably attack a single market at a time. Both these factors make the task of gathering market information easier because it is more specific.

However, these circumstances also mean that published statistics tend to be too general to be of great use. Therefore a number of EU and UK government organisations exist with the specific task of providing information for SMEs and helping them in other ways. There are also private consultancies and market research organisations with the expertise to assist.

Planning the information-gathering process

Information-gathering can be classified as 'desk research' and 'field research'.

Desk research makes use of publicly available sources, and data from market research agencies and other organisations. Such research usually helps to determine what is needed, and it should, therefore, be carried out before field research. *Field research* involves 'going and looking' and is achieved either by visits or by commissioning market research activities such as surveys within the export market. It tends to be expensive and it is necessary to be quite specific about the information needed.

Part of the planning process for information-gathering should be the setting of a budget and a timescale.

Sources of general information

Before undertaking any investigative work, it is desirable to take stock of what information is already available. Within the company there may be people who have visited the target area, or who have relatives or friends there. A good local contact is the most effective way of finding out about an area and market.

Background information

Apart from personal contacts, books offer the most readily available source of information. It is possible to find out from books about the geography and economics of the target area and industrial sector. The business section of most large public libraries often has a good range of relevant books and other publications. Types of useful publications are as follows:

- Travel books, like the guides published by Baedeker, Michelin, the Automobile Association, and Berlitz, provide background information and include maps and town plans. These books are of use later when planning visits.
- Magazines and journals.
- A number of guides for exporters have been published, many by banks and quality newspapers. These are particularly valuable as sources of names, addresses and phone numbers of EU, national and industry specific organisations.
- Company information in trade directories, together with market research reports, provide more detailed information on specific regions, industrial sectors and specific companies.
- Some of the professional bodies have also published guides to assist their members with transnational activities, and their journals often include articles on EU business activities.
- The Department of Trade and Industry (DTI) publishes a wide range of general information for exporters, and information on specific markets and industrial sectors.

- The European Commission publishes a vast amount of material, much of it aimed at helping SMEs. Eurostat, in particular, is an excellent source of statistical data. Most of the EU data is free or available for a nominal charge.
- Very many publications and videos were issued as part of the '1992' campaign that accompanied implementation of the SEM. Some of these are useful for background information, although the figures they contain are becoming somewhat dated.

The timescale of publication usually means that information in books is generally one to two years old. Magazines and business journals have a shorter timescale for publication and potentially are more up to date. Time-sensitive data is best obtained through one of the increasing number of computer-based systems which give access to data on CD-ROM and on-line databases. Examples include 'Pharos' (Nat-West Bank database of EU legislation), 'BC-NET' (an EU database for finding business partners, accessible through European Information Centres) and 'TED' (Tenders Electronic Daily – an EU database of public sector invitations to tender).

Getting more specific information

Armed with background information it should be possible to move on to the next stage of desk research, which involves acquiring a more detailed knowledge of specific topics. The main sources of information include:

- European Commission – publications, databases, advice and small firms services.
- The Department of Trade and Industry (DTI) and British Overseas Trade Board (BOTB) – market opportunities, country profiles.
- Chambers of Commerce – links with chambers in target region.
- Export clubs – local businesses with similar needs.
- Universities and business schools – links with industry and other academic institutions elsewhere in Europe, access to on-line data, expertise in research, students trained in EU and international business.
- Professional and trade bodies – information on specific business sector and specialist activities.
- Information centres and private organisations – expertise in locating appropriate information, advice on transnational business trading techniques.

Later in this chapter we examine the activities of two organisations who provide industry with information and advice. In Chapter 16 we consider the broader area of support services and funding that can assist organisations engaged in business within Europe, and in particular with market entry and marketing.

ACTIVITY 10.3

Identify the large shoe manufacturers in Spain and obtain as much data on them as possible.

Field research

Having done the necessary desk research, the organisation should now have sufficient data to decide which region and market sector to attack.

Hopefully, it will also have identified potential customers and organisations that may be suitable agents, distributors or trading partners. If it has not been possible to reach this stage, then it will be necessary to undertake research to identify them. This can be done by the organisation itself, or it may commission a market research agency or a consultancy to do the task on its behalf. Alternatively, the company can attend a trade show or conference and hope to make contacts in that way.

It is now time to visit the market, but who should go? In the Keepdry case study the owner initially visited potential markets himself. Later, when a person had been employed specifically to undertake marketing activities it was she who undertook these visits. In both instances, language, technical knowledge, and sales and marketing skills were essential. The authority to negotiate on behalf of the company is also important, the potential customer/partner will not be impressed if the visitor is continually having to hedge and refer back to the office for instructions.

What is the purpose of the visit? The aim is to visit possible customers, and potential agents, distributors and partners. There is no substitute for face-to-face contact, especially in the early stages of building a business relationship.

The visit needs to be carefully planned. Holiday periods should be avoided. So should periods when the person to be visited is likely to be very busy. Arrangements should be made in advance, agreeing the time of the visit and the agenda. Since travel to and from the region is likely to be the most expensive and time-consuming part of the activity, it is desirable to fit in visits to as many organisations as possible during the one trip.

For a senior member of a company, time away from the office is costly. There is likely to be a backlog of work when he or she returns. Nevertheless, it is vital that there is prompt follow-up of the visit. At the very least there should be a letter of thanks and confirmation of what was agreed. If prices, specifications or other data were to be provided, these should be despatched as soon as possible. The same promptness should be present when, hopefully, the first order is received. As it said in the TV commercial, 'You never get a second chance to make a first impression.'

ACTIVITY 10.4

Draw up a schedule for visiting shoe manufacturers in Spain. The aim is to discover whether they would be interested in a piece of machinery that would increase productivity by 10 per cent.

What marketing data is needed?

The aim is to identify the target population, and ideally to identify potential customers.

In business-to-business selling it might be possible to get an available list of all possible customers (e.g. from an industrial directory). When selling to the public it is more difficult to be specific. Demographic and other data has to be used. Examples of such data are:

- *Population*   Male–female, age groups, births, deaths, life expectancy.
- *Employment profile*   Blue collar–white collar, management–other, remuneration analyses.
- *Social profile*   Live births, marriage, divorce, suicide, house ownership, health-care provision, schooling, crime.
- *Consumer demand*   Sales value per head of population by product category, ownership of consumer products.

Other factors which require research are as follows:

- It is necessary to determine what similar products are available. A good way of assessing them is to buy, test and dismantle samples.
- At the same time it is desirable to find out about competitive companies.
- Approaching the market from the viewpoint of a potential buyer will allow the organisation to gather information on prices and discover what discounts are available.
- Investigating suitable methods of distribution and assessing the quality of communications is more complex. The aim is to identify organisations who can provide good-quality distribution and transport services.

The aspect of marketing with most variation between EU member states is promotion and selling. Again, there are major differences in strategy, depending on whether the exporter is involved in business-to-business selling or sales to the public. First, for business-to-business selling, trade shows, advertising in the trade journals, mailshots and sales calls are the most effective. Obtaining information on these is relatively straightforward for many products because the number of journals and customers is fairly small. However, making the appropriate sector of the public aware of the product is more difficult. Exhibitions are likely to reach only a small proportion of the potential market.

Employing an agent or distributor may be the most cost-effective method. Once the product is on sale through a retailer there are opportunities for in-store promotions and other advertising methods.

Advertising on TV, radio or the cinema, in the regional and national press, and on outdoor displays (hoardings) requires detailed knowledge of their penetration.

Which of the 8 major TV stations received in Italy, or the 15 received in the Netherlands, is best for your product? TV viewing patterns are fairly similar across Europe, with a penetration of over 30 per cent (across all stations) between 6pm and 10pm and a peak at 8pm. However, listening patterns for radio vary significantly. Some peak at 7am, others at 9am, while only in Ireland and Spain is there a major peak in listening at around 1pm.

In the Netherlands, 11 newspapers have coverage of over 1 per cent of the population. By contrast, in Germany, Italy and Portugal there are 3 or less, and in Spain only 1. However, Germany, like the Netherlands, has more than 30 magazines which reach over 1 per cent of the population; Greece and Portugal have less than 10 comparable magazines.

France has, by far, the largest number of poster sites (over 450,000), well ahead of Germany (300,000), while Ireland has fewest with less than 7000).

Thus an organisation considering an advertising campaign directed at the general public would be well advised to seek professional advice.

ACTIVITY 10.5

What methods of advertising would you consider in promoting your productivity-improving device for shoe manufacturing in Portugal, and in Italy?

European business information services

A number of organisations have been established to assist businesses, especially SMEs, to establish a European dimension to their trade. The key year in the history of these organisations was 1992 – the deadline for implementation of the Single European Act. They worked hard to raise awareness amongst business people, publishing regular bulletins reporting progress.

Some 276 important measures had to be implemented by the end of 1992. For each measure there had to be agreement at Council of Ministers level and it had then to be transformed into legislation in each of the member states. At the beginning of 1993 a significant number of the SEM measures had not been implemented – 5 per cent of the measures had still to be agreed as EU legislation, and between 20 per cent and 30 per cent of EU legislation had still to be converted into legislation in at least one member state. Denmark and France had made most progress, with less than 10 per cent of the measures still to be put into legislation; Spain, Italy and the UK were the furthest behind with 20 per cent still to be done.

It will therefore be some time before all the measures arising from the Single European Act are fully implemented. Businesses will need help and advice for some time to come. The business information services still have work to do.

Nor is that the end of business-related developments in Europe. The 1992 action plan to strengthen and expand the SEM had other key elements, included the following:

1993   Creation of the European Economic Area (EEA) comprising the 12 member states of the EU, together with the EFTA countries – Austria, Finland, Iceland, Liechtenstein, Norway, Sweden and Switzerland – with legislation on public procurement, competition policy, and consumer protection.

1994   Higher education diplomas to be recognised throughout the EU.

Open competition will be established for public authority and utility contracts.

1996   Stockbrokers able to operate in any member state.

1997   Agreement for the implementation of a single system for VAT, based on harmonisation of rates.

1999   Duty-free sales on internal flights and ferry crossings to end.

2000   A free internal market in cars, and the removal of controls on Japanese imports.

Local organisations

Many large towns and cities in the UK have a **European Office**. Its function is to provide information and advice to local companies, particularly those with limited resources such as SMEs. Their activities are mirrored by similar organisations throughout the EU.

One of these offices, located in the north-west of England produces a regular publication, appropriately titled *EBIS* (*European Business Information Service*), containing topical information. A recent copy provided an 'Update on EU legislation', a country profile on Portugal, the latest information on European funding opportunities, and an explanation of the new tender opportunities in public procurement.

This office also advertises the launch of any new publications that might be useful to local businesses. Recently, for example, it announced the publication of a report on the restructuring of the European defence industry and handbooks covering: mechanical engineering; electrical engineering; plastics and plastic packaging; pulp, paper and board; chemicals; and construction – all published by the local **Training and Enterprise Council (TEC)**.

Chambers of Commerce are also very useful sources of information. Via their national and international network they are able to provide local business-es with personal contacts in other locations.

Closely associated with Chambers of Commerce and the TECs are **Export Clubs**. These bring together local business people with a common aim – to trade transnationally within the EU.

National organisations

The **Department of Trade and Industry (DTI)** was the key organisation in preparing the UK for the Single European Market. Its high-profile 'Europe Open for Business' campaign was designed to raise companies' awareness of SEM legislation. A natural sequel was the 'Business in Europe' service to assist companies to succeed in Europe (the EU *and* the EEA). It includes an informa-tion hotline signposting to experts, guidance and support on specific regional and industrial sector issues, and a range of publications.

DTI Country Desks are the focal point for all information and advice on trading with each country in Europe. They have a wide range of information on trading practices, rules and regulations, and the do's and don'ts of trading within each country.

The **DTI European Task Force** co-ordinates a focused attack on specific com-mercial targets, identifying potential UK suppliers and assisting them to take advantage of the opportunities. The Department also organises **trade missions**, allowing UK companies to explore prospects for their goods and services at first hand, and it assists UK companies to exhibit at **trade fairs**.

The **Export Credits Guarantee Department** provides insurance against the main commercial and political risks that arise between taking an order and obtaining payment. It also provides guarantees of payment to banks providing export finance at favourable interest rates.

Because small firms are faced with a bewildering range of advice and infor-mation from a confusing maze of support agencies, the DTI is contributing towards the cost of **'one-stop shops'**, managed by the **TECs**. Each 'shop' pro-vides core services of advice, diagnostic work, counselling and information.

European Information Centres (EICs)

The European Commission believes that the Single European Act will only truly result in a Single European Market if businesses are kept fully briefed on how it can affect them. To this end, the **European Information Network (EIN)** was established by the European Commission to help SMEs recognise and understand the opportunities and threats that the 'new Europe' presents. Its objectives, in line with the Commission's enterprise policy, are to inform; to assist with the making of business contacts; to encourage co-operation between businesses across Europe; and to simplify administration (particularly accounting and taxation).

There are 211 **European Information Centres (EICs)** in the EU, 23 in the UK. As 'satellite' offices of the European Commission they are in daily contact with Brussels, and they can therefore obtain up-to-date information for their client companies. The centres are located to support regions rather than countries. Thus, each EIC has a good knowledge and understanding of the types of business that are most common in its region.

EICs can provide information on the following topics:

- EU grants and loans.
- EU law (on such matters as environmental, health and safety).
- EU institutions (who to contact in the Commission).
- EU statistics and market information (e.g. GDP, trade, labour costs).

The majority of centres operate the **Business Co-operation Network**, a kind of 'dating agency' for companies seeking business partners, such as agents and distributors, in other countries. They can also access **Tenders Electronic Daily (TED)**, a database which is an essential tool for firms interested in public sector contracts, with details of invitations to tender for works and supply contracts across Europe and beyond.

The EICs obtain their income partly from patrons such as TECs, Chambers of Commerce, and private and public sector companies, partly from annual membership subscriptions from smaller businesses, and partly from charging fees for services. An EIC may deal with a simple enquiry without making a charge. A business person could, for example, make occasional use of an EIC in the same way as they would use a reference library. For a more complex enquiry, however, where the EIC staff undertook some investigative work on behalf of the business, a charge would be made.

Membership is an attractive option for a small business. The subscription varies according to the size of the business and the amount of enquiry time they expect to require.

ACTIVITY 10.6

Because EICs are largely dependent on income from work they do for businesses they are not likely to be able to spare much time to deal with enquiries from students, however much they might wish to. They are, however, generally prepared to provide a college with information about their activities and charges, because it helps to raise awareness and ultimately add to business demand for their services. Using any such information, and the description of EIC activities given in the preceding pages, write notes on how an EIC could assist in marketing productivity improving machinery to shoe manufacturers.

SUMMARY

1 Customers who have placed unsolicited orders can be very useful as sources of marketing information.

2 Marketing information for business-to-business selling can generally be more clearly identified than that for sales to the public.

3 Market research can be expensive and time-consuming. Careful planning is needed so that effective use is made of generally available information and desk research; and visits and field research are then undertaken with specific objectives and limited scope.

4 The primary purpose of marketing data is to identify potential customers, but it also provides information on competitors and competitive products, prices and discounts, distribution and promotional methods, suitable agencies to assist with distribution, promotion and selling, and possible business partners.

5 Local, national and EU organisations (such as Chambers of Commerce, Export Clubs, Universities and Business Schools, EICs, TECs, professional and trade bodies, the DTI, BOTB and European Commission) all have a role to play in providing information on opportunities in the EU, grants and loans, EU law and institutions, market information. Many have access to networks of contacts within the EU and elsewhere.

6 European Information Centres offer a cost-effective way for SMEs to get up-to-date information on Europe. They are especially useful in finding trading partners for businesses who wish to establish a European dimension to their operations.

Assignment 10

BACKGROUND

The activities in this chapter have been very specific in terms of the product that is being manufactured, and the target group. Now reread the case study on Airpower Limited, about industrial compressors. The company's product range is quite narrow but there is a much wider potential target group.

ACTIVITY

1 Assume that Airpower Limited aims to achieve 3 per cent of its £10 million turnover in each of three new markets – Spain, Portugal and Italy – and decide on an appropriate budget.

2 Plan the programme for gathering marketing information for entry into each of the markets.

3 Undertake whatever desk research you can using all the resources available to you.

11 Innovation, quality and safety

OBJECTIVES

1 **To identify ways of gaining EU assistance with Europeanisation: for example by identifying the innovative features of a company's operations.**

2 **To understand the different perceptions of quality that arise from various cultures and business practices.**

3 **To understand the equivalence of ISO, EN and BS standards.**

4 **To gain an up-to-date knowledge of health and safety at work regulations, following the 1993 changes made at the instigation of the European Commission.**

Introduction

Three key areas in which UK businesses need to be strong to maintain competitiveness in EU and world markets are innovation; quality; and health and safety. The European Commission recognises the importance of having businesses that are competitive and successful because these qualities create the wealth and employment and help to fulfil the EU's goals. The Commission has therefore introduced many schemes to facilitate progress in these three areas, and a legal framework is being developed to ensure that consistently high standards are adopted throughout the member states.

Innovation

Innovation is the successful exploitation of new ideas. For example, it may involve devising a new product, making an existing product more attractive or more user friendly, finding a more efficient way of making the product, finding a new market or market strategy, exploring new ways of financing a venture, developing information systems such as a marketing database, or establishing a new company culture (e.g. Investors in People, Total Quality Management).

Innovation is often forced upon a business by threats to its survival (e.g. when the existing products are approaching the end of their life cycle, when there is a declining market, when there is fierce competition, when there is a downturn in economic conditions). Equally, it is a way of taking advantage of opportunities such as the removal of barriers arising from the Single European Market (SEM) and the potential to extend the 'home' market. Moreover the benefits of innovation are potential for high profit, high growth, and a high company or brand profile, and innovation is usually associated with high levels of job satisfaction and motivation, new methods and new jobs.

EU funding is most readily available for innovation that provides technology that is transferable, and employment in socially deprived regions.

There are risks associated with innovation. A delay in reaching the profitable stage of a project can threaten other parts of the business. Development costs are difficult to predict and a business may find it has not the expertise to carry through the ideas. Traditional funding agencies (e.g. banks, development agencies) prefer short-term returns and are unhappy about investing in projects where there is high risk. EU funding is aimed at longer projects where the outcome is more difficult to predict, and it insists on good project management and regular reviews of progress to prove that its investment is being used wisely.

It is always good practice to prepare and use a business plan when introducing change into business activities and particularly when considering innovation. A business plan helps the company to evaluate the risks, and is an essential part of any application for funding.

To help in identifying potential areas of innovation, to plan its implementation, and, in particular, to gain outside assistance and funding, innovation is normally classified as being:

- a new product;
- an enhancement of an existing product;
- a new process; or
- a new market.

EU and national schemes usually relate to innovation in one or more of these categories.

Funding innovation

The Regional Enterprise Grants – development scheme

Support for innovation can be obtained, in certain circumstances, through the DTI Regional Enterprise Grants scheme. Through this scheme 50 per cent of eligible costs, up to a maximum of £25,000 may be obtained.

Any development work on a new product leading up to the point of commercial production, including a feasibility study, development of the technical specification, and design and manufacture of prototypes, can be funded. The work may be done by the company developing the product, or it may be subcontracted.

To be eligible for the grant, the business must be located in an area that has Development, Intermediate, Objective 2, Task Force, or City Challenge status and must employ less than 50 people. The DTI will need to be satisfied that the project involves genuine innovation as well as technical risk.

It is possible to apply for more than one grant, provided each application relates to a different project, but it is not usual to fund more than one project at the same time.

SMART

SMART is an annual competition to encourage innovative technology in firms with fewer than 50 employees. Entrants with the best commercially viable ideas are awarded up to £45,000 towards the cost of the first year's development. In a second stage of the competition, the most promising ideas from the first stage may be awarded up to £60,000 more to exploit the ideas commercially.

SPUR

SPUR is a scheme to help firms of up to 500 employees develop new products and processes that involve significant technological advance for the industry. A flat-rate grant of 30 per cent towards eligible costs is offered, up to a maximum of £150,000.

Regional Enterprise Grants – investment scheme

Grants for investment projects are available under the Regional Enterprise Grants scheme for projects in most manufacturing and some service sectors. Up to 15 per cent of expenditure on fixed assets, with a maximum of £15,000, may be granted. The business must be located in a Development or Intermediate area, have less than 25 employees and be able to demonstrate the need for such assistance. Only one grant is available to an organisation.

Regional Selective Assistance

In the Development and Intermediate areas, grants of up to £25,000 may be negotiated for projects that are commercially viable, create or safeguard employment, and contribute to both the regional and national economy.

ACTIVITY 11.2

Assess the likelihood of obtaining an innovation or investment grant for the project defined in Activity 11.1 (assume the company's base is in your locality):

1 How does the project represent a departure from the company's current practice?

2 Is the innovation a new product, a product enhancement, a new process, or a new market?

3 What technical risks are there?

4 How many people does the company employ?

5 Is the company located in an area that is eligible for regional aid?

6 Will the project create or safeguard jobs? How can this be proved?

7 What will be the impact of the project (a) locally, and (b) nationally?

Protecting an innovation from imitation

Society accepts that there is a need for industrial, commercial and intellectual property to be protected, in order to encourage creative effort, innovation and investment. However, in some ways the restrictions imposed by this protection can be viewed as a limitation on free competition. A careful balance has therefore to be achieved.

Protection is provided by patents, trade marks and copyright. Traditionally these were national measures which varied from one country to another, and were only effective within the country where the idea was registered. Those who wanted to have the benefit of a trade mark, for example, were obliged to take legal measures in every one of the countries in which guaranteed rights were wanted. The rights thus acquired, after multiple procedures that were often long and costly, would vary from one country to another. In some cases access to a national market would not be possible because rights had already been assigned to a competitor.

The EU is now introducing schemes that apply in every member state and will require only a single application. Furthermore, to prevent unfair limitations on competition, the European Court of Justice has been given power to prohibit the use of a patent or trade mark that is unfair because it disguises illegal agreements between companies, allows national discrimination, or attempts to restrict trade between member states. The benefits of a unified EU system are:

1 Fuller, consistent protection.
2 Simpler administration.
3 The possibility of businesses operating policies better suited to the scale of the EU, free of national barriers.
4 Easier adaptation of the rules to cope with ever faster technological change, for example, in biotechnology and computing. This adaptation could be done by states individually, but that would mean doing the work 12 times with the risk of creating new disparities.

European patents

A patent is an official registration which can be requested by the author of an industrial invention or discovery and which gives that author the exclusive right to use the invention for his or her own benefit for a specific period. The author can license a third party to exploit the discovery.

Two conventions have been drawn up:

1 The Munich Convention (1973) came into force in the EU and other western European countries in 1977 and can be used instead of or in parallel with a national patent. The European patent is relatively expensive but is less onerous and involves fewer procedures than obtaining three or four national patents. The number of applications rose from 1500 per month in 1980 to over 4000 per month in 1992.
2 The Luxembourg Convention (1975) supplements the Munich Convention. Amongst its provisions is a restriction of the exclusive rights conferred by a European patent. If, for example, a company holding a patent delays the marketing of a product in prejudice of the general interest, then a compulsory licensing system can be forced on it.

Community trade marks

A trade mark is one of the most common ways of protecting a consumer product. There are several million trade marks in the EU. Usually they are registered when they are created but some arise out of usage. Trade marks have no time limit.

Put simply, a trade mark enables the holder to prevent another person or business using an identical or similar distinguishing sign where there would be the risk of confusion in the public mind.

The EU aims to reduce differences in national legislation and has introduced an EU trade-mark system. This will provide for:

- A ten-year registration, renewable for another ten years.
- Refusal of registration if the proposed trade mark is already held by another owner or is unlawful (for example likely to mislead the public).
- A procedure for settling legal disputes in the case of counterfeiting or contested validity.

Copyright

'Works of the intellect' are not subject to patent or trade mark, but they do benefit from national and various international copyright conventions. However, there are many gaps and disparities, particularly in publishing contracts and duration of copyright protection. These are particularly troublesome in fields where the speed of technological progress calls for massive investment – for example, the design and production of integrated circuits and computer programs, data banks, and the development of new audio and audio-visual formats such as digital recording.

The Community aims to deal with:

- Piracy (unauthorised reproduction for commercial purposes) of films, disks, cassettes and computer programs.
- Private copying.
- Distribution rights.

Piracy and copying are serious problems in the music sector, where digital recording makes it possible for anyone to produce a copy as good as the studio master-recording. The EU proposes to guarantee the rights of authors to renumeration, permit technical limitation so that originals cannot be copied, and the introduction of a levy on recording material and equipment.

Television stations, video libraries and cinemas are keen to introduce new titles. However, the producer may wish to commercialise the title in stages. The problem is growing rapidly with the increasing amount of cross-border access to TV programmes. The Commission proposes to allow authors to control the release of the work by licensing, and so ensure that there is fair remuneration from rental and other methods of showing the film. The Commission also aims to protect the author's exclusive rights of reproduction, adaptation and distribution of computer programs and data banks for a period of 50 years.

There is, moreover, provision for legal protection on the topography of semiconductor products. This is vital because the development of a sophisticated microchip can require an investment of 100 million ECU, while it costs only 50,000 to 100,000 ECU to plagiarise an existing topography. Similar measures have already been taken in Japan and the USA.

Quality

Quality concepts

Quality is fashionable, and there is a host of jargon associated with it – 'right first time', 'zero defects', 'quality culture', 'quality circles', 'quality assurance' and so on. This book is not the place to investigate these in detail. However, it is appropriate to examine how the EU countries approach the concept of quality.

Quality is often defined as 'fitness for purpose'. A 'quality product' is valued and respected. German cars and French wine are generally considered to be 'quality products', but a less subjective judgement of quality is needed for cross-border comparisons.

It proved extremely difficult to gain agreement on what constitutes a quality product or a quality service. The Germans, for example, had very definite ideas about alcohol content of beer and imposed severe restrictions on additives. The English and Belgians had their own different belief about what produces 'quality' beer. Another example is that of 'mince meat'. Initial EU proposals for quality standards for this product involved a specification that would have classified all UK mince meat as substandard. Detailed examination revealed that this arose from different national perceptions of the nature of 'mince meat'. In France 'mince meat' is steak, eaten raw. In the UK it is an ingredient for cooking in pies and other dishes. They are, in fact, two quite different products.

Attempts to control the use of names (often much misrepresented in the UK media) proved impossible because of long-established use of names in the various member states. The solution, therefore, was to ensure that the ingredients of products were clearly shown on the labels. There is, for example, an EU requirement that the additives in food are identified by the 'E number' system. In addition, there has been a levelling-up in standards of hygiene. This has often favoured British manufacturers and retailers, but on other occasions they have been involved in additional costs to match the hygiene criteria for the same or very similar product in other countries.

The concept of harmonisation – similar regulations for similar products – is vital to implementation of the SEA. Harmonisation has preserved national differences. It is a concept that applies to all products. There will, for example, continue to be national differences in building products, electrical fittings, VAT rates, professional qualifications, and many other items.

Harmonisation is based upon giving the consumer a better knowledge of the similarities and differences. This encourages value and respect for products to be based on knowledge rather than prejudice and ignorance. This *might* lead to a 'standard' product (or a 'standard' method or service) if one product is clearly and considerably better than the others. It is more likely, however, that national or regional differences of need and preference will maintain the distinction.

The following are two key criteria for quality.

1 Information for the consumer.
2 Health.

An additional criterion was introduced in 1992 – the effect on the environment of the production, use, and disposal of a product, method, or service.

ACTIVITY 11.3

1 Examine the packaging of (a) fresh meat (b) frozen food, and (c) eggs in your local supermarket.

2 What information do they contain that is helpful to the consumer and/or relevant to health?

3 What information do they contain that can help the supermarket improve the quality of its service to customers? (Think carefully about how 'quality of its service' can be measured.)

Quality standards

The development of standards

Perhaps the clearest indicator that a UK business has recognised the importance of quality is the fact that it has gained, or is working towards gaining, BS5750 certification. Since BS5750 was first published in 1979, well over 15,000 organisations in the UK have been assessed and registered against BS5750 or directly equivalent standards. A number of other countries have introduced their own quality standards, many of them essentially copies of BS5750, and some with amended or additional requirements.

In 1983 the International Standards Organisation (ISO) initiated work on international standards for quality. This led to the publication of the five standards in the ISO 9000 series in 1987. The ISO standards are largely based on BS5750:1979. However, they reflect international requirements and eight years of UK experience. They were published in the UK as BS5750:1987, effective from 29 May 1987. The equivalent European standard is called EN29000:1987.

The Consumer Protection Act 1987 provides an additional incentive for businesses in the UK to implement the standards. It requires products to be safe, and produced and supplied in such a way as to minimise the likelihood that they could give rise to liability.

The EN29000 standard, and its equivalent national and international standards, tells suppliers and manufacturers what is required of a quality-orientated management system. They explain how a company can establish, document, and maintain systems for managing quality. All these standards are practical standards, the principles of which apply whether the company employs 10 people or 10,000. They identify the basic disciplines and specify the procedures and criteria that ensure that products and services meet the customers' requirements.

EN29000 is not, in itself, a guarantee of quality. It does, however, mean that the organisation has procedures and documentation which define how quality can be achieved and measured. It is, therefore, much easier for quality to be improved and sustained within an organisation that has adopted EN29000.

What exactly are the standards?

EN29000 has two components:

1 The first component (also known as ISO9000 and as BS5750 part 0, section 0.1) is a guide to the selection and use of the appropriate parts of the standards.
2 The second (also known as ISO9004 and as BS5750 part 0, section 0.2) is a guide to overall quality management and the quality system elements in other parts of the standards.

EN29001 (ISO9001 and BS5750:part 1) relates to quality specifications for design/development, production, installation and servicing when the requirement of goods or services are specified by the customer in terms of how they must perform and which are then provided to the supplier.

EN29002 (ISO9002 and BS5750:part 2) sets out the requirements where a business is manufacturing goods or offering a service to a published specification or to the customer's specification.

EN29003 (ISO9003 and BS5750:part 3) specifies the quality system to be used in the final inspection.

What aspects of quality do they cover?

Elements of the quality system, as defined in the EN29000 standards are set out in Table 11.1.

Companies gain EN29000 certification when they have been inspected by an organisation that has been accredited to carry out the quality audits by the Secretary of State for Industry, and have satisfied this organisation that suitable quality procedures and supporting documentation are defined and are in use within the company.

Why is it important to have quality standards?

First and foremost, customers are always concerned that they get value for money. Thus a company can make itself more attractive to potential customers by proving that is concerned about quality. EN29000 certification does exactly that. Indeed some organisations will only buy from suppliers that have EN29000 certification (or the equivalent BS5750 or ISO9000).

Table 11.1 Elements of the quality system, as defined in the EN29000 standards

	EN29001	EN29002	EN29003
1 Management responsibilities	3	2	1
2 Quality system principles	3	3	2
3 Internal auditing of the quality system	3	2	1
4 Quality-related cost considerations	0	0	0
5 Quality in marketing	3	3	0
6 Quality in specification and control	3	0	0
7 Quality in procurement	3	3	0
8 Quality in production	3	3	0
9 Control of production	3	3	0
10 Material control and traceability	3	3	2
11 Control of inspection and testing	3	3	2
12 Product inspection and testing	3	3	2
13 Control of measuring and test equipment	3	3	2
14 Control of non-conforming products	3	3	2
15 Corrective action	3	3	0
16 Handling, storage, packing and distribution	3	3	2
17 After-sales servicing	3	0	0
18 Control of quality documentation	3	3	2
19 Quality records	3	3	2
20 Personnel and training	3	2	1
21 Product safety and liability	0	0	0
22 Use of statistical techniques	3	3	2
23 Purchaser-supplied product	3	3	0

Note: Scale of stringency ranges from 3=high to 0=none.

Second, concern about quality is good for the company. Staff who are properly trained and motivated, and who have clear procedures to follow to ensure that products and services are of a high quality, are likely to be proud of the company. Faulty products and poor service are less probable, and when something does go wrong it is probable that it will be spotted and rectified earlier. Preventing problems is almost invariably cheaper than fixing them, while problems spotted earlier can be fixed at lower cost, and with less disruption to normal operations, than those that are not discovered until later.

ACTIVITY 11.4

1 Evaluate the benefits of gaining accreditation against quality standards for UK trade.

2 Discuss to what extent the same benefits would be gained when trading trans-nationally in Europe, and whether there are any additional benefits.

Health and safety

EU directives

At the end of 1992, as part of the implementation of the Single European Act, new EU directives came into effect covering health and safety. These EU directives form a code of practice covering:

1 Management of health and safety.
2 Health and safety in the use of display screens.
3 Manual handling and operations.
4 Provision and use of equipment.
5 Workplace health, safety and welfare.
6 Personal protection equipment.

The directives arise chiefly from Article 100A of the SEA, which relates to the removal of barriers to trade, and Article 118A, which sets minimum health and safety standards throughout Europe. They incorporate good practice identified in one or more member states and prevent a business gaining competitive advantage by adopting sub-standard practices and producing sub-standard products that threaten consumers, customers, employees and the public.

Few, if any, extra burdens are incurred by UK businesses as a result of these directives. The new framework for health and safety brings together items from a variety of sources, most from the 1974 Health and Safety at Work Act. However:

1 Penalties for offences against health and safety regulations have been increased. The situation now is that an offence against the Health and Safety at Work Act 1974 relating to sections 2 to 6, improvement notices, prohibition notices, and court orders can be penalised in a magistrates' court by a £20,000 fine and/or up to six months' imprisonment, while other offences against this Act can be penalised by a £5000 fine. Offences against other regulations can also be penalised by a £5000 fine in a magistrates' court. If an offence is referred to a Crown Court, then unlimited fines and up to two years' imprisonment can be imposed.

2 From 1 January 1993 BS5750 has a section covering health and safety.
3 Visual display units (VDUs) are now a common feature in offices, shops, factories, and even in the high street. The new regulations, which came into effect on 1 January 1993, affect employed and self-employed workers who habitually use VDUs for a significant part of their normal work. Employers have to analyse workstations of employees covered by the regulations, ensure that workstations meet minimum requirements, and assess and reduce risks.

Health and safety policy

The EU favours self-regulation in the management of health and safety.

Employers clearly want to achieve the very best levels of health and safety at minimum cost. To achieve this it is necessary to identify and evaluate the risks. Appropriate, cost-effective measures can then be adopted by determining priority, preparing an action plan, and monitoring progress as the plan is implemented. A manager can easily demonstrate that good practice has been followed in developing and implementing health and safety policy by producing simple documentation at each stage.

There are six key features of good health and safety policy:

1 *Define procedures and set standards*   For example, agree targets with managers and supervisors, and make health and safety a component of purchasing practice.
2 *Train the staff to adopt healthy and safe methods*   Raising awareness encourages a 'health and safety culture' and develops self-regulation, which is more cost effective than the 'add on', which is totally dependent on the company's safety officers.
3 *Organise staff so that hazards are recognised, reported and dealt with promptly*   The Health and Safety Executive suggests an approach that encompasses four c's – competence, control, co-operation and communication. You may wish to add a fifth – commitment.
4 *Monitor and measure performance*   It is important for a company to know how well it is doing and, if there are any problems, what caused them. The more time that goes by before an incident is investigated, the more difficult it is to determine the causes.
5 *Learn from experience*   The last thing that should happen is for accidents and mistakes to be 'swept under the carpet'. That only allows the same thing to happen again.
6 *Carry out regular audits*   Although it is important for health and safety improvements to be continuous and ongoing, it is useful for management periodically to pause and reflect on where the company is, where it wants to be, and what difference there is between the two. New targets can then be set.

The following is a suggested starting point for preparing an audit check-list specific to your own organisation. During the audit, answers and other comments should be made against each question. Subsequently the answers and comments should be analysed and an action plan prepared with clear responsibilities and deadlines.

1　Health and safety (H & S) policy

1.1　Are H & S responsibilities defined and allocated to staff?
1.2　Are H & S procedures defined and implemented?
1.3　Are H & S audits undertaken regularly?
1.4　Is there a H & S committee?

2　Training

2.1　Is H & S included in the induction programme?
2.2　Is on-the-job H & S training given?
2.3　Is there any H & S awareness training (off the job)?
2.4　Are hazards associated with specific tasks identified (e.g. lifting equipment), and is there special training to avoid/deal with accidents?
2.5　Are there fire/evacuation drills? Are they effective?
2.6　Are H & S spot checks carried out? Are the results analysed and do they lead to action if necessary?
2.8　What records are kept of training specifically relating to H & S?

3　Statutory records

3.1　Of plant and equipment checks (e.g. lifting tackle, pressurised containers)?
3.2　Of accidents?
3.3　Of fire alarm, extinguishers testing, etc?
3.4　Of radiation levels?
3.5　Of safety critical items (e.g. abrasive tools)?

4　Incident and accident analysis

4.1　Monthly analysis undertaken?
4.2　Injuries analysed?
4.3　Fire alarms analysed?

5　Statutory notices

5.1　HASAWA – 'What you should know' information on display?
5.2　Are warnings and advice on good practice on display for all hazards relevant to the organisation's premises, equipment and processes?
5.3　Are electricity regulations on display?
5.4　Is electric shock resuscitation and other first aid information on display?
5.5　Is Health & Safety Policy displayed?
5.6　Is Employer's Liability Certificate on display?

6　Fire precautions

6.1　Fire certificates up to date?
6.2　Fire exits marked, freely accessible and unlocked?
6.3　Fire extinguishers and other appliances ready for use?
6.4　Battery-charging ventilation clear?
6.5　No smoking notices present and legible?
6.6　Conditions for storage of flammable liquids at and preferably above minimum safety levels?

7　Environment

7.1　Does space per person meet statutory requirements?
7.2　Is heating adequate?
7.3　Is ventilation adequate?
7.4　Is fume extraction effective?
7.5　Is dust extraction effective?
7.6　Is lighting adequate and suitable?
7.7　Is the area clean, and in a reasonable decorative state?
7.8　Is the work-space adequately delimited?
7.9　Are access and evacuation routes adequate, marked, and unobstructed?
7.10　Are all the necessary warning signs (including no smoking if appropriate) present and legible?

8　Welfare

8.1　Is there adequate first aid equipment? Does it match the contents list, is it up to date, is it sterile?
8.2　Are there sufficient first-aiders for the number of personnnel employed and the nature of the work and conditions? Are their certificates up to date? Do they have opportunities to update them?
8.3　Is there access to drinking water?

Fig. 11.1　Health and safety audit

8.4	Are toilets and washing facilities adequate for the number of personnel, the nature of the work, and the working conditions?
8.5	Are toilet and washing facilities clean and in good order – with soap, towels, etc?
8.6	Is there appropriate locker space?
8.7	Is there a suitably equipped rest room?

9 Protective clothing

| 9.1 | As necessary, for:
  ● eyes;
  ● face;
  ● feet;
  ● hands;
  ● hearing; and
  ● head? |
9.2	Adequate protection against cold, heat, fumes, dust, glare, etc?
9.3	Is work-wear (including footwear) appropriate, and readily available?
9.9	Do employees use the protective clothing provided?
9.10	How is usage of protective clothing controlled?

10 Housekeeping

10.1	What is the level of tidiness?
10.2	What is the level of cleanliness?
10.3	What arrangements are there for refuse disposal (particularly oil, degreasers, batteries, etc)?
10.4	Are there separate receptacles for sharp and dangerous objects?
10.5	Are there separate receptacles for hot or flammable objects (e.g. cigarettes)?

11 Access and workplace

11.1	Access roads adequate and clear?
11.2	Floors suitably surfaced and in good condition?
11.3	Stairs in good condition, adequately lighted, and marked to highlight treads?
11.4	Paths adequate and clear?
11.5	Pits in good condition with safe access and evacuation?
11.6	Building and structures sound and in good repair?
11.7	Ladders and steps well maintained?
11.8	Passageways and gangways adequate in width, unobstructed, and reasonably straight?
11.9	Vehicles in good condition and well maintained?
11.10	Platforms, scaffolding, etc, in good condition and properly erected?

12 Storage

12.1	Racks sound and not overloaded?
12.2	Stacks in stable condition and not overloaded?
12.3	Floor loading within tolerances?
12.4	Chemicals in suitable containers, suitable locations, and not susceptible to damage or disturbance?
12.5	Flammable products protected against heat and flash risks?

13 Work systems

13.1	Operations defined with evidence of H & S considerations?
13.2	Handling, lifting and movement defined with evidence of H & S considerations?
13.3	Maintenance procedures defined to support H & S policies?
13.4	Equipment life assessd with H & S considerations included?
13.4	Noise reduction programme in operation.
13.5	Emergencies anticipated and contingency plans defined and practised?

14 Plant and equipment

| 14.1 | Fixed electrical equipment safe, checked and protected physically and electrically? |
| 14.2 | Portable electrical equipment registered and regularly checked? |
| 14.3 | Checks, repairs and replacements undertaken and records kept, for:
  ● pressure equipment;
  ● lifting equipment;
  ● mechanical handling equipment;
  ● ladders and staging;
  ● fixed machinery; and
  ● extraction equipment? |
| 14.4 | Provision to cut off or isolate electricity, gas, water, etc? |

Fig. 11.1 continued

ACTIVITY 11.5

1 Undertake a health and safety audit of your own organisation (college or company), using the check-list given in Figure 11.1.

2 Identify what changes to current practice (if any) have resulted from the 1993 directives.

SUMMARY

1 Innovation may be defined in several ways (e.g. new products, new processes, new marketing or distribution methods).

2 The European Commission provides assistance, in the form of support funding and expertise, for innovation, especially where they involve SMEs or are in regions identified as eligible for EU aid.

3 National preferences are more easily retained while achieving high-quality standards by harmonisation, rather than standardisation.

4 The guiding principles of European quality regulations are information for the consumer, health and safety, and protection of the environment.

5 There are equivalent European (EN) and international (ISO) standards for the well-known UK national standard BS5750.

6 Within the range of standards it is possible to select those that suit the different types of business – manufacture, distribution, service, and so on.

7 Health and safety directives aim to identify examples of good practice in member states and promulgate them throughout the EU.

8 The EU is concerned to prevent companies gaining competitive advantage by adopting substandard practices which threaten consumers, employees and the public.

Assignment 11

BACKGROUND

A key element in gaining EN9000 accreditation is the preparation of manuals that describe the company's procedures. Having procedures and manuals describing the procedures does not guarantee their quality but it does open them up to scrutiny and, with the right approach from management, encourage a business culture that strives to achieve ever improving quality. The manuals must be comprehensive. They must describe not just normal operations but also the procedures for dealing with errors and exceptional situations. Manuals are needed for every part of the business – sales, purchasing, technical, personnel, accounts, production, and so forth.

In the European context, quality includes informing the customer by labelling and other methods, considering the health and safety of customers and workers, and ensuring that the product and production processes do not harm the environment.

This assignment focuses on health and safety.

ACTIVITY

Work with two or three other people on the first activity. Work individually on the preparation of the manual.

1 Choose one of the items in the 'six pack' code of practice arising from EU directives (page 204) and apply it to your own organisation (workplace or college). Consider:

(a) What targets are appropriate to the measurement of standards.

(b) How a 'health and safety culture' can be established involving everyone.

(c) What procedures are needed to ensure that hazards are recognised, reported and dealt with promptly.

(d) How to ensure that health and safety standards are continually improved, building on experience.

2 Prepare a health and safety quality manual for the selected part of the code of practice. Remember, the manual must be comprehensive, dealing with errors and exceptional conditions as well as normal situations, and must be consistent with the relevant EU directives.

Part Four

BUSINESS SUCCESS IN EUROPE

12 Distribution and logistics

OBJECTIVES   1 To understand the size, importance and characteristics of the distribution industry in the EU.

2 To explain the role of EU legislation in liberalising, harmonising and removing barriers to transnational transport.

3 To analyse the contribution to intra-EU transport by the main modes of transport.

4 To recognise the increasing importance of air freight, and of independent carriers in European freight operations.

5 To describe the characteristics of a modern transnational distribution system.

Introduction

The distribution chain begins with raw materials and ends with consumers. Between these extremities materials, components, assemblies and finished products have to be transported from location to location. Often it is necessary to store items to provide a buffer between the supplier and the customer which compensates for fluctuations in production and usage. Distribution systems, therefore, have two components: transport and storage.

Inadequate distribution systems increase costs and cause business to fail to meet local customers' service expectations. Poor systems may result from: using the wrong methods of transport; storage systems that are badly located or that do not have efficient ways of entering and removing goods; or a lack of control over the distribution function.

The transport industry has, in the last 10 to 15 years, undergone rapid changes. The principal changes are the increased use of multi-modal transport, containerisation, and the growth in the number of highly efficient carriers offering next-day delivery throughout the EU.

The 1970s saw significant progress in stock control and materials handling methods. In turn, the 1980s and 1990s have seen emphasis placed on the location of warehouses, together with the development of 'just in time' and other techniques aimed at smoothing the flow of goods from original source to final destination. However, the most important development in distribution systems has been the improvement in control that arises from computer-based control systems which make it possible to locate unallocated storage and transportation capacity and track the movement of goods .

It is estimated that the European distribution market amounts to some £81 billion. The European Commission therefore recognises the importance of logistics to the EU economy and has introduced a wide range of measures to improve its efficiency and competitiveness.

ACTIVITY 12.1

List the items of information you think is needed to locate a consignment in transit, and to trace its movement from source to destination.

The EC legislative programme

The European Commission has contributed to the improvement in distribution systems by deregulating much of the transport industry, and by providing a better infrastructure.

The Single European Act, implementation of which was scheduled for completion at the end of 1992, included proposals specifically to make transport easier and subject to less regulation. It also provided for a liberalised and harmonised environment for transport companies to operate in. This environment is not only to the benefit of transport companies, it also allows a whole range of companies to examine their distribution strategies and put into place more efficient systems. They can, and should, plan their distribution on a European scale.

The removal of physical barriers

Historically, national boundaries were convenient places to carry out checking procedures. These included inspection of goods, checking of paperwork, collection of VAT and excise duty, anti-smuggling activities, checking of vehicle safety standards, checking of hauliers' licences, collection of trade statistics, checking of animal and plant health, and calculation of monetary compensatory amounts for agricultural produce.

The majority of these checks could be carried out anywhere. The Single European Act was the opportunity to eliminate the checks that were inappropriate to a single market, to simplify those that needed to remain, and to shift them to the most efficient place. The effect was to speed up the movement of goods and to allow transport users to predict transit times more accurately.

VAT collection

To avoid unnecessary red tape at EU frontiers a transitional system has been introduced that will continue until the full system, based on the destination principle, can be implemented in all the member states. The EU's VAT systems are described more fully in Chapter 14.

Excise duty

There are proposals to harmonise excise duties throughout the EU. The effect on tobacco, alcohol and petroleum products sold in the UK will be dramatic. An assessment of the probable effect includes a 40p reduction on a packet of cigarettes, and an increase of 20p on a pint of beer, with fuel prices remaining more or less unchanged. Health lobbies are opposing the proposals, and they may not be politically acceptable either.

ACTIVITY 12.2
Why would harmonisation of excise duty be opposed by health lobbies and be politically unacceptable?

Customs procedures and physical checks

Border checks have been replaced by roving customs officers. Concerns that the removal of frontier checks would assist drug smugglers and terrorists have been unfounded. In fact the detection rate has risen because Customs personnel, released from routine checks, have been able to target their activities more precisely.

Prior to 1993, intra-EU freight movements were based on the use of the Single Administrative Document (SAD) introduced in 1988, and the Community Transit (T-form) system. They have been retained temporarily for Spanish and Portuguese traffic under the transitional membership arrangements. Generally, however, formalities are now handled by the Direct Trader Input (DTI) system.

EFTA

Since EFTA countries have removed customer barriers to EU traffic and received reciprocal treatment for their exports to the EU, common transport rules seem a logical consequence. However, Switzerland and Austria have tax penalties to deter road transit traffic and Switzerland has a 28-tonne gross weight limit on trucks. All six EFTA members are 'environmentally aware' and their rules on exhaust emissions, weights and noise are currently more stringent than those of the EU.

Other countries

The principle on which the EU works is that goods imported from countries that are not members (or are covered by special arrangements such as EFTA) must be cleared with the authorities in the EU country they first enter. They are then deemed to be in 'free circulation' and can travel between EU countries without any further formalities.

However, there are a few product sectors where national quotas are still allowed. For example, steel and textiles are subject to international agreements limiting the volume of imports. Also, some voluntary restraint agreements exist, including a limit on the number of Japanese cars that can be sold in the UK. The EU hopes eventually to remove quotas totally, or at least arrive at a EU quota so that goods are cleared against that quota rather than against individual national quotas.

The EU is committed to international arrangements such as the General Agreement on Tariffs and Trade (GATT) and the Organisation for Economic Co-operation (OECD). The EU subscribes to the view that international trade negotiations should take place on the principle of broad reciprocity of benefits.

The 'origin of goods' system will continue. It provides a means whereby preferential treatment for specific countries, or embargos, can be operated. Existing anti-dumping duties are also protected under the terms of the Single European Act.

Countries outside the EU stand to benefit from the single market. For instance, there is only one frontier to cross; product standards and certification are harmonised, or at least are universally recognised; and economies of scale may be possible because of the size of the market.

Animal and plant health

A new set of borders was created at the beginning of 1993 to deal with animal and plant health regulations. Some are in line with national boundaries (e.g. the border for checking animals for equine horse fever which equates with that of

Spain because Spain was the only country affected). On the other hand, the border for rabies checks is in mid-France because northern France is believed to be clear of the disease.

ACTIVITY 12.3

Investigate what animals and plants are controlled by customs and excise, and the reasons.

Trade statistics

The European Commission was keen to ensure that the collection of important statistical information should not increase the number of indirect checks or the burden on tax payers. The information is now collected through the VAT system.

ACTIVITY 12.4

Why is the statistical information collected by Customs and Excise in the EU member states so important?

Liberalising the transport system

Road transport is the dominant mode of transport within the EU. Over 85 per cent of goods by weight that cross intra-EU borders are carried by road. National regulations define criteria which limit the entry of new companies into the road haulage business and cover operational aspects such as operating hours and environmental issues.

Prior to 1993, each member state had a number of permits under which its hauliers could perform international work. The number of permits was agreed between every pair of EU member states. Countries such as the Netherlands and the UK set the number so high that it never represented a practical limitation. However, between the UK and France, and between the UK and Italy, the numbers were much lower. If a haulier was unable to get a permit, he or she would have to travel empty for some parts of a trans-European journey. The removal of this permit system opens up opportunities for UK companies to transport goods to and from some member states that were previously not accessible.

Table 12.1 Transport of goods within the EC by mode of transport[1]

Mode	Millions of tonnes			
	National	Intra-EC	Extra-EC	Total
Road	9,114.8	236.4	24.3	9,375.4
Rail	700.1	81.6	72.8	854.5
Inland waterway	249.3	240.8	25.8	515.8
Total	10,064.1	558.8	122.8	10,745.6

Mode	Percentages			
	National	Intra-EC	Extra-EC	Total
Road	84.8	2.2	0.2	87.2
Rail	6.5	0.8	0.7	8.0
Inland waterway	2.3	2.2	0.2	4.8
Total	93.7	5.2	1.1	100.0

Note: [1]estimates for 1994 based on Eurostat data.

Domestic road transport

Applicants for an 'O' licence need to satisfy a number of requirements, such as good repute, financial standing, professional competence, satisfactory vehicle maintenance arrangements, and environmental suitability. Most of these conditions arise from national legislation; several are supported by EU directives.

Cabotage

Under the Treaty of Rome, the EU Transport Council decides the conditions under which domestic road transport in one member state may be undertaken by a haulier registered in another member state. This practice is known as 'cabotage'.

Vehicles engaged in cabotage work are subject to many of the regulations of the state where the work is carried out. This can cause complications because the host country's laws apply to pricing, contracts, vehicle weights and dimensions, and work and rest hours, but other matters such as social security, vehicle registration and taxation come within the jurisdiction of the operator's home country.

Transit countries

Negotiations have taken place between the EU, Switzerland, Austria, and the former Yugoslavia. The EU wants transport 'corridors' for trucks of up to 40 tonnes and an end to restrictions on night-time journeys. Both of these concepts have been resisted by the other countries on environmental grounds.

Switzerland and Austria argue that greater use should be made of rail–road combined transport.

Shipping

Traditionally, 'third country' shipping companies have been allowed to carry goods between any countries. This led to the dominance of the UK merchant fleet in the nineteenth century. However the UK fleet has declined to a very great extent since the 1950s as a result of the growth of 'flags of convenience'. Shipping registered in 'flag of convenience' countries have the benefit of low taxation and less stringent regulations governing the operation of ships.

EU policy is to protect the fleets of member states from this 'unfair' competition. Central to this policy are plans for a European Register of Shipping (EUROS).

The EUROS scheme proposes the formation of a single European flag to replace the separate national flags. This will affect some of the countries closely associated with the EU which are 'flag of convenience' countries (e.g. the Isle of Man and Gibraltar). At the same time, the scheme will involve subsidies and will thus interfere with the tax-gathering policies of individual EU countries. Under the scheme European sailors will become exempt from paying personal income tax, reducing shipowners' crewing costs. Taxation is one of the most sensitive areas of national 'sovereignty', and this aspect of EUROS has been highly controversial.

The anticipated benefits of the EUROS scheme include tough safety standards, with technical and safety certificates acceptable throughout the EU. It also guarantees jobs for European nationals: cargo ships must have 100 per cent European officers and 50 per cent European ratings; passenger ships must be entirely European-crewed; and minimum crew sizes are stipulated. Finally, grants from the EU's research and development fund will be available to produce more efficient ship designs.

ACTIVITY 12.5
Identify the main 'flag of convenience' countries.

Air cargo

The EU has been able to introduce common criteria for airline and route licensing, cabotage (enabling an airline based in one country to operate domestic services in another), the phasing-out of capacity restrictions, and other liberalising features. The schemes give preference to EU-based operators, which has, understandably, caused a fierce reaction from airlines that operate in the EU but are based elsewhere.

The EU is nevertheless keen to negotiate more liberalised air transport agreements with countries outside Europe, particularly the USA. The goal is a 'mutual benefit' agreement whereby US airlines can operate within Europe, provided European airlines have more freedom to operate on US international and domestic routes.

The EU hopes to achieve the phasing-out of noisy aircraft over a seven-year period starting in 1995. This has considerable implications because it is reckoned that up to 75 per cent of airfreight is currently carried by 'noisy' aircraft. The move could be expensive (in the short term) for airfreight operators, but good for aircraft manufacturers.

ACTIVITY 12.6

Investigate which airlines operating into and out of your local airport are: (a) passenger only; (b) freight only; (c) passenger and freight.

Harmonisation of transport regulations

The EU's aim is to create the same transport regulations and conditions throughout the Community, which should produce, in theory, equality of operators' costs. Construction and use regulations ensure that vehicles have the same minimum quality standards and have the same weight and dimensions limits throughout the EU. They also cover drivers' hours, safety equipment, road tax, fuel duty, and member states' licensing systems.

EU standards only apply to vehicles operating international routes. For domestic transport, for example, most countries have a weight limit of 40 tonnes, but some countries allow 44 tonnes, and Belgium and the Netherlands allow up to 50 tonnes. The UK was able to get a postponement of the international regulations for 15 years to deal with the 1200 bridges that need strengthening. It will be 2003 before the current 38 tonne weight limit is raised to 40 tonnes in the UK. Maximum vehicle length is now 16.5 metres. The debate over allowing heavier vehicles in the UK has been bitter. Some argue that heavier vehicles damage the roads and the environment; others say that heavier trucks reduce overall fuel consumption and mean fewer vehicles on the roads.

Harmonisation of EU transport regulations may lead to a change in the type of vehicle we see on UK roads. Drawbar rigs – a truck with two or more axles towing a trailer with road wheels at each end – are already appearing. They are very common elsewhere in Europe. Piggyback operation, where a standard articulated semi-trailer drives straight onto lightweight rail cars, is a form of multi-modal transport that may become common.

Vehicle excise and fuel duties are completely fragmented between member states. The French impose low vehicle excise duties but operate road tolls. UK operators pay 14 times more vehicle excise duty than the Italians.

UK regulations state that drivers must take rest breaks totalling at least 45 minutes for each rolling period of 4.5 hours' driving, and other rules cover rest periods. EU regulations aim to harmonise driving time, breaks, and daily, weekly and fortnightly rest periods. In particular, via the Social Charter, they will limit the working day to 11 hours, with a limit of 8 hours for night driving.

With the difference in hauliers' costs becoming less and less between countries, operators are likely to look for cost savings by employing drivers from low wage (generally eastern European) countries.

ACTIVITY 12.7
Obtain details of the regulations covering drivers' hours and rest periods, and explain the tachograph system for recording vehicle usage.

Environmental issues

A vital concern is the risk arising from the carriage of hazardous goods. In this respect, rail and water transport are considered to be safer than road. It is estimated that roughly 80 per cent of dangerous goods are transported by road. Of these 75 per cent of the dangerous goods transported are carried in tankers. They include gas, inflammable liquids, and toxic and corrosive substances. With an accident rate of 1 in 6.6 million kilometres (resulting in injury), tankers are safer than conventional commercial road vehicles (1 in 1 million kilometres).

Several different agencies exist, each with responsibility for a mode of transport. The quality of packaging is crucial to safety. The EU intends to introduce standards on compatibility and leak-proofness and to replace the separate regulations of the various safety bodies, using United Nations standards as the basis to avoid duplication of work.

Some parts of Europe have introduced special routing systems for freight, particularly freight involving hazardous goods. Cleveland in the north-east of England is one example. A large fire in Salford, Lancashire, in the late 1980s, focused attention on the need for special storage requirements for hazardous substances.

Vehicle noise is a significant issue in some parts of the EU, notably in the UK, and has led to time limits on operations. Some airports close at night. On the road, more noise is produced by rubber on tarmac than by engines. Research is being carried out on both tyre design and road surfaces.

Construction of road vehicles continues to improve. Rear under-run barriers, side-guards, and spray suppression equipment have been introduced in the last few years. The EU introduced new exhaust emission regulations in 1990. The increasing popularity of slim cabs to maximise load space has led to the EU introducing more stringent crush prevention requirements to protect drivers. However, there is still no legal requirement to fit and use load restraint equipment on many vehicles. Those carrying containers have ISO (International Standards Organisation) twist-locks, but many operators rely on ropes and sheets to secure their loads. Load retention is principally a safety feature, but it also protects the environment from dust and other pollution.

ACTIVITY 12.8

1 What road, rail and waterway routes, if any, are designated as suitable for hazardous consignments through your area?

2 Plan a route that minimises risk to the public for: (a) an explosive load; and (b) a load that would be hazardous if spilled.

Overview of the European transport market

Three modes of transport dominate the movement of goods within the EU:

Road services

Three member states, Germany, the UK and France, account for 67.5 per cent of the total Community tonnage transported by road. This is not surprising since they are the three main producers and consumers of goods.

Germany, the Netherlands, France and Belgium are the primary countries for intra-EU trade. Manufactured articles, foodstuffs and agricultural products account for the majority of intra-EU transport by road.

ACTIVITY 12.9

As well as being the main countries involved in intra-EU trade, Germany, the Netherlands, Belgium and France are the main users of inland waterways. Why?

ACTIVITY 12.10

Why is a disproportionate amount of manufactured goods carried by road, as compared with other product groups?

Table 12.2 Transport of goods within the EU by country and mode (million of tonnes)[1]

Country	Road	Rail	Inland waterway
Belgium	38.6	13.6	49.6
Denmark	5.0	1.4	0.0
France	46.1	16.6	13.7
Greece	0.7	0.2	0.0
Germany	64.9	17.9	118.5
Ireland	1.4	0.0	0.0
Italy	12.2	17.1	0.0
Luxembourg	3.2	7.2	1.4
Netherlands	46.4	5.4	57.6
Portugal	1.8	0.3	0.0
Spain	8.5	1.3	0.0
UK	7.6	0.6	0.0
Total	236.4	81.6	240.8

[1] Estimates for 1994 based on Eurostat data.

Source: AA Scott

Most of Europe's haulage is currently in the hands of small firms or owner drivers. Economies of scale are likely to lead to a consolidation, however, because a company that can serve the whole of Europe – with a range of delivery services, using different modes and operating in all directions – can expect to win much of the traffic. There have already been many instances of cross-border partnerships, takeovers and mergers.

The best strategy for operating in this market for organisations that are not already multinational is as follows:

1 Find partners in other member states.
2 Find niche markets in which to trade – refrigerated transport, for example.
3 Offer an enlarged service.

Table 12.3 Transport of goods within the EU by product group (million of tonnes)[1]

Category	Road	Rail	Inland waterway	Total
Agricultural products	32.2	5.6	11.3	49.1
Foodstuffs	35.9	3.7	15.4	55.0
Solid mineral fuels	3.1	8.6	14.4	26.1
Petroleum products	4.0	2.2	44.1	50.3
Ores and metal work	4.0	10.2	47.9	62.1
Metal products	20.1	17.8	12.5	50.4
Minerals and building materials	34.8	5.9	62.1	102.7
Fertilisers	3.1	2.9	8.2	14.2
Chemicals	33.8	5.9	18.3	58.0
Manufactured articles	65.5	18.8	6.5	90.8
Total	236.5	81.6	240.7	558.7

[1] Estimated for 1994.

Value-added services are an attractive form of enlarged service. Packing goods for shipment, labelling, holding transit stock, and warehousing are all possibilities, but total supply-chain management is the most attractive.

Probably the biggest difficulty for operators is back-loads. UK operators, for example, operate in a market that has many imports but relatively few exports. Consequently they find it difficult to get full rates for export because operators from other countries, who find it easier to get work importing to the UK from their local manufacturers, are offering low rates to get back-loads. Within the UK domestic market own-account fleets have carried a large proportion of goods. As they increase their amount of intra-EU trade, with longer journeys, they need to look for back-loads to keep their costs down. It is possible that they may contract out their deliveries, and perhaps even the whole of their distribution. On the other hand, they may decide that they should go for full haulier status.

Rail services

Three countries dominate the domestic rail transport sector – Germany, France and the UK. They are the countries that most need to transport bulk mineral fuels and metal products, and they have major extractive and heavy industries.

For intra-EU movement, the main users of rail are Germany, France and Italy. There is, however, a general decrease in rail freight, with only two countries – Denmark and Greece – reporting increases. Rail is still a viable alternative for local transport of raw materials and postal parcels, although in the UK the railways have, to a large extent, lost these markets. Rail transport in Europe is likely to receive two boosts:

1 The Channel Tunnel makes rail a more attractive mode of transport for UK goods.
2 Rail is seen as an environmentally attractive alternative to road transport.

The UK and much of Europe has a standard rail gauge. Ireland has a broader gauge, and Spain and Portugal have an even wider gauge (which is also the gauge used in Finland and the CIS); Spain intends to convert to the European standard. Moving down in gauge is easier than moving up, when platforms, bridges and tunnels might have to be modified.

The ferry companies have a strong position in the movement of surface freight between the UK and the continent. Even rail traffic has to cross by ferry. However, the Channel Tunnel is a considerable benefit to rail transport. It offers the opportunity for fast transit times for heavy or bulky goods without the need for transshipment. Several new depots are being planned in the UK. The aim is to have 8 depots in the UK linking with 15 to 20 depots in continental Europe.

The railways have purchased half of the Tunnel's operating capacity. The other half will be used to carry road vehicles by its shuttle services. For the time being existing railway lines between Folkestone and London will be used. A fast link is planned, to be opened in 1998. The new line will be used for non-freight traffic, freeing capacity on the existing line for Tunnel goods. In France massive public investment has been put into developing a TGV line for passenger trains, linking with Paris via Lille, and then on to the Mediterranean. From Lille there are plans for a high-speed line to Brussels and Cologne.

Businesses in the south-east of England will benefit from the Tunnel, but the area will undoubtedly suffer from increased congestion. Congestion pushes up costs – fuel consumption increases and relief drivers are needed. It also means that transit times are unpredictable. This becomes critical with the growth of just-in-time (JIT) policies. Companies may find it worthwhile to site their distribution centres in northern France, where there is no congestion. The traffic would then pass through the south-east of England by the rapid routes. A precedent for this was the Seven Bridge between England and South Wales.

EU assistance

There are plans to build a high-speed rail link in Europe between 1995 and 2015. Over 30,000 kilometres of track will be laid, of which at least 19,000 will be usable by high-speed trains. The EU also encourages the use of multi-modal transport such as piggy-back services.

In the UK there are plans to privatise the railways. Support for socially desirable services will become a contractual obligation. In Switzerland and Sweden, where the railways have been privatised, the management of the infrastructure has been separated from the operations, as is planned for the UK.

At present, trains are handed over at frontiers and there is no end-to-end control of international transit. The French, German and Belgian railways administration have set up a joint management team. Other countries are likely to follow. Co-ordinated end-to-end control offers significant advantages, synchronising services and reducing delays.

Inland water services

Inland waterways offer the cheapest form of transport, but they are often neglected in the UK. Elsewhere in Europe, notably in France, Germany, Belgium and the Netherlands, it is a more significant mode of transport.

The new Rhine–Danube canal creates a 3500 kilometre waterway capable of carrying barges of up to 3300 tonnes from the North Sea to the Black Sea. This opens up a viable route to Hungary, Rumania, Bulgaria and the former Yugoslavia. Ultimately it will provide a route to the Balkans and Middle East. UK operators are looking at the Rhine–Danube waterway with interest. P & O have taken over a German company which operates 33 barges on the Rhine, and has entered into a partnership with a Rhine 'roll-on, roll-off' shipping company.

Sea services

Some Channel ports may lose their ferry links completely after the Tunnel opens. Northern ports could lose out too as Channel ports look for extra deep-sea traffic to replace the cross Channel ferry services. There appears to be over-capacity in the UK ports industry, and their trust status makes it difficult for them to diversify.

The trend is towards smaller vessels providing a frequent service, with smaller delays while loading and unloading takes place. The emphasis has to be on a high-quality, reliable service, capable of supporting just-in-time procurement policies.

Ferry operators are very concerned about losing the very lucrative duty-free sales business and have negotiated for it to be prolonged.

ACTIVITY 12.11

Investigate prices at your nearest 'duty free' shop (airport or port). How do they compare with the best prices for the same products elsewhere? You cannot visit such a shop unless you are travelling abroad, so if you cannot persuade the shop to send you a price list you may have to wait until you or a friend is travelling abroad to carry out this activity.

Air and airfreight services

Passenger travel to, from and within Europe is about one-third of the world-wide total. Although the market continues to grow, price and quality competition is increasingly fierce.

Airfreight offers very fast transit times. However, the cargo often ends up well away from the end user. Time spent on the ground is usually more than four times as long as the flight time. At present, freight traffic is an add-on for many airlines. Airfreight is restricted to high-value goods that can justify the high transport costs. The premium market is for mail. In fact, there is currently a shortage of air cargo capacity.

Better infrastructure around airports and more fuel-efficient aircraft with reduced maintenance requirements are some of the factors that are making air-lines think about freight-only aircraft. A slump in the package holiday market would probably precipitate an early decision.

Airlines enjoy six types of freedom, which govern the service they can offer:

1 Freedom to fly across the territory of another state.
2 Freedom to land for non-traffic purposes (e.g. for refuelling, mechanical problems).

3 Freedom to transport passengers, mail or freight from the airline's 'home' country to another country and deposit them there.
4 Freedom to collect passengers, mail or freight from a country and transport them to the airline's 'home' country.
5 Freedom to transport passengers, mail or freight between two countries that are not the airline's 'home' country.
6 Freedom to transport passengers, mail or freight between two countries, via the airline's home country.

Because of the structure of the industry, most airlines operate predominantly from a single country. This is likely to change, principally by takeovers.

A critical problem facing air traffic is the efficient use of airspace. Some redistribution between military and civilian space is taking place. EU countries are re-examining the present use of fixed corridors for aircraft and instead considering the increased use of area navigation to route aircraft.

ACTIVITY 12.12

Investigate the sources of goods in your local supermarket. Which of them do you think have been flown in to the UK?

Integrated delivery services

Express delivery services offer on-demand collection and delivery of time-sensitive documents and parcels. The service is fast, reliable, and easy to use. Senders are not concerned with how the goods travel.

The key feature of many services is the promise to deliver next day to the main European centres, and to all other areas within two days. This is of particular importance in opening up eastern bloc countries that do not have good surface transport systems. This level of service can only exist if the operator has total control of the door-to-door movement, and this implies using its own equipment and employees.

The evolution of the industry has been heavily influenced by regulatory laws covering postal services, customs formalities, and transport. It is a very competitive market, and the cost of entering this market is high. Those wishing to enter need to invest in a depot network, vehicle fleets, aircraft, and above all a sophisticated computer system.

It was the growth in integrated services, and their complaints about inefficient customs and clearance systems, that led to the inland clearance depot system, and pre-entry customs clearance. The widespread introduction of EDI (electronic data interchange) means that many loads moving within the EU can

```
Air                              Sea
    Airfreight                       Conventional services
    Air consolidation                Container
    Air charter                      Roll-on, roll-off
    Postal/parcels services          Lift-on, lift-off
    Couriers                         Charter
                                     Liner services
                                     Tramps


Road
    Trailer services             Rail
    Small packet services            Conventional
    Groupage                         Freightliners
                                     Channel Tunnel
Factors to consider:
    Transit time.
    Frequency.
    Estimated time of arrival.
    Flag of carrier.
    Increased use of multi-modal operations.
```

Fig. 12.1 Freight-forwarding options

obtain customs clearance before they arrive in their destination country, subject to random checks on cargo and paperwork.

Most express operators have adopted a hub system. Brussels and Cologne are the most favoured locations for hubs. All goods collected in a country are flown nightly to the hub. There they are sorted according to their destination country, and are then sent out on the aircraft returning to the destination country. For example, a parcel would be flown from Manchester to Cologne, and from Cologne to Marseille. The system makes cost-effective use of aircraft and allows for late collection times and early deliveries.

Operators use computerised information systems, based on high-speed, international private data networks. Systems include parcel tracking, vehicle routing and scheduling, customs clearance, fast-response enquiries, billing and proof of delivery.

ACTIVITY 12.13

Collect information about the large carriers that have bases in your area.

- Track record and reputation among clients.
- Credit worthiness.
- How sound and capitalised is the company?
- Does it own its vehicles? What condition are they in?
- To what extent does the company subcontract?
- How does it store and handle cargo before shipment?
- How do its rates and charges compare?
- What are its trading terms and limits of liability?
- What are its arrangements for insurance, particularly when there is a need for special clauses or cover for special risks?
- Once instructed to ship, how long does it take the company to despatch goods?
- How good is it at progress chasing?

Fig. 12.2 Selecting a freight forwarder

Distribution logistics

Strategy

The concept of mass marketing of a limited product range to maximise market share is giving way to segmented marketing. The Single Market will reinforce this trend. Making the right product available to the right customer encourages customer loyalty. Distribution logistics is concerned with achieving this.

Logistics is the discipline of managing the supply chain from raw material sourcing to delivery of the finished product to the final customer. There is more to it than the mode of transport, routes and costs. The strategy should encompass order processing, the flow of materials and components into manufacturing, warehousing, inventory levels, transport, and customer service.

One way of reducing costs is to reduce the total amount of finished goods in stock. This may be achieved by using fewer warehouses and having a good information system. Admittedly, goods have to be moved further from warehouse to outlet or customer, with the attendant danger of increased transport costs. However, with a good information system this problem can be overcome by larger loads and better routing. Marks & Spencer is a good example. The company uses one centralised distribution centre at Aulnay-sur-Bois, just north of Paris, to serve eight stores in France and two in Belgium. Goods are shipped to this centre from three supply depots in the UK.

In planning the distribution strategy a number of additional factors need to be considered. Is it wise to have everything on one site? Is it politically sensible to have a presence in a country? Does the scale of operations make it impractical to have one depot?

Finally, an important consideration in planning distribution strategy for the EU is the reduction in customs clearance work. It has been estimated that this has reduced the work associated with transnational trade by up to 85 per cent where both source and destination are within the EU.

Channels of distribution

The key objective in distribution is to get the right product, to the right place, at the right time, in the right condition. To achieve this objective four channels of distribution come easily to mind – road, rail, air and sea. Many of our European neighbours would also include inland waterways more readily than we do; for mainland Europe is well provided by inland waterways, including the Rhine–Rhône and the North Sea–Danube routes. But for long-term, high-volume transportation of fluids and gases, pipelines offer a better solution than tankers (road, rail or sea). Increasingly, too, goods are transported by multi-modal methods (i.e. a combination of several methods during the journey). Often the exporter leaves the exact method of transportation to the freight company.

The key factors governing the method of shipment are:

1 *Cost.*
2 *Contract terms* Where some or all of the carriage and insurance are the responsibility of the customer, the contract may specify the methods to be used.
3 *Type of goods* A long, heavy, or hazardous load may preclude some choices. Mercury, for example, cannot be transported by air because a spillage would rot the airframe. Porcelain and other fragile cargos would need special treatment. Pharmaceuticals need special protection against theft.
4 *Availability.*
5 *Packaging costs* It might, for example, be financially better to send some products by airfreight to avoid the special packing necessary for transportation by sea.
6 *Urgency.*
7 *Quantity and regularity* For example, full containers at regular but less frequent intervals might be a better solution than paying the premium for part-filled containers or taking risks of theft that might arise from less secure forms of groupage.
8 *Insurance* Insurance for transportation by air is generally cheaper than for transportation by sea.
9 *Capital tied up in transit.*
10 *Unpacking, refurbishing, recalibration.*
11 *Overall marketing policy* Many organisations prefer to keep control of the

shipment throughout the journey, or consign it to a freight company that has this total control.

Table 12.4 Freight cost comparison

	Air	Sea
Transit time (days)	4	35
	£	£
Ex-works cost	2,600	2,600
Freight	120	20
Packing	20	60
To port	10	30
From port	14	53
Insurance	6	7
Duty	130	130
Capital in transit	3	22
Unpacking	5	10
Total cost	2,908	2,932

ACTIVITY 12.14

Investigate the comparative costs of shipping (a) 100 pairs of shoes, and (b) 100 dozen roses, by air and by road from your home town to central Madrid.

SUMMARY

1 Distribution is one of the largest industries in Europe. It encompasses transport and storage.

2 Multi-modal freight, containerisation, integrated services, and computer-based control systems giving end-to-end control of distribution are the key developments in transportation techniques.

3 EU legislation has liberalised and harmonised distribution operations.

4 Road transport is the main mode of transport for manufactured goods. Air-freight is increasing in importance, especially for high-value and perishable products. Inland waterways offer a cost-effective way of transporting goods in bulk and is a major mode of transport in some EU countries.

5 Logistics strategies should aim to minimise the total cost of distribution (transport and storage) and provide a high level of reliability to the final destination.

6 Businesses must choose between having their own in-house distribution organisation and employing the services of an independent carrier. Both can provide a high level of service and reliability, using multi-modal transport, hub-based distribution networks, and computer-based information systems.

Assignment 12

BACKGROUND

Superfreight is a growing independent carrier with a turnover of £12 million. It has bases in Manchester, Newcastle, Bristol and Reading which act as hubs for its operations in the north-west, north-east, west and south-west, midlands and south-east respectively.

Increasingly it is asked by its customers to provide a European delivery service. Most of the customers want their goods to be delivered in northern France, Belgium, north-western Germany, and the Netherlands. It is increasingly difficult to ignore their requests.

ACTIVITY

1 Prepare a report considering the issues associated with entering the trans-national carrier market.

2 Formulate an action plan.

13 Administration and documentation

OBJECTIVES   1 To distinguish between procedures for transnational trade within the EU and those required for trading elsewhere in the world.

2 To describe the purpose and content of official, financial and commercial documentation used in transnational trade.

3 To distinguish between the various international delivery terms and understand the purpose of INCOTERMS.

Trade between EU countries

Documentation can be divided into three classes: official; financial; and commercial.

Official documentation

From the beginning of 1993, EU customs services adopted integrated procedures for carrying out their EU and national responsibilities, and discontinued systematic intervention in legitimate trade at national borders. Many of the restrictions and prohibitions on the transfer of goods were eliminated, and those that remain are controlled at the traders' premises, rather than at borders.

Customs personnel are now free to target their activities more precisely, using intelligence-based anti-smuggling checks. There is evidence that they are now more effective in preventing contraventions of the laws and regulations. The drugs menace remains their primary concern. In 1991 over 60 per cent (by weight) of drugs seized were in transit between EU countries.

Another primary concern is the maintenance of high standards of animal and plant health. Preventing the spread of disease is achieved more effectively by defining boundaries appropriate to a specific threat, rather than by arbitrary national boundaries.

Since the implementation of the Single European Act (SEA) there are no import duties on goods transferred between EU countries, except for some transitional duties relating to Spain and Portugal. However, there are still differences in VAT rates between member states, and consequently the source and destination countries have to be identified so that VAT adjustments can be made.

Those goods that are subject to excise duty (e.g. alcohol, tobacco, and petrol) are moved under duty-suspension between bonded warehouses. The individual member states set their own conditions for authorisation of warehouse keepers. In the UK there is also a system of registering traders to operate outside the warehouse scheme known as REDS (Registered Excise Dealers and Shippers). Duty becomes due on release of the goods from the warehouse, or in the case of REDS, on receipt of the goods.

ACTIVITY 13.1

Investigate what bonded warehouses and REDS shippers are located in your area.

Allowances of tax and duty-paid goods for travellers within the EU disappeared at the end of 1992, but the liability for duty is waived when goods are for personal use. Indicative levels are used to distinguish between alcohol and tobacco goods for commercial purposes (on which duty is payable) and those for personal use. Logically there is no place for 'duty-free' shopping within the single market. However, the size and extent of intra-EU 'duty-free' trade is such that member states have agreed that the system will continue until 30 June 1999. Duty-free sales for travellers between EU and non-EU countries will continue indefinitely.

A logical consequence of the single market is the disappearance of the Single Administrative Document (SAD) for trade within the EU. Documentation is needed for any goods that come under the Control of Export Goods Act 1989, and there is still a need for documentation and controls where goods travel via a non-member country from one member state to another. Even where there is a straightforward transfer of goods from one EU country to another the recipient will often ask for a certificate of origin (although one is not needed for intra-EU trade) because it is necessary if the goods are subsequently exported to a non-EU country. The certificate of origin relates the *original* source of the goods.

EU regulations concerning intra-EU trade statistics link the VAT and statistical systems so as to minimise the burden on businesses. Since January 1992, all UK traders have been required to complete two new boxes on their normal VAT return, declaring the value of their intra-EU exports and imports. From January 1993, there have been some changes to these boxes to take account of single market VAT requirements for supply and acquisition. Businesses with intra-EU trade above a threshold (of about £140,000 per annum) are required to complete a monthly statistical return. Customs and Excise are keen to receive statistical data on magnetic media (e.g. computer disks) and through telecommunications devices so as to minimise data collection costs to businesses and themselves.

ACTIVITY 13.2

Obtain copies of the form used by businesses to make their quarterly VAT return, from your local Custom & Excise office.

Financial documentation

There are still several factors that make trade between EU states more complicated than trade within a single country. For example, language differences, especially the use of special business terminology, make it essential that terms and conditions of payment are clearly defined.

Business practices vary from country to country. In particular, the length of the credit period, usually one month in the UK, may be different in other member states.

While each EU country continues to have its own currency there will be a need for many businesses to maintain bank accounts in several currencies. Despite the Exchange Rate Mechanism (ERM), which limits variations in exchange rates, currencies can rise or fall against one another, and some countries do not belong to the ERM system. It is important, therefore, for the seller and buyer to be clear as to the currency in which payment is to be made, and when payment is due. This information must appear along with a description of the goods, and the quantities, on the invoice.

ACTIVITY 13.3

Conduct a survey to establish what terms of payment and currencies (own or customers') are used by local businesses engaged in trade with other EU countries.

Commercial documentation

Transportation of goods is often much more complicated when distances are great, and multi-modal transport (e.g. road, then rail, then sea, then road again) is therefore quite usual. Documentation is needed to indicate which transport operators and freight forwarders are handling the consignment, and the route it is to follow. It is necessary to establish who pays for the carriage and include this on the invoice.

When the goods are in transit for longer, and when perhaps they have to be loaded, unloaded, and stored several times, the risk of damage or loss is greater. Various types of insurance are available, according to who is responsible for the safety of the goods at successive stages in their transportation and storage. The documentation must indicate how the goods are insured and who is responsible for paying the premiums.

Packing has to be more robust and the cost of this is another item that has to be considered to a greater extent than for local deliveries. The weight, size and markings of the packages in which the goods are consigned are usually included on the documentation.

ACTIVITY 13.4

Choose one of the companies described in previous activities (e.g. shoe manufacturer, company making hospital supplies, snail farmer):

1 Decide what type of packaging would be needed for delivering the goods to another EU country. How, if at all, would it be different from domestic deliveries?

2 Investigate packaging costs.

Movement of goods outside the EU

Although the movement of goods within EU member states has been simplified, it is often the case that goods are transported via non-EU countries, or they may be ultimately destined for a non-EU country. For this reason it is important to have some understanding of the documents of international trade. The principal classes of document are:

1 Documents used to obtain payment.
2 Documents relating to the sale and specification of goods.
3 Receipts issued by transport operators and freight forwarders.
4 Official documents to meet the requirements of customs and licensing authorities.
5 Documents relating to insurance.

The documentation must be adequate, not just for the final country of destination, but also the countries through which the goods will pass in transit.

Croner's Reference Book for Exporters is the definitive source of information on the necessary documentation. Chambers of Commerce, embassies and consulates are also excellent sources of information.

It is important that documents are correct and complete so that transportation and delivery take place smoothly. This is especially important if the documentation, particularly the guarantees of payment, have a time limit, or if costs accrue while goods are stored in transit.

SITPRO, an independent agency sponsored and endorsed by the DTI, has done much to achieve simpler international trade. It attacks red tape, encourages the use of information technology in transportation and payment procedures, and provides help and advice.

The documents most commonly encountered in international trade are bill of exchange; invoice; certificate of origin; bill of lading, airway bill, railway consignment note (CIM) and road consignment note (CMR); and insurance documents.

Bill of exchange

A bill of exchange is 'an unconditional order in writing addressed by one person to another, signed by the person giving it, requiring the person to whom it is addressed to pay on demand, or at a fixed or determinable future time, a sum in money (or to the order of) a specified person (or the bearer of the bill)'.

Invoice

A commercial invoice is the basic document required by the buyer and must be in a form that meets the requirements of the customs authorities in the original country, the final country, and any intermediate countries. It should contain:

1 A full description of the goods.
2 Details of the shipping and packaging marks as they appear on the bill of lading.
3 The price of the goods and the currency.
4 Details of the terms of contract (e.g. CIF Cairo, FOB).
5 Details of freight and insurance costs where payable.
6 Details of import licences and exchange permits where applicable.
7 In some cases, separate weight lists and specifications.

The importing authorities of some countries require *consular invoices*. These are specially printed invoices, obtainable from the consulate of the appropriate country.

Certificate of origin

This indicates the original source of the goods.

Bill of lading

The bill of lading is used when goods are despatched by sea, and fulfils the following three functions.

1 It is the receipt issued to the exporter by, or on behalf of, the shipping company for goods accepted for carriage.
2 It is evidence of a contract between the two parties and will include an undertaking that the shipping company will deliver the goods in the same condition that they were received.
3 It is the document of title of the goods.

The bill of lading is usually prepared by the exporter or freight forwarder. It should contain a description of the goods, the terms of carriage, the name of the vessel, and the port of discharge. It is signed by the shipping company and issued in sets of one or more, known as negotiable bills of lading. Any one of the set gives title to the goods, the number of copies comprising the full set being shown on each.

If the carrier receives the goods in apparent good condition a 'clean' bill of lading will be issued. If the shipping company considers there is a defect in the goods or packing then it will issue a 'claused' or 'dirty' bill of lading. This may provide the buyer with a reason for refusing to accept the goods.

The importer will normally expect to receive a bill of lading from the exporter marked 'shipped on board'. If it merely states 'received for shipment' then there is a risk that the goods are awaiting the next vessel.

Title to the goods passes on endorsement and delivery of an original bill of lading. In the past, consignments were often traded while still at sea. The bill of lading was evidence of ownership. It is now much more likely that a bank will hold the bill of lading until the buyer has paid and then release it so that the buyer can claim the goods. The shipping company will release the goods at the port of destination when the first original bill of lading is presented to it.

If goods are shipped CIF (carriage insurance freight), then the shipping company must endorse the bill as evidence that the freight charge has been paid.

Airway bills

These are receipts issued by an airline for goods despatched by air. Unlike the bill of lading they are not documents of title. Once the goods have been cleared through customs the consignee can claim them without further formalities. Because transit times are shorter, the airway bill is usually faxed to the buyer or the buyer's agent.

Railway consignment note (CIM)

This is not a document of title. It is a receipt for the goods, issued by the railway organisation when the goods are to be transported to a foreign destination, similar in operation to an airway bill.

Road consignment note (CMR)

This is an international road consignment note, again similar in operation to an airway bill. If a journey begins by road then the CMR conventions apply throughout the journey. In particular, the compensation for loss or damage to the goods by carrier negligence is at the agreed rate for road transport, which is about three times higher than the sea-freight rate.

It is interesting to note that goods transported through the Channel Tunnel will be covered by CMR (road) rules since the carrying vehicle drives onto the train.

ACTIVITY 13.5

Obtain samples of each of the key export documents mentioned above.

Insurance documents

It is important that goods are covered by insurance at every stage from the time when they leave the supplier until the buyer takes delivery. Responsibility for arranging insurance is a matter of negotiation between the supplier and the buyer. The arrangements must be set out in the contract of sale. The two key points to be considered are:

1 *Insured value* This should include not just the goods and packing, but also the cost of transport, which might be significant.
2 *Risk to be covered* This will include transport from the supplier to the port, railway station or airport; storage while awaiting loading; the journey by sea, rail or air; off-loading and storage on arrival; and final transport to the buyer.

It may be necessary to extend the insurance if there are delays in transit. Cargo and credit insurance can be very complicated. Expert advice is essential.

Other documentation

Certificate of quality

This may be requested by the buyer but is more likely to be a requirement of the destination country's government. They are commonly required by Japan and some African countries. Rejecting goods that are of 'inferior quality' is sometimes used as a covert method of controlling imports.

ATA carnet

Goods exported temporarily, for example to be used at an exhibition or trade fair, or as samples that will later be re-imported, can pass through customs without payment if covered by an ATA carnet, obtainable from UK Chambers of Commerce.

Blacklist exemption certificate

Freedom of UK companies to trade, in certain goods, with other countries is restricted by a blacklist, drawn up by the UK government. Most countries have blacklists.

Generally, this is to prevent trade with a country with whom they are at war, or with whom they have a poor relationship. The 'arms for Iraq' case in 1993–4 was a well-publicised example of restrictions on the export from the UK of machine tools that could be used in weapon-making. It illustrated the difficulty of defining products, and the highly sensitive and political nature of blacklists.

The DTI and Customs and Excise are responsible for the administration and enforcement of the blacklist. A company carrying out international trade may need to provide the authorities with evidence that the goods involved do not originate from (or are not destined for) blacklisted countries and/or are not banned products. An exemption certificate will then be issued.

The blacklist is also a way of preventing the use of carrying vessels registered in particular countries, or shipment routes that include ports-of-call in banned countries.

Dangerous goods

Certain goods – those which are highly imflammable, explosive, toxic or corrosive, etc – are subject to stringent EU regulations in respect of packing, handling and carrying. In the UK these regulations are administered and enforced by the Home Office and the Department of Transport.

ACTIVITY 13.6

1 Investigate the range of countries/products that are blacklisted.

2 Investigate the regulations covering the transport of hazardous goods, such as liquid petroleum gas (e.g. butane).

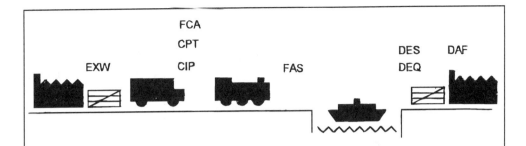

The terms are grouped into four classes:

E terms	EXW	ex-works
F terms	FAS*	free alongside ship
	FOB*	free on board
	FCA	free carrier
C terms	CFR*	cost and freight
	CPT	carriage paid to ...
	CIF*	carriage, insurance and freight paid
	CIP	carriage and insurance paid
D terms	DES*	delivered ex-ship
	DEQ*	delivered ex-quay
	DAF	delivered at frontier
	DDU	delivered duty unpaid
	DDP	delivered duty paid

Notes:
* suitable only for sea or inland waterway

1. Multi-modal terms. FCA is the multi-modal equivalent of FOB. CPT is the multi-modal equivalent of CFR. CIP is the multi-modal equivalent of CIF.
2. FOB, unless adapted in the contract, is a strict FOB (i.e. buyer is responsible for contracting and paying for freight).
3. Payment of carriage. In EXW there is no obligation for an international contract of carriage. Such an obligation exists in all the other terms. In F tems the main international carriage is unpaid by the seller. In the C and D terms the main carriage is paid by the seller to the specified point of delivery e.g. CIF New York (INCOTERMS 1990)
4. Risk. In FOB, CFR, CIF, the risk passes to the buyer at the place of loading. In FCA, CPT, CIP, the risk passes to the buyer once the goods are delivered into the hands of the carrier or his or her agent. In other terms, risk passes at the point of delivery.
5. Ownership. The passing of ownership is determined by the contract of sale, not the INCOTERMS. In most contracts, ownership passes on payment for the goods.

Fig. 13.1 INCOTERMS, 1990

Delivery terms

Use of standard terms of delivery evolved from traditional sea-freight operations based on FOB (free on board) and CIF (carriage, insurance and freight) terms. Problems of interpretation sometimes arose and terms based on sea voyages became progressively less representative of actual transportation practice, particularly with the development of multi-modal operations and the increasing amount of end-to-end responsibility accepted by carriers.

The international Chamber of Commerce attempted to overcome these difficulties by producing internationally agree terms called INCOTERMS. These are periodically revised and updated. The current terms are INCOTERMS 1990. These terms do not have the force of law unless they are adopted in the contract of sale. It is also possible to use other than the latest terms, so it is important to quote the date (e.g. FOB UK port (INCOTERMS 1990)). The latest INCOTERMS offer the following advantages:

1 Both buyer and seller are clear as to their responsibilities and obligations.
2 They reflect modern shipping techniques (typically multi-modal).

Method	Documents	Convention
Sea Inland waterway	Bill of lading, or seaway bill	Hague Visby rules
Rail	CIM note	CIM convention
Road	CMR note	CMR convention
Pipeline	None	None
Air	Airway bill	Warsaw convention

Fig. 13.2 Transport modes and conventions

SUMMARY

1 Documentation for trading within the EU is much simpler than that needed for exporting elsewhere, but it retains some features that are additional to what is needed for domestic trade.

2 Documentation is required for official purposes (e.g. VAT and duty, controlled products, statistics, movement to, from and via non-member countries).

3 For financial reasons the invoice must show the terms of payment, value and currency.

4 Documentation must indicate who is responsible for transporting and storing the consignment, what route it will follow, who is responsible for various payments, and the physical characteristics of the goods and packaging (e.g. description, markings, quantity, weight, size).

5 Insurance has particular significance because of the increased time and distance involved in international operations. Insurance sometimes includes the cost of freight as well as the cost of the goods if it is a significant amount. The nature of the risk, and duration of the insurance, must be defined.

6 INCOTERMS offer a way of clarifying the conditions covering transportation, storage and insurance. They were revised in 1990 to accommodate multi-modal methods of transport.

Assignment 13

BACKGROUND

In the 1930s, when the UK was suffering a severe economic recession, several members of a UK family emigrated. They took with them several portraits and landscapes painted by their father.

An attempt has recently been made to trace these paintings and return them to the family home near Birmingham. The task is almost complete. There are now four paintings in Melbourne, Australia, and another three in Marseille. They vary in size from 0.5 m x 0.7 m to 0.8 m x 1.0 m and weigh between 2 kg and 5 kg each. They will need careful packing to avoid damage. The packaging will probably form a significant part of the shipment weight and dimensions.

The paintings are valued very highly by the family, for sentimental reasons. It is believed that they have little market value and there is (at the present time) no intention of selling them.

ACTIVITIES

Plan the transportation of the paintings, considering the arrangements for shipment, and the formalities when they arrive in the UK.

14 Risk and financial management

OBJECTIVES 1 **To investigate the risks that are enhanced by long distances and transnational trading and design a strategy for managing risk.**

2 **To describe the various methods of making payment, and the possible arrangements for short-term financing of transnational transactions.**

3 **To calculate the effect of various currency management techniques.**

4 **To compare the pre-1992, transitional, and proposed final methods of VAT collection within the EU.**

What types of risk are there?

- Physical risk (i.e risk of loss of or damage to goods despatched).
- Non-payment arising from poor credit worthiness of buyer, theft or fraud, and political events affecting flow of funds.
- Currency risk arising from fluctuations in exchange rates, and from controls on currency in some countries.

Dealing with risk – a procedure

1 Evaluate risk.
2 Choose low-risk options (but there may be cost or time disadvantages).
3 Insure against loss through cargo insurance; or through financial risk insurance.
4 Monitor the situation and adopt strategies to manage changing circumstances (principally currency variations).

Methods of payment

There are three basic methods of payment, which are described below in sequence of increasing risk.

Advance payment

This is the method often used for unsolicited business from unknown buyers.

Documentary credits

A letter of credit is a written undertaking given by a bank on behalf of the buyer, to pay the seller an amount of money within a specific period of time, provided the seller presents documents strictly in accordance with the terms laid down in the letter of credit.

With an irrevocable letter of credit the obligations of the parties to the credit cannot be altered without the agreement of them all. This is a source of protection to the exporter and is more common than a revocable letter of credit.

A confirmed letter of credit is one which has been confirmed by the bank. The exporter can therefore be assured of payment. Unconfirmed letters of credit are used where there are controls over foreign currency dealings and the bank may be unable to guarantee that sufficient currency will be available to meet its obligations.

Open account

Where an established buyer–seller relationship exists and where foreign currency availability is not a problem, business can be conducted on an open account basis. This is normal practice for domestic trade, and competitive pressures often make it a necessity for EU trade and exporting.

The buyer may pay by cheque, but it is sometimes cheaper and less risky for payment to be made by banker's draft. Because of postal delays it is often bet-ter to use electronic methods of transfer (telex, fax or electronic funds transfer).

Choosing the method of payment

In choosing the most appropriate method of payment, three factors must be considered:

1 The needs of the seller are security of payment; good cash flow; and avoidance of currency exposure.

2 The needs of the buyer are the goods he or she is paying for must be received on time and in good condition; and an acceptable period of credit.
3 Market norms are method of payment; credit period; exchange controls; and political stability.

When trading within the EU there is considerable competitive pressure for exporters to adopt the open account method. Buyers do not want to be troubled by the complexity, cost and delays associated with letters of credit, and also expect a period of credit that advance payment does not offer.

Short-term financing

Ideally, the seller would like to be paid for the goods before they are manufactured so that materials and labour can be paid for. On the other hand, the buyer would like to have as long a period of credit as possible in order to sell the goods before payment falls due. In each case the business is trying to manage its cash flow.

In practice, some form of short-term financing is often needed where there are long delivery times and extended credit, both of which are more common with export transactions. Some of the more common methods of financing are described below. All except the overdraft provide the exporter with funds *after* shipment has taken place (i.e. to cover the period of credit).

Overdraft

The seller takes an overdraft with a bank and uses the money to pay for materials and labour. When payment is received from the buyer, the overdraft is paid off.

Documentary advances

When shipping documents are forwarded through a bank to the buyer, the seller gets a loan based on a percentage of the value of the goods. The loan is repaid when payment is received for the goods.

Confirming finance

Where an agent acts for the overseas buyer, payment is made to the exporter on shipment of the goods. Thus, any risk or period of credit will be borne by the agent, not by the exporter.

Both documentary advances and confirming finance relate to payment on the basis of letters of credit.

Export factoring

The exporter uses the sales-accounting and debt-collection services of factoring agencies (including most banks). The exporter can receive prepayment of up to 80 per cent of invoiced sales in anticipation of payments to be collected by the factoring company. This method is suitable for transactions based on open account payment.

Forfaiting

The forfaiting agency purchases deferred trade debt from the exporter, usually evidenced by bills of exchange or promissory notes. Forfaiting has the advantage of turning debtors into cash with no recourse to the exporter in the case of bad debts.

Currency management

The currency in which a transaction takes place has to be agreed between the buyer and seller. Each prefers the transaction to be in the currency of his or her own country, for the following reasons:

1 The company that has to trade in another currency is faced with additional effort and the cost of arranging for currency exchange. There is also the risk of fluctuations in rates of exchange between the time the price is agreed, and the payment date.
2 In a politically or economically unstable situation, foreign currency controls or devaluation are a considerable risk. In some countries the availability of 'hard' currency is limited.
3 A transaction in the seller's currency enables him or her to match income precisely against costs without any risk from currency exchange fluctuations. The buyer, on the other hand, wants to know precisely how much the goods will cost compared with local sources.

Within the EU the dominant pressure is competition. The buyer is usually able to insist that the transaction is in his or her currency. The seller would be risking a serious competitive disadvantage to insist on trading in his or her currency.

Currency accounts

Where regular trading takes place with another country, it will be advantageous to have an account with your own bank in the currency of that country.

This has the following three advantages.

1 It facilitates the transfer of funds between your account and the buyer's account.
2 It avoids the cost of exchanging each individual transaction into your own currency.
3 It allows you to transfer funds between this currency account and your main account at a time when exchange rates are advantageous.

A further option is to have an account with a bank in the country where you are trading. This gives you a stronger presence there, it facilitates dealings with the buyer, and it allows you to take advantage of higher interest rates by transferring funds in bulk to an account in the country with the higher rate. Conversely, if you need an overdraft it should be in the country with the lowest interest rates.

It is generally worthwhile to have local currency accounts once the level of sales exceeds £10,000–£20,000 per year. It may be worthwhile having currency accounts even if the level of trading is less than this if you also buy from that country – the total value of transactions is the key figure.

The spot rate

Banks always quote two prices for the present exchange rate, called the 'spot' rate. The bank buys currency at the higher rate and sells at the lower rate against sterling; for example:

the French franc (FF) spot price against the pound has low 8.09 FF, high 8.10 FF

starting with £1000

if you buy francs you receive:
    1000 x 8.09 = 8090 FF

if you then sell the 8090 francs you receive:
    8090 / 8.10 = £998.77

You may also pay the bank a fee for each transaction.

ACTIVITY 14.1

1 Determine the transaction charge on foreign currency dealings made by your bank.

2 Determine the spot rate on Deutschmarks.

3 How much would you receive if you changed 10,000 DM into £?

Currency exposure management

Risks arise where receipt of a foreign currency occurs some time after the price was originally agreed; for example:

price agreed 10,000 FF

exchange rate when price agreed £1 = 8.04 FF

expected income 10,000 / 8.04 = £1243.78

exchange rate when 10,000 was received £1 = 8.52 FF (a change of about 6%)

actual income 10,000 / 8.52 = £1173.71.

It is prudent to guard against such changes (e.g. by forward exchange contracts described below).

ACTIVITY 14.2

1 Using the bank charges for currency dealings obtained for Activity 14.1, determine the spot rate that applied two months ago, and look up today's.

2 Calculate the income you would have derived from selling goods for 10,000 DM two months ago and receiving payment at the time of sale.

3 Calculate the income derived from selling the goods two months ago for 10,000 DM but receiving payment in DM today.

Forward exchange contracts

This is a legally binding agreement between the bank and its customer to the effect that one currency will be exchanged for another at a specified future date, at an exchange rate that is agreed now. The customer may benefit from the agreement, or suffer by it. However, the risk of financial loss is removed because the customer knows precisely how much he or she will receive in his or her own currency.

Forward rates are arrived at by an adjustment of the spot rate, mainly reflecting the difference in interest rates between the two currencies; for example:

interest rates	UK 9%	Germany 4%
spot rate	£1	3 DM
3-month forward rate	£1	2.963 DM

difference in interest rates is 9 – 4 = 5% per annum

this corresponds to 5 x 3 / 12 = 1.25% in 3 months

hence the 3-month forward rate for DM is
3 x 100 / 101.25 = 2.963.

VAT and excise duty

VAT collection

A common VAT system applies throughout the EU, although rates vary considerably. As part of progress towards European Monetary Union (EMU) these rates are likely to become less disparate.

Under the original system of VAT, all exports are zero-rated. VAT is payable on all imports at the point of entry into the country, at the importing country's rate. To pay VAT there are two systems:

1 An importer or a transport company sets up a deferment account, backed by a bank guarantee, with the customs authorities. All VAT monies due are debited against this account, which is topped up on a regular basis.
2 Alternatively, an importer can pay any VAT monies due by a banker's draft or cash before the goods are released from customs.

The European Commission proposed a new system under which VAT would be charged on goods before export (i.e. in the country of origin) and recovered in the country of destination. This is the logical system within a 'single market' because it is exactly the same as domestic trade.

In domestic trade, the amount a company has to pay to the customs authorities is the amount of VAT arising from its sales, less the amount of VAT paid on its purchases. In transnational trade, the principle would be the same. For example, a UK business would charge VAT (at the UK rate) on goods sold to a French customer. Provided the customer was registered for VAT with the French authorities, he or she would reclaim VAT (at the French rate).

The system needs a clearing house for adjustments between member states that arise from their different VAT rates. Once rates are harmonised the adjustments will no longer be needed. Consider two examples:

Example 1

A UK wholesaler sells to a French company goods valued at £1000, adding VAT of £175 (assuming a standard rate of 17.5%).

The French company pays £1175 for the goods.

The UK company is liable to pay HM Customs and Excise £175 less whatever the goods cost to buy from the manufacturer.

The French company must pay the French customs authorities the VAT arising from the sale of the goods, less the equivalent of £200 from the French customs authorities (assuming a VAT rate of 20% on this class of goods).

Overall, the EU customs authorities have lost £25 on the transaction.

Example 2

A German company sells goods valued at £1000 to a UK company, adding VAT of £250 (assuming the German VAT rate is 25%).

The UK company is able to claim £175 from HM Customs and Excise (assuming a VAT rate of 17.5%).

Overall, the EU customs authorities have gained £75 on the transaction.

The proposed system was not acceptable to some of the member states and a transitional system based on the destination principle was introduced. This works as follows:

1 Exports continue to be zero-rated and VAT is paid by the importer at the importing country rate.
2 Registered businesses account for VAT on supplies from other EU countries as part of their normal domestic VAT system, eliminating the need for border delays.
3 A more sophisticated, electronic data interchange (EDI) system will be introduced to monitor the payments.

Both new systems simplify the VAT collection system. Under the clearing-house system, it is the responsibility of the seller and buyer to collect and pay VAT. The transporter would no longer be involved.

Excise duty

It is proposed to harmonise excise duties throughout the EU (see p.51).

Customs procedures and physical checks

Border checks have been replaced by roving customs officers (see p. 215).

SUMMARY 1 Loss arising from damage to or loss of goods can be minimised by careful choice of freight method and by insurance.

2 Financial risk can arise from delayed or non-payment, and from currency fluctuations. They are addressed by choosing safer terms of business, by short-term financing, and by currency management.

3   There is often no practical alternative to trading with customers on the same terms as local suppliers.

4   There are moves to harmonise rates of VAT and excise duty and to introduce simplified procedures. These moves are opposed by some powerful lobbying groups.

5   VAT and excise duty are dealt with by suppliers and customers, removing the need to delay goods at frontiers to carry out VAT and duty formalities.

Assignment 14

BACKGROUND

Select one of the companies used in previous activities or assignments, or a local company engaged in EU trade.

ACTIVITY

1   Monitor fluctuations in exchange rates between the UK and target countries.

2   Compare insurance rates for various countries and methods of transport as they relate to the selected company's products and markets.

3   Obtain details of costs of various methods of short-term financing from the international division of one of the large banks.

4   Find out VAT and excise duty rates (if any) for the company's goods in the EC countries you have targeted.

15 Human resource management (HRM)

OBJECTIVES   1 To describe the differences and similarities in industrial relations in the EU countries.

2 To analyse current trends in EU human resource management policies.

3 To examine individual aspects of human resource management in the EU, including recruitment, conditions of employment, worker protection, trade unions, consultation and industrial democracy, training, taxation and social security issues, and equal opportunities.

Introduction

The EU decision to introduce a 'Social Charter' is having an impact on human resource management (HRM) in the member states that have adopted it. There is debate as to whether it should be the basis of a single model for HRM in the EU.

Some people argue that accepted and finely tuned patterns of industrial relations behaviour, arising from the historical, cultural and political background of individual countries, would be disrupted and the result would be chaos rather than a well-functioning system across Europe. They conclude that industrial relations should be left at the margins of European integration.

However, at any given time, the same issues are generally being addressed by personnel and human resource managers across Europe. Increasingly, multinational businesses and unions are tackling problems from a transnational perspective. The amount of intra-EU trade is rapidly increasing. It is suggested, therefore, that the common factors already present should be the basis of a European system of HRM.

Certainly there is considerable diversity in the approach to HRM among the member states and moves towards a uniform system would displace existing institutions and practices. However, certain common trends appear in the operating methods of businesses within Europe and these will undoubtedly develop as a result of the SEM. There are clear indications that HRM systems adapt to accommodate the needs of employers and employees. Therefore, the choice appears to be not whether to change industrial relations frameworks in the EU, but how best to ensure that the changes benefit the whole European Union.

ACTIVITY 15.1

What do you consider to be the principal issues that have to be addressed by personnel and HRM managers in the UK at the present time?

Industrial relations differences in the EU

There are very significant differences between EU member states in four key areas:

1 *Unionisation* Levels of trade union membership vary significantly across the EU. In France, for example, union membership is around 15 per cent of the total workforce, while in Denmark it is over 80 per cent. Germany and the UK are about average with 40 to 50 per cent.
2 *Centralisation* In countries like Italy and the UK, industrial relations agreements are reached mainly at company level. In other countries there is more centralisation, with employers, unions and government addressing issues like pay and working conditions.
3 *The role of law* In Belgium and France industrial relations are underpinned by employment law. In Denmark, Ireland and the UK there is very little legislation specifically covering relations between employers and employees.
4 *Ideology* In Belgium, Denmark, Germany and the Netherlands the approach to industrial relations is based on consensus. There is a high level of agreement on values and beliefs among employers, employees and government. In other countries there are acknowledged to be distinct and even opposing views. In Italy and the UK, for example, there is an 'us and them' mentality in many industries, which is reflected in the political system. Some EU countries have mitigated the conflict by developing legislation and clear procedures for resolving disagreements so that they do not become confrontational.

Specific aspects of employment conditions and working practices differ considerably. In some countries there are no legal statutory limitations on maximum working hours; in others there is detailed legislation. There are also differences in the extent of employee participation in decision-making, termination of employment formalities, minimum holiday entitlements, and so on.

Common features of EU industrial relations

The labour market is undergoing change throughout Europe. For example:

1 There is an increase in the proportion of the workforce employed in service industries.
2 An increasing number of people are employed to work part-time, on a temporary or seasonal basis, and on fixed-term contracts.
3 There is a shift away from industry-wide collective bargaining towards negotiation at enterprise level. There are many more agreements on productivity, technology, consultation and participation, and single-union recognition.
4 There is increasing flexibility in work practices. Job demarcation is much reduced as businesses find they have to adapt quickly to changing market conditions, and this is reflected in workers' conditions of employment.
5 There are many more multiskill tasks, and this demands better training. Skilled employees are recognised to be a valuable asset and organisations are seeking ways of retaining them.

Human resource management policies are tied in with these changes. There is an increasingly close match between HRM policies and the commercial needs of the firm.

ACTIVITY 15.3

Choose a local company and investigate: (a) the proportion of employees that are temporary, on fixed-term contracts, and so on; (b) the nature of pay bargaining and special agreements; and (c) how much flexibility is written into job descriptions.

The effects on HRM of production methods

Mass production

To a large extent the underlying production system determines the style of industrial relations in an industry. As well as giving rise to working conditions and methods of supervision, it also influences the business culture and social framework of companies.

In the 1940s, 1950s and 1960s there was a trend in the major industrialised European states towards mass production and consumption of consumer goods, particularly cars and consumer durables. Mass production is usually based on the assembly-line principle, first introduced by the Ford Motor Company in the USA. This production method results in the replacement of skilled craftsmen by semi-skilled workers, each worker doing relatively simple, specialist and repetitive tasks which require little training. In many ways this production system is highly efficient. However, there are a number of basic consequences.

1 There is a trend towards large companies – to provide economies of scale and to finance the large capital investment needed to establish the production facilities.
2 Finely balanced production lines are most efficient when they are producing high volumes of the same product because set-up times tend to be long.
3 Raw material, intermediate parts, assemblies, and finished goods are stocked, both to avoid disruption to the production line, which could arise from hold-ups or breakdowns at specific points in the line, and to guarantee customer delivery. Holding stock is expensive when interest rates are high because stock ties up capital.
4 Quality procedures are distinct from the production process. Supervision and management structures tend to be hierarchical. Productivity is encouraged through work study and incentive bonuses.
5 Union structures also reflect the production system. Unions tend to be industry-based and agreements on wages and working conditions are arrived at by collective bargaining. Although pay bargaining is essentially centred on the company, the size of the company, competitiveness, and the fact that there are often just a few, dominant, companies in an industry sector means that an agreement in one company frequently becomes the national norm.
6 Management's concern is to ensure that increases in pay are 'paid for' by increases in productivity or reductions in costs.

The main function of the personnel department in this environment is to maintain industrial peace, participate in rounds of negotiations, and undertake the administration associated with a large workforce. In some companies it also participates in work study.

ACTIVITY 15.4

Obtain information from two companies – one a large business with assembly-line production and one which is in an industry sector that demands rapid changes to its product mix – on the activities of the personnel/HRM department.

Trends towards flexibility

Since the mid-1970s businesses have found it difficult to achieve the levels of sales that are needed to sustain economies of scale and productivity increases. The problem has been mitigated to some extent by aggressive exporting, but stagnant world markets and protectionist policies by governments (needed to protect domestic industry) have limited the scope of this approach. However, it has resulted in an international dimension to many industries: joint ventures, marketing consortia, and licensing agreements have produced globalisation of several industries.

In these circumstances most companies have undertaken a re-appraisal of their activities, with plant closures, rationalisations, and a massive number of redundancies. The result is 'smaller and fitter' companies but at the cost of higher levels of long-term unemployment throughout Europe.

Another crucial influence on industry which has affected patterns of industrial relations has been the fragmentation of demand. Customers increasingly want differentiated instead of standard products. Product life cycles have shortened considerably and there are many more competing products on the market.

To remain competitive, businesses have developed the ability to make smaller batches cost effectively, moving from one product to another quickly and cheaply. Another development is re-usability – parts and assemblies that are common to several products. This trend towards 'economies of scope' has been helped by developments in technology.

Changes in demand and production have been reflected in changes to work patterns. Small teams of workers produce functional and testable units. These teams can be thought of as working in parallel towards multiple products, rather than sequentially towards the production of a single product. Moreover, quality control is 'built into' the production process, with individual workers and small groups taking responsibility for making, testing and rectifying faults in their own work.

Smaller batches and frequent changes in the product mix mean that there is an increased risk associated with holding material and parts stock. Techniques based on the 'just in time' principle have become common. Products are 'pulled through' the plant by demand for output rather than according to an overall long-term plan. Computer-based systems that provide instant feedback on the location and status of material, parts and assemblies facilitate such techniques.

The demand for skilled labour increased significantly between 1980 and 1990. An EU labour market survey indicated an overall increase of 26 per cent in demand for skilled workers and a drop in demand for the unskilled. The trend was strongest in the Netherlands (53 per cent), Ireland (44 per cent) and Belgium (41 per cent) and weakest in Germany (11 per cent) and Denmark (15 per cent). Nevertheless, figures on changes in demand for skilled labour must be treated with care. In Greece, for example, where the change is about the average of EU states, there has been only limited exploitation of economies of scale in production and low levels of labour productivity. Also de-skilling associated with assembly-line production has only been significant in the relatively few but very large multinational companies, and consequently a move away from assembly-line production is not numerically large enough to be reflected in national statistics.

Job demarcation in this post-assembly-line era is much reduced, with workers performing multiple tasks. Training is sharply increased and provided on a continuing basis. Consultation is increased, reflecting the autonomy and discretion that many skilled workers enjoy. Payment systems tend towards individual or small-group performance-related pay – bonuses, incentives, profit-sharing and equity schemes. Clear career paths and schemes to improve job satisfaction are offered to valued workers.

In an economy that some believe will always have uncertainty, volatility and market fragmentation, some European companies have adopted HRM strategies that can be described as 'competitive flexibility' – in which employers aim to manage human resources in a way that closely links them with market conditions. To achieve this, they believe it is necessary to eliminate external constraints such as government regulations and trade union power, both of which are seen as causes of labour market inflexibility. The view was widely accepted during the 1980s, and many statutory provisions on minimum wages and maximum hours were removed, and regulations covering the recruitment and dismissal of workers were diluted. As a result, there are now many more temporary and fixed-term contract employees who are not covered by employment protection legislation. However, a ruling in the UK House of Lords in March 1994 that such workers *were* covered by the legislation, challenges this trend.

A feature of *competitive flexibility* is the trend towards categorising workers as 'core' and 'peripheral' (or 'insiders' and 'outsiders'). Skilled and specialist workers who are vital to the successful operation of the company often have conditions of employment that are superior to the rest. They are likely to be offered pay and conditions that are better than any agreement negotiated nationally by trade unions and that are highly competitive with those offered by other employers. Core employees are likely to be involved in consultation and participation procedures, and may be offered high levels of employment security. Surveys indicate that there is a movement towards a two-thirds to one-third ratio, where core employees enjoy good conditions at the expense of the underclass minority.

Proponents of a *constructive flexibility* HRM policy believe that competitive flexibility encourages confrontation in industrial relations and produces social divisions that are ultimately destructive. They argue that the whole organisation should be committed to and engaged in innovation and improving quality and productivity, and that this cannot be achieved if some employees are discriminated against. They also propound the view that a company cannot, and should not, attempt to operate in isolation. Government, trade unions, and other bodies have a role to play in providing strong and competitive industry. The suggested components of employer–employee relations within a constructive flexibility HRM system are:

- Employment security.
- Fair share of success (and fair share of failure).
- Co-determination between employer and employee.

- Work organisation for co-operation, creating a sense of community and purpose.
- Skill enhancement should have a broad content.
- Training at work should allow workers to maintain their value in the labour market as well as supporting the company's aims.
- Working hours must retain freedom of choice over the agreed maximum basic hours.
- Equal opportunity in the workplace, with positive discrimination where necessary.
- Working environment without health risks and accidents.

This model has much in common with the EU Social Charter.

ACTIVITY 15.5

1 Prepare a list of the factors that you think are the important differences between 'competitive flexibility' and 'constructive flexibility'.

2 What are the advantages of each, from the viewpoint of: (a) the company; and (b) its employees.

Human resource management in the EU

Advertising a vacancy

The personnel manager needs to find where there are potential sources of labour. In Greece, for example, there is a shortage of finance and personnel staff and also skilled white-collar workers. How can he or she discover that there is a pool of well-educated graduates, frequently with second degrees from UK and US universities, who would be interested in working for international companies?

Matching job seekers with employers varies from country to country. In Italy, for example, newspapers regularly include columns of personal information on new graduates, classified according the type of job they are seeking. Employers contact them directly. In France, the Minitel information system (similar to Prestel), which is used regularly by over 40 per cent of households, is used by employers to provide more details on jobs they have advertised in newspapers. The system is interactive and permits the employer to carry out a pre-selection test via the Minitel system prior to issuing the job details and inviting a formal application. In Germany, the state-run employment placement system covers all grades of employee – executives, white and blue-collar workers, while in Greece the most used system of recruitment is still personal introduction.

In Italy private employment agencies can only 'advise' potential employers about candidates because all recruitment is state-controlled, while French and German employment agencies are prevented by law from dealing in full-time appointments, and can deal only with temporary jobs. Employment exchanges throughout the EU can help job seekers to find vacancies using the 'Sedoc network'. This is a system that allows unemployment offices to exchange information on jobs. Some UK employment exchanges specialise in advertising overseas jobs and in finding appointments for clients. These tend to be jobs where there is a specific skill shortage.

Occupations for which there is a professional association usually feature a significant proportion of international job advertisements in their professional journals. Marketing, media, catering and computing are better served than law and banking. Increasingly the better quality newspapers have days when they concentrate on European affairs and include a modest amount of job advertising. However, an employer seeking applicants from a particular country would find it best to advertise in the newspapers and magazines of that country.

ACTIVITY 15.6

Choose one EU country and investigate what methods of advertising job vacancies are available.

Employing EU citizens

Citizens of every EU country have the same rights to be employed in another EU country as nationals of that country. There is, however, one important exception to this freedom. Public service organisations may have rules which stipulate that only nationals of their country may undertake certain jobs. Often this is for reasons of national security.

Many UK organisations have been recruiting from other countries for a long time. Often this has simply been due to shortages of suitably qualified people in specific occupations. For example, hospitals in the West Midlands have recruited doctors from Germany, the Netherlands and Italy; schools in the south-east have recruited teachers from Germany, the Netherlands and Denmark.

Increasingly, recruiting from other countries is part of a policy of 'Europeanisation'. Cross-border mergers, acquisitions and joint ventures have made it necessary for businesses to set up operations in other countries. For example, an Italian company that has formed a subsidiary in the UK may want a mix of Italian and British staff to manage and operate its office in Birmingham. It may also recruit British staff to work in its main office in Milan to provide language skills and knowledge of the UK, and to help with liaison.

Employers considering employing nationals of another EU country must not discriminate against applicants on the basis of their nationality. The normal recruitment procedure, used for nationals of the company's own country, should be adopted. The employer does not need to make any special arrangements to overcome any inherent disadvantages the applicant may have – language difficulties for example.

There are different procedures and practices for recruitment throughout Europe. Very few personnel managers in the UK, for example, have to consult employee representatives before appointing a new member of staff. In Germany this is a statutory requirement.

The extent to which the nationals of EU countries work in other than their own country varies. In border areas people often live in one country but work in another. Belgians, the Dutch, and Greeks are those most likely to seek overseas employment. Danes often work in other Scandinavian countries. Italians and Germans tend not to work abroad, except where they come from areas that have declining industries. Portuguese and Spanish graduates tend to stay local. There are some occupations where overseas working is quite common – consultancy and engineering, for example.

Recruitment procedures

The *interview* is the most used method of selection throughout Europe. In some countries, such as France and Germany, it is not permitted to ask questions on some personal matters that are normal in UK interviews. Some topics which the British would wish to explore, like previous salary, is considered irrelevant to the candidate's acceptability in several countries. Other methods of selection are now used, including *aptitude tests* and *personality tests*. *Hand-writing analysis* is sometimes used as a component of the selection process in Belgium, France and Italy.

It is forbidden to have an upper age limit for a job in France. In the UK age discrimination is legal and common, even though discrimination on grounds of gender, ethnic origin, and so on, are not permitted.

There are also differences in procedure once a job offer has been made. In France, for example, all employees are required to have a medical check at the time of their appointment, and again each year. Refusal to undergo the examination is a valid basis for dismissal. In several countries, notably Germany, employees have the right to see all the information that goes into their personnel file and to add their own comments if they wish. In the UK employees can insist on seeing the content of their personnel file only if the file is held on computer.

ACTIVITY 15.8

1 List the selection techniques that could be used to determine the suitability of applicants during recruitment.

2 For each technique, identify the problems you might encounter when using it on the national of an EU country in which that technique was not common practice.

Temporary employment

A growing number of organisations employ people on temporary and fixed-term contracts. This is attractive to many young Europeans who 'take time out' to work abroad, either between school and college or after graduating and before going into a career, and it is an effective way to learn the language and life-style of another country. Employing such a person may be an attractive option for a company because the employee will generally be academically sound. They will normally only be suitable as short-term 'casual' labour because they often wish to spend short periods in several locations during their 'time out'.

Exchange programmes

A company wishing to have the benefit of employees with a knowledge of another EU country, and perhaps skills in a particular business activity, may consider taking part in a work exchange scheme.

There are several schemes, designed for people between the ages of 18 and 28, who are already in employment or about to enter it, who have basic vocational training or first-hand work experience and who can usually offer vocational skills (e.g. accounting, marketing, practical skills). These 'young worker' exchanges can be as short as 3 to 13 weeks, or longer (4 to 16 months). The European Commission gives financial aid to institutions entrusted with the task of running the schemes.

ACTIVITY 15.9

Young people who take 'time out' to work in another country do so either between school and college or between college and a career. What are the advantages and disadvantages of each? Consider the question from the employer's viewpoint, and from the young person's.

Qualifications

One of the first things that a potential employer needs to consider is the applicant's qualifications.

Graduate and postgraduate qualifications are the best recognised levels of academic achievement throughout the EU, although there are differences both in the period of study and the actual level of attainment they represent.

In the UK and Ireland, higher academic education is broadly at two levels: the first level (bachelor's degree) of three years followed by the higher level (master's degree). The best-known higher level vocational qualifications are BTEC Higher National Diploma courses. Professional bodies (accountancy, banking, computing) have their own specialist examinations. Most people begin their higher education courses at the age of 18 or 19.

Elsewhere in Europe it is more common to find that degrees approximate more to the UK's master's degree, that the period of study is 4–6 years or more, and that students start later. Their studies may be interrupted by military service, but students can usually defer it to the end of the course.

UK higher education courses are mainly based in universities and institutes of higher education. Some establishments are perceived to be superior to others, but distinctions between the quality of courses and qualifications tends to vary from subject to subject.

In many parts of Europe there is a functional distinction between academic universities and technical universities. The academic universities deliver 'pure' subjects such as languages and science, and are particularly appropriate for those wishing to progress into research or teaching. The technical universities deliver 'applied' subjects such as engineering, business studies, law, and so on.

There are also non-university higher education colleges that provide technician and vocational education such as the IUT (*Instituts universitaires de technologie*) in France, Higher Vocational Schools in the Netherlands, and *Fachhochschulen* in Germany. In these colleges, the courses tend to be shorter and lead to different awards. The level of the qualifications is as high as a degree but covers a more limited scope. Education systems are by no means standard, however, and these shorter, vocational courses are delivered in the university system in Spain. In Spain, and in Germany, the education system has a strong regional bias.

Within the EU, recognition and acceptance of professional qualifications gained in another country have been established only for some of the occupations – doctors, pharmacists, dentists, nurses, midwives, veterinary surgeons, and architects. A general system for the recognition of higher education diplomas which are awarded following training lasting at least three years has applied since 1991. The system covers, for example, such occupations as surveyors, accountants, physiotherapists, psychologists, and opticians. Qualifications offered by BTEC, RSA, and City and Guilds are not generally familiar to employers elsewhere. Even where they are, employers have difficulty in equating them to vocational qualifications in their own country. There is some recognition of the fact that BTEC National and A-levels are of a slightly lower standard than the French baccalaureate but there is still a lot to be done before most qualifications have acceptance in other EU countries.

The introduction of GNVQs, replacing the main vocational qualifications of the UK awarding bodies, provides a benchmark for comparison within the UK and eventually also with other EU qualifications. GNVQs also represent an attempt by UK authorities to demonstrate to employers how vocational qualifications compare with essentially school-based qualifications like GCSE and A-levels.

Accreditation of prior learning (APL)

The establishment of National Vocational Qualifications (NVQs) in the UK provided a framework to which all vocational qualifications could be related. The necessary knowledge and skills can be acquired by both on-the-job and off-the-job training. Assessment of NVQs is predominantly in the workplace. Another key feature of these qualifications is that they allow the trainee to undertake assessment without the requirement to attend classes. In other words they allow for the accreditation of prior learning (APL).

This principle has been taken further by the Management Charter Initiative (MCI). MCI recognises that there are very many UK managers who are competent in their jobs but who have arrived at their present status without gaining formal qualifications. They are, therefore, disadvantaged if they wish to move to another employer. In the European context, this lack of qualifications severely restricts the mobility of competent but unqualified UK managers. The MCI qualifications M1 and M2 (managers and managers-of-managers) fit within the NVQ framework. They were devised by industry and the scheme is strongly supported by the UK government. They recognise that in order to be competent it is necessary for every manager to be able effectively and efficiently to manage operations, finance, people and information.

The elements within each of these components are shown in Figure 15.1. The 'managing people' elements are of special interest in this study of human resource management.

ACTIVITY 15.10

Decide what qualifications would be appropriate for a specific job in the UK and investigate the equivalent qualifications in one or two other EU countries.

MANAGING OPERATIONS

1. **Maintain and improve service and product operations**
   1.1 Maintain operations to meet quality standards.
   1.2 Create and maintain the necessary conditions for productive work.

2. **Contribute to the implementation of change in services, products and systems**
   2.1 Contribute to the evaluation of proposed changes to services, products and systems.
   2.2 Implement and evaluate changes to services, products and systems.

MANAGE FINANCE

3. **Recommend, monitor and control the use of resources**
   3.1 Make recommendations for expenditure.
   3.2 Monitor and control the use of resources.

MANAGE PEOPLE

4. **Contribute to the recruitment and selection of personnel**
   4.1 Define future personnel requirements.
   4.2 Contribute to the assessment and selection of candidates against team and organisational requirements.

5. **Develop teams, individuals and self to enhance performance**
   5.1 Develop and improve teams through planning and activities.
   5.2 Identify, review and improve development activities for individuals.
   5.3 Develop oneself within the job role.

6. **Plan, allocate and evaluate work carried out by teams, individuals and self**
   6.1 Set up and update work objectives for teams and individuals.
   6.2 Plan activities and determine work methods to achieve objectives.
   6.3 Allocate work and evaluate teams, individuals and self against objectives.
   6.4 Determine feedback to teams and individuals on their performance.

7. **Create, maintain and enhance effective working relationships**
   7.1 Establish and maintain the trust and support of one's subordinates.
   7.2 Establish and maintain the trust and support of one's immediate manager.
   7.3 Establish and maintain relationships with colleagues.
   7.4 Identify and minimise interpersonal conflict.
   7.5 Implement disciplinary and grievance procedures.
   7.6 Counsel staff.

MANAGE INFORMATION

8. **Seek, evaluate and organise information for action**
   8.1 Obtain and evaluate information to aid decision-making.
   8.2 Record and store information.

9. **Exchange information to solve problems and make decisions**
   9.1 Lead meetings and group discussions to solve problems and make decisions.
   9.2 Contribute to discussion to solve problems and make decisions.
   9.3 Advise and inform others.

Fig. 15.1 MCI standards

Conditions of employment

The principle of equal treatment applies to all employees who are nationals of other EU countries. An employer should not discriminate between them in terms of pay or conditions (e.g. hours, holidays, training, promotion, pension entitlement, discipline, termination of employment).

An employer may not, for example, dismiss an employee who is a national of another EU country on grounds that would not also apply equally to nationals of the employer's country. In the case of a dispute over dismissal (or any other employment issue) the EU national has the same statutory protection as other employees. This may mean the right to reinstatement or compensation in the case of proven unfair dismissal. There are similar EU regulations that prevent discrimination against self-employed EU nationals who wish to set up business in an EU country other than their own.

The employee's responsibilities to the company, and the employee's liability to pay tax, social security contributions, and so on, are identical to those of nationals of the EU country in which the place of work is located. (Rights and responsibilities continue, subject to some conditions, if the person becomes unemployed through no fault of their own.)

It is important to remember that the rights of an employee are the rights applicable in the country where they live and work. These may be different from the rights that an EU national would be entitled to in his or her own country. One exception to the 'live and work' rule is military service. For example, a Greek working in the UK would have to return to Greece to do military service if liable for it, even though the UK does not have compulsory military service.

EU nationals living in another EU country who embark on vocational training (and who have the same rights to do so as nationals of that country) must not be required to pay fees that are different from those charged to nationals of the country. An EU national also has similar rights and obligations as nationals of the country in terms of home ownership, borrowing money, and entering into contracts, payment of tax, payment of social security contributions and receipt of benefit. Moreover, all employees have the right to join (or not join) a trade union and have the right to vote and hold office in the union, except where it is a position governed by public law or management of a body governed by public law.

In 1991 the European Commission proposed, as part of the Social Charter, regulations that limited the working week to 48 hours, and prevented Sunday working except in special circumstances. The UK did not agree to the Charter and consequently is not bound by its content, including those relating to working hours. In fact, the UK is almost unique in not already having laws covering these two areas. Most EU countries have legislation that is tougher than the European Commission's proposals. In France, for example, the legal limit is 39 hours and workers are entitled to five weeks' paid holiday plus 11 public holidays. The legislation protects employees against exploitation. In practice extra hours and Sunday working do take place where it is with the agreement of employer and employee.

Holidays

Although no single country has more than 15 public holidays during the year, there are over 40 weekdays during the year when businesses in one or more of the EU countries are 'out of action' because of public holidays. Some of the holidays are familiar to us in the UK – Easter, Christmas and New Year. Other days with religious significance are widely observed, as are national days, royal birthdays, Labour Day, and so on.

As in the UK, particular industries have their own patterns of holidays. EU statistics reveal that most European employees have four or five weeks of holiday in addition to the public holidays.

ACTIVITY 15.11

How would you deal with the situation of employees who are the nationals of another EU country wanting to take holidays to coincide with friends or family in their home country?

Employee protection

Within the EU, employee protection covers the following areas:

1 Several 'EU Action Programmes' have resulted in improved protection for workers against illness and accidents at work. The protection includes standards for safety-markings, and identification of dangerous physical, chemical and biological hazards (asbestos, lead, noise).

2 There is agreement on the provision of preventative, protective and emergency services, on the training and information that should be available on health and hygiene, and on workers' consultation and participation in improving the workplace.

3 An EU directive relating to collective redundancies compels the employer to give notice of at least 30 days.

4 In the event of a company takeover, the new employer cannot unilaterally change or cancel employment contracts or the arrangements for employer–employee relations.

5 EU regulations also safeguard, in the event of a takeover, employees who have retired and receive company pensions.

6 Persons employed in an EU country other than their own who have lost their jobs through no fault of their own do not lose their rights. They must ask the

employment office where they are resident for a certificate testifying that they have lost their jobs. If the insurance payments they have made in the various EU countries where they have worked are sufficient, they will be eligible for unemployment benefit.

Trade unions

Throughout the EU employees have the right to belong, or not to belong, to a trade union.

The role of the trade unions varies from country to country. In Germany, for example, wage bargaining is carried out on a *Länder* basis, between the employers' federation and a trade union. If a company is not a member of the relevant employers' federation, then it is not directly involved in the wage bargaining that will subsequently apply to the company. The affluence of the various *Länders* has an influence on the negotiations so that wages within an industry vary in different parts of the country.

In the UK, much union reorganisation took place in the late 1980s and early 1990s, notably in engineering and the public sector, and a number of unions have gone ahead with single-union agreements and no-strike deals with employers. Membership has also fallen, due to the decline in industries with a strong union tradition (e.g. mining, steel, heavy engineering), and the shift towards part-time working and service-sector jobs.

ACTIVITY 15.12

Trade unions have responded to the proliferation of multinational companies and transnational joint ventures by developing their own international links. Choose one of the big UK unions and investigate how it liaises with organisations representing workers in the same industry sector in other EU countries.

Consultation and industrial democracy

Employee involvement in decision-making and representation on management committees is strongest in Germany, where it is under-pinned by laws passed in 1971 and 1976. For example, in German public limited companies (AGs), which have a two-tier management structure, the supervisory board comprises shareholders' and employee representatives, and, depending on the size of the company, employee representation may be one-third or one-half of the number of members. The supervisory board appoints an executive committee comprising full-time senior managers of the company which initiates policy and runs the company. The chairperson of this committee has to be approved by the majority of the employee representatives on the supervisory board.

At a lower level within the organisation is the works committee. All companies, not just those engaged in manufacturing, have these. The works committee:

- Gives consent to the appointment of workers to new positions, internal transfers between work groups, dismissals, adjustments to the working day, the introduction of overtime or shift working, canteen prices, and so on.
- Is consulted on plans to open or close plants, on investment decisions, and on business policy issues.
- Receives information on the company's economic performance and prospects.

ACTIVITY 15.13

What are the functions of the works committee in organisations in your locality? Are there any differences between SMEs and large companies?

Training

There are three main barriers for people who wish to continue their studies: finance; getting existing qualifications accepted as entry qualifications; and coping with studies in a foreign language.

An employer who wishes an employee from another EU country to continue studying on a part-time basis would normally be expected to provide financial assistance and to assist in convincing the institution that the employee's qualifications and/or other qualities are appropriate for acceptance on the course. The employer has, after all, found the qualifications acceptable for recruitment and has knowledge of the person's competence.

The EU's COMETT programme is aimed at trainees, including new graduates, persons in active employment, and training officers. It assists co-operation between universities and businesses in training for new technologies.

Taxation and social security payments

Income tax is a complex system even for people who live in one country, because of the allowances and tax bands, and methods of assessment and payment, especially if they have unearned as well as earned income. A person with assets in more than one country, such as property or shares, will probably need the help of a specialist in transnational taxation to avoid paying more than they need to.

Although personal taxation is the responsibility of the individual employee, it may be good practice for an employer to help a valued employee in dealing with the tax authorities. Some understanding of the tax system in the company's 'own' country and competence in the language when dealing with tax officials is likely to be much appreciated by the employee.

The industrially advanced countries of Europe all have well-developed social security systems, providing a wide range of benefits. Both the employer and the employee make contributions which are based on the employee's wage. Usually a contribution is a percentage of gross pay, which in some countries is quite high: in France, for example, it amounts to about 15 per cent of income, compared with about 10 per cent in the UK.

Unlike the UK, where benefits are generally a flat rate, many EU countries pay a percentage of the claimant's former salary, subject to a minimum and maximum. For example, in France unemployment pay is 40 per cent of last salary, and sick pay is 50 per cent of salary.

As in the UK, the pension that derives from social security contributions is generally considered inadequate and employees usually belong to a superannuation or pension scheme arranged either by the employer, the trade union, or the employee's professional association.

A person working in another EU country is treated in the same way as a national of that country for social security purposes. If they have not made adequate contributions in the current country of residence then contributions made in other EU countries should be taken into account. However, liaison between the various social security organisations in different EU countries is not strong at present.

People who work close to a frontier and live across the border in another EU country enjoy the benefits of the country in which they reside, even though their contributions are not made there. They will have registered at a social security office in the country where they work when they first took up employment (or started to search for work there). They must obtain form E106 from this office, and this entitles them to medical care, medicines, hospital treatment, and so on. The E106 is valid only for a limited period, and its validity must be extended as necessary.

The UK Department of Social Security at Newcastle upon Tyne has a section that specialises in providing details of social security, health care and pension rights in the EU.

Private medical schemes for core employees are at least as common in other EU countries as they are in the UK. The principal advantage is that treatment can be arranged at times to suit the employer and employee, rather than to suit the medical authorities.

Equal opportunities

Women tend to be concentrated in certain sectors of employment, often those requiring fewest skills and which are lowest paid. They are the most vulnerable group as regards unemployment. They suffer from discrimination in two areas: occupational equality and equality of opportunity in society.

A woman within the EU is entitled to equal pay for equal work. 'Pay' refers to basic wage and all other benefits, in cash or kind, directly or indirectly. She is also entitled to participation in vocational training, have equal opportunities for promotion, equal working conditions, and so forth.

EU directives seek to ensure that men and women have equality in all areas covered by social security laws, banning discrimination in contributions and benefits in the areas of sickness and invalidity; accidents at work and occupational diseases; old age and retirement; and unemployment. Special directives address equality in self-employment and agricultural work.

Legal framework of industrial relations

There are significant differences between EU countries in the amount of legislation specifically relating to industrial relations. At one extreme is the UK with very little legislation. On the other hand, Germany has a great deal of legislation: federal legislation covers topics such as the establishment of works councils, and there is a system of labour courts to which employers and employees may resort.

German companies often treat their internal rules and procedures as though they were laws. Issues are invariably resolved by formal processes and the outcomes are recorded in writing. There is also an absence of informal procedures (e.g. unofficial channels of communication, improvised working methods and standards, accepted but undocumented ways of behaving).

By contrast, Greece, where the legal framework for business is complex, and the state approach to its application appears to be inconsistent and unpredictable, there are extensive informal channels of communication and improvisation. There are also basic differences within Greece between the HRM policies of the influential multinational businesses and Greek-owned companies.

ACTIVITY 15.14

List the main Acts that affect HRM in the UK and summarise the main provisions of each.

SUMMARY   1   Industrial relations differ in four main areas between EU countries: unionisation, centralisation, the role of law, and ideology. Arguments in favour of Europe-wide HRM systems make reference to the similar approach adopted throughout Europe to many industrial relations issues, and the increasing amount of transnational business activity.

2   There is a trend throughout the EU towards flexibility in work practices, individual and small group agreements, and HRM policies that closely match the commercial needs of the enterprise.

3   In the countries that had production methods aimed at achieving economies of scale, there is a trend towards methods offering economies of scope. This is reflected in HRM policies that are based on 'competitive flexibility' or 'constructive flexibility'.

4   The trend towards part-time and fixed-term contract employment and service-sector jobs has an impact on trade union and other HRM issues.

5   EU nationals have the right to compete for and take jobs in all EU countries on equal terms with nationals of that country. However, applicants may still find themselves disadvantaged in countries other than their own by lack of language skills and poor knowledge of business practices.

6   Different methods exist in each country for advertising job vacancies. There are national differences in the methods of selection and recruitment.

7   There is currently no EU-wide recognition or comparability of qualifications, except in certain of the professions, but there is a commitment to establishing transferability of qualifications as part of progress to the SEM. Programmes that assess the trainee in the workplace and give accreditation to prior learning are in the forefront of progress towards comparability of qualifications.

8   An increasing number of young EU citizens seek temporary work and participate in exchange schemes that involve employers and universities.

9   Although all EU nationals have the same worker protection, equal opportunity, social benefits and unemployment rights as a national of the country in which they live and work, there are, and will continue to be, differences in salaries, tax and social security contributions, medical care, working hours and holidays.

Assignment 15

BACKGROUND

Management practice, particularly that relating to HRM, differs throughout the EU. However, there appears to be more and more commonality, particularly as a result of increasing transnational trade and the SEM.

The MCI standards, devised in the UK by industrialists, are a model of management activities that, it is believed, can be applied to any business anywhere in the UK.

ACTIVITY

1 Study the MCI standards given in Figure 15.1.

2 Interpret them as they apply to a local UK business with which you are familiar (if necessary undertake investigative work).

3 Decide, element by element, to what extent they could be applied to management in another EU country.

16 Support services and funding

OBJECTIVES
1 To describe the financial and other assistance that is available from UK institutions.

2 To review European sources of financial and other assistance, particularly those specific to regions and SMEs.

3 To identify possible projects that would attract support, and suggest an outline proposal from which a full submission could be prepared.

ACTIVITY 16.1

At the end of each section of this chapter, pause and carry out the following two tasks:

1 Seek out a local organisation that is receiving funds in the categories you have just read about. Identify the characteristics of the company and its project that make it eligible for funding and strong enough to succeed in competition with other bids.

2 For one of the organisations that have been mentioned in previous case studies, activities and assignments, suggest a project that you think would be eligible for funding and other assistance.

Government support of international trade

The Department of Trade and Industry (DTI) provides help and advice to firms wishing to enter, or already operating in, export markets, chiefly by means of its 'Export Initiative', as follows:

1 It provides export information to help firms prepare marketing plans and set up exporting and distribution operations.

2 It helps businesses set up a presence in the market through a range of promotional activities.

3 It provides help to reduce the financial risks associated with international trade.

4 Its Export Market Information Centre maintains a database on over 150,000 overseas businesses, nearly 100,000 articles, cuttings and reports on markets and products, and details of DTI-supported trade fairs and exhibitions.

5 It publishes a range of country profiles, economic reports, research information on specific market sectors, and hints to exporters.

6 It has information on selling opportunities, such as foreign buyers looking for suppliers, agents who wish to represent British companies, and companies inviting tenders for projects.

7 DTI-supported trade fairs offer opportunities for UK companies to promote their goods, at subsidised rates for space, stands and travel. They also assist in overcoming language difficulties.

Other forms of assistance for the exporter include the following:

8 Trade missions, sponsored by trade associations and Chambers of Commerce, give opportunities for businesses to travel with 10 to 20 other exporters in the same sector to make contact with agents and customers. The DTI provides financial support for a number of visits.

9 The Export Credits Guarantee Department (ECGD) helps individual companies to minimise financial risk by providing insurance and financial guarantees.

10 Insurance may be taken out against the possibility of insolvency of the foreign customer, political occurrences that delay payment, cancellation of import or export licences, and the sudden introduction of exchange controls.

11 The British Overseas Trade Board (BOTB) is also a source of help to exporters. Through its European Trade Committee it promotes awareness of export opportunities in particular market segments. As well as the EU countries it has information on the EFTA countries – Iceland, Norway, Sweden, Finland, Austria and Switzerland.

Finance from the EU

Throughout its history, the EU has adhered to the principle of providing funds to help economic development in member states. More recently it has also begun to tackle social problems. Any attempt to tackle such complicated and important issues is bound to be complex. Very often the causes of economic and social problems are interrelated and only partially understood. A variety of measures are needed to tackle them and the outcomes of a course of action are often difficult to predict.

Many schemes are therefore within the areas of responsibility of more than one Commission Directorate. Funding under a scheme is usually available for a fairly limited period (often two–five years) and new schemes are being introduced all the time. Furthermore, understanding a scheme and how it can be applied to the needs of a particular business or community has become a specialist job and many organisations (e.g. private-and public-sector businesses, local authorities, educational institutions) employ staff to analyse new schemes and prepare bids for funding.

For some time the Commission operated the various funds independently, but it is now better organised to co-ordinate the use of the funds and to ensure they are used effectively to achieve specific Community objectives. Funding can be divided into six categories: structural funds; business and industry; research and development; education, training and exchange schemes; cultural and social issues; and development aid.

Structural funds

These are intended to help those regions that are disadvantaged and are targeted on geographical areas and industrial sectors. Grants are available from three separate funds: the European Regional Development Fund (ERDF); the European Social Fund (ESF); and the Guidance Section of the European Agricultural Guidance and Guarantee Fund (EAGGF). These funds are known collectively as the Structural Funds.

Financial assistance from all three funds is focused on five complementary objectives:

1 To assist regions whose development is lagging behind.
2 To revitalise regions affected by serious industrial decline.
3 To combat long-term unemployment.
4 To integrate young people into the job market.
5 To adjust agricultural structures and develop rural areas.

The Regional Development Fund deals mainly with objectives 1 and 2, the ESF with objectives 3 and 4, and the EAGGF with objective 5.

Because the five objectives are designed to reduce the gap between the advanced and the less developed regions, and to promote a more balanced economic development of the EU, most of the funding is restricted for use in designated geographical areas. The importance attached to the reduction of regional imbalance can be judged from the fact that between 1987 and 1993 the resources available to the Structural Funds were doubled in real terms to 14 billion ECU (based on 1988 prices).

The impact of EU structural funding is increased by the fact that they are usually conditional on the national authorities providing at least the same amount.

Regional aid

Regional aid is provided principally through the ERDF. Recent projects initiated under objective 1 have dealt with:

- The physical and social environment, including urban regeneration, environmental improvement and community reconciliation.
- Improving land, sea and air transport.
- Industrial development, including help to both new and existing businesses, and assistance with research and technological development.
- Measures to assist tourism through improved facilities and marketing.
- Measures to promote agricultural development.
- Schemes to tackle long-term unemployment and integrating young people into employment.

Projects under objective 2 include:

- Developing industrial and business premises, especially on disused sites.
- Improvements in the road, rail and inland waterway networks, and improvements to public transport to assist business development and tourism.
- Provision of business advice centres, assistance in introducing new technology, the provision of shared business services.
- Improvements to the image and environment of regions by reclaiming derelict land, landscaping and cleaning up town-centre and urban areas where there is potential for the development of business or tourism.
- Support for research, development and training to overcome shortages of skills and manpower.

Originally funding was provided on a year-at-a-time basis for specific projects. Very large and longer term projects are now funded. Government departments, local authorities and publicly funded organisations are the main recipients, but SMEs are targeted for some support. Investment projects of over 10 million ECU and infrastructure projects of over 15 million ECU may bid for this type of funding.

A number of Commission-initiated programmes have been set up where a community rather than a national level is more appropriate. Among the many schemes are:

ENVIREG is concerned with the disposal of household waste and sewage in urban areas, the disposal of effluent from ships, and methods of dealing with toxic and dangerous waste.

REGEN assists with the creation of networks for the transportation of energy, particularly gas and electricity.

RENAVAL began in 1988 to assist shipbuilding areas that have suffered large-scale job losses, providing support for job creation and SMEs.

REGIS is designed to assist the integration of peripheral EU areas.

STAR and **TELEMATICS** provide support for the development of telecommunications in the most disadvantaged regions.

Employment and training grants

The aim is to expand employment opportunities and improve job prospects. Funding is mainly through the ESF under objectives 3 and 4. The whole of the UK qualifies for assistance under these objectives.

The two principal target groups are:

1 *Long-term unemployed* Persons over 25 who have been unemployed for more than a year.
2 *Young people* Job seekers under 25 who have completed their full-time education.

Priority is given to workers who have special employment difficulties, notably women, migrant workers and the disabled, and this includes schemes to help women return to employment after a long break.

Two complementary strategies are adopted:

1 *To provide training opportunities* Cash is provided for vocational guidance and for training. Training is specifically in new or improved skills demanded by a labour market that is undergoing rapid technological and economic change. In areas seriously affected by industrial decline funding is provided to support schemes to introduce new management and/or production techniques in SMEs.
2 *To stimulate the job market* Subsidies are offered for recruitment into newly created and stable (i.e. at least six months' duration) jobs, and there is start-up aid for the self-employed.

Agricultural development

The EAGGF is divided into two sections. First, the Guarantee section, by far the larger, finances various intervention schemes to stabilise internal markets, and export rebates to bridge the gap between EU and world prices.

Second, the Guidance section is concerned with objective 5 and has the following aims:

- To reorganise agriculture in some regions.
- To find alternative ways of marketing and processing agricultural products.
- To find ways in which farmers can diversify or find alternative activities.
- To ensure a fair standard of living for farmers.
- To develop the social fabric of rural areas, protect the environment, and preserve the countryside.

Business and industry

Loans for economic development

The European Investment Bank (EIB) is the EU's banking institution, providing long-term finance for investments which further the balanced development of the EU. One minister (usually the Finance Minister) from each member state sits on its board of governors.

The EIB raises most of its funds on the capital market and provides loans to assist in the following areas:

- For economic development in less-favoured regions, industries that are recognised as needing special help, such as textiles, steel, shipbuilding and fishing, and projects furthering urban renewal.
- To improve telecommunications and infrastructure (e.g. roads, rail links, urban transport systems, ports, airports, aircraft and aerospace).
- To protect and improve the environment and the quality of life (e.g. reducing air and water pollution, waste treatment schemes, ensuring security and purity of water supplies, land conservation, and safeguarding Europe's heritage).
- To improve the competitiveness of European industry, promote modernisation and the introduction of new technology, and develop co-operation between companies in different member states.
- To support SMEs, regardless of location, in industries and related services, agriculture and fisheries.
- To support the EU's energy policy by improving security of supply, rationalising energy use, and developing alternative energy sources.

Social investment such as health, general education and welfare *cannot* be financed by the EIB.

While the bulk of its activity is concentrated in the EU, the EIB also participates in the EU's development policy, involving co-operation agreements with 12 Mediterranean countries and 69 African, Caribbean and Pacific states. It is also funding projects in Bulgaria, Slovakia, Hungary, Poland, and Romania.

Projects have to be technically and commercially viable and the EIB also has to be assured of the lasting effectiveness of the investments it supports. The EIB is allowed to finance up to 50 per cent of a project's cost, but usually lends between 25 per cent and 30 per cent. For SMEs the loans are arranged through 3i or Barclays Bank.

Loans may be at fixed or fluctuating interest rates. The interest rate reflects the Bank's borrowing costs. The term of the loan is set according to the nature of the project. Industrial loans are generally between 4 and 12 years. Financing for infrastructure and energy projects are often up to 20 years. They may be in a single currency (including ECUs) or a mix, according to the project's needs. Currencies are not restricted to those of EU member states.

Support for SMEs and business innovation

Increasingly, the EU is concerned to promote a favourable business climate in which enterprise can flourish, and it is especially sensitive to the needs of SMEs. A number of schemes are directed specifically at SMEs and innovation. For example:

1 **EUROTECH** encourages private firms to provide finance for high-technology transnational projects and the SMEs taking part in them.
2 The **Venture Consort** scheme makes it easier for SMEs to get venture capital for innovative projects.
3 **Business Information Centres (BICs)** have been created using EU funds to provide services such as training, financial advice, marketing support, business planning and technology transfer for SMEs.
4 The **Business Co-operation Network (BC-NET)** is a computerised European network, linking over 350 advisers, to encourage cross-border co-operation and joint ventures.
5 The SPRINT programme aims to encourage the transfer of new technologies to SMEs by:
   (a) strengthening transnational networks of specialist intermediaries to help SMEs find technological partners in other EU countries;
   (b) supporting projects that transfer innovation across national boundaries; and
   (c) building an 'innovation culture' by encouraging the exchange of experiences.
6 **BRITE** offers grants to test the feasibility of using advanced materials and innovative industrial manufacturing methods.
7 **IMPACT** provides funds for projects that help information to flow freely across national boundaries with the aid of data transmission services, databases, CD-ROM, electronic bulletin boards, multi-media technology, and so on.

Finance for coal and steel regions

Business organisations, public bodies and local authorities may bid for funding in the form of grants, loans and guarantees to improve economic and social conditions in the coal and steel producing regions of the EU that have suffered particular hardship as a result of industrial decline and contraction. In particular:

1 Funding may be provided for the building or improvement of housing and has been used, for example, to modernise housing estates.
2 Assistance is provided to workers made redundant as a result of plant closures in the form of a supplement to unemployment benefit for a transitional period, resettlement allowances, and vocational retraining.

Research and development

The primary aim of funding in this area is to increase the competitiveness of the EU in world trade. Consequently the funding is concentrated on 'enabling' technologies, such as telecommunications, information technology, and materials research. The EU does not fund product development except where it needs international co-operation is needed because of its large scale.

The management of natural resources is seen as vital to the EU's future. Funding is therefore provided for many environmental and marine science projects. There are also projects in biotechnology, agricultural and agro-industrial research, bio-medical and health research, life sciences and technologies for developing countries.

Human resources are also recognised as an essential component in the EU's future prosperity. Schemes which assist the transfer of knowledge and expertise are, therefore, supported by EU finance. Collaborative research between industrial companies and educational institutions is encouraged, particularly where it involves SMEs. Because a major objective is to encourage cross-frontier collaboration, many of the bids in this field have to be made jointly by partners in at least two member states.

The Commission selects projects to be funded with the aid of advisory bodies. Projects are selected on the basis of criteria such as scientific merit, technical feasibility, potential application, the transnational constitution of the research team, their qualifications, and the types of organisation involved. Priorities are shifted periodically, reflecting changes in EU policies. Expenditure on information technology schemes (such as ESPRIT), telecommunications projects (e.g. RACE) and the development of industrial and materials technology (e.g. BRITE) attract up to half of total funding. Since 1990, environmental research, biotechnology and research staff mobility have been given increased priority, while energy research has been reduced.

Education, training and exchange schemes

The EU finances exchange schemes to encourage co-operation and the transfer of ideas between scientists, researchers and other academic staff. Grants are also available to allow students to undertake periods of study in universities elsewhere in the EU.

For example, **ERASMUS** encourages co-operation between universities. It began in 1987 and from 1987 to 1990, with its help, 40,000 students and 8000 members of staff from more than 1000 educational institutions spent time abroad. By 1992 it was estimated that one in ten students were benefiting from exchanges. The scheme provides financial support to allow students to spend periods of study between 3 and 12 months in another member country, to allow academic staff to teach in partner institutions, to develop new curricula, and to organise short, intensive, joint teaching ventures. Grants of up to 5000 ECU (but typically 2000 ECU) are provided to students who carry out part of their course in another member country. The grant is intended to cover only the expenses arising from living abroad such as travel, and higher living costs. Students are expected to be exempt from registration and tuition fees at the host university.

Another aim of EU funding is to develop training that enhances the skills and qualifications of employers and employees. Such schemes include: **CEDEFOP**, which provides information on vocational training across Europe, and undertakes comparative studies on training in member states; and **LINGUA**, which aims to improve the teaching and learning of foreign languages by providing grants for language teacher-training, for the development of teaching materials and self-learning methods, and to encourage the inclusion of language training in courses, particularly those that are vocational.

ACTIVITY 16.2

In many of the funding schemes you have just read about it is essential to have international partners.

1 Identify the ways in which one of the organisations you have studied could acquire an international partner.

2 Prepare a plan for establishing the partnership.

3 What benefits would the partner gain from the relationship?

Cultural and social issues

The EU recognises that the 'quality of life' is an important aspect of the Union – in its own right and as a factor in the development of other EU aims. It is active, therefore, in the following areas:

- Funds are available for the conservation and promotion of Europe's architectural heritage.
- A number of projects have been funded under the MEDIA scheme to stimulate the European film and television industries.
- There is an annual award of 20,000 ECU for the author of the literary work that is judged to have made the most significant contribution to contemporary European literature. Another prize of 20,000 ECU is awarded annually to the translator who achieves outstanding quality in translating a contemporary item of European literature. Financial assistance is provided for the translation of literature into minority languages.

- The EU provides support for cultural and sporting events.
- Funding to combat poverty and related social issues has led to UK projects in Toxteth (Liverpool), Pilton (Edinburgh) and Brownlow (Northern Ireland).
- A number of projects are funded to assist with equal opportunities, the social integration and greater independence of the disabled, and voluntary services for the elderly.
- The European Foundation for the Improvement of Living and Working Conditions was established in 1975. It operates as an EC research centre and recently has focused on six themes: industrial relations; restructuring of working life; promoting health and safety; protecting the environment, the worker and the public; raising the standard and quality of life for all; and assessing the technologies of the future.

Development aid

As the world's largest trading block, the EU recognises its obligations to assist former dependencies of its member states and other countries in the course of economic development. EU aid consists mainly of grants for development projects to encourage trade, promote rural development, combat food shortages, and assist with emergencies and natural disasters.

Sub-Saharan Africa has traditionally been the principal recipient of EU aid. More recently, considerable assistance has been channelled towards the emerging democracies in central and eastern Europe to assist in their transfer to market economies. The European Development Fund (EDF) was set up as long ago as 1958 to develop co-operation, trade and aid agreements and is the most important method by which technical and financial assistance is provided.

A substantial number of development activities are undertaken as part of the various Lomé Conventions. Sixty-eight African, Caribbean and Pacific (ACP) countries are eligible for aid, and they themselves determine the priorities and projects to be supported, under the overall financial management of the European Commission.

In 1991 the European Bank for Reconstruction and Development was formed to support the development of free market economies, particularly in central and eastern Europe, by providing finance for the development of infrastructures and the environment. The EU also provides finance, and economic and social assistance, to this area directly through the Commission budget, and through the European Investment Bank, the European Training Foundation, and the Poland and Hungary Assistance in Restucturing (PHARE) programme, which, despite its name, assists any country that has moved far enough towards democracy and free market economy.

Getting financial help

The regional nature of many schemes, the focus on innovation, the enthusiasm for SMEs, and many other features of EU funding mean that small business should not ignore the opportunities for financial assistance.

As indicated at the beginning, the scope, and variety, of European funding schemes is vast. Yet, although some schemes are long-lasting, many of them are available only for a short time. When a new scheme is introduced there is usually a comparatively short period after it has been announced in which bids can be made. The bids are then considered and successful applicants subsequently receive funding. Many funding schemes are oversubscribed and, in consequence, a number of bids are unsuccessful.

The assessment panel is normally multinational and the bids have to be translated. It is important, therefore, that a bid should be clear, easily translated, and relate closely to the criteria used to match it against the scheme's aims. Some large organisations employ staff specifically to prepare bids, and their expertise enhances the bid's chance of success. However, it is generally acknowledged that without external help a small business is unlikely to be very successful in bidding for European finance.

The Commission is a fairly open organisation, and information about new schemes can usually be obtained prior to its formal announcement, increasing the time period in which a bid can be prepared. Many large organisations have employees or agents, often based in Brussels, to gather information about each new scheme and to analyse its appropriateness to the organisation's needs.

A number of organisations exist which have the expertise to seek out schemes suitable for a business and to assist in preparing a good bid. Some of these organisations are EU-funded; others are fully or partly funded by local authorities, Chambers of Commerce, the Department of Trade and Industry (DTI) and Training and Enterprise Councils (TECs). There are also many independent consultants and agents who provide this service, but at a price.

SUMMARY

1 The DTI is an important source of help for organisations seeking financial assistance (and other support) for EU projects. Local sources include Chambers of Commerce and TECs.

2 The ECGD and BOTB are able to offer practical help in specific areas of EU trade.

3 EU funding is in six categories: structural; business and industry; research and development; education, training and exchange schemes; cultural and social issues; and development aid.

4 EU funding for businesses is prioritised on the basis of objectives, and is principally aimed at:

(a) tackling problems arising from the disparity between regions and industrial decline;

(b) promoting the transnational activities of SMEs;

(c) promoting competition, innovation, and research and development;

(d) providing transitional protection for threatened industries;

(e) reducing unemployment; and

(f) encouraging vocational training and employee mobility.

5 Bids for funding must be matched closely with the criteria for the scheme if they are to have any chance of success, and the bid must be explained in a way that can be easily translated to other languages and understood by the assessment panel.

6 There is generally a very short lead-time between announcement of a new scheme and the deadline for bids.

7 Many schemes require organisations to have international partners.

Assignment 16

BACKGROUND

EU and other funding makes an important contribution to transnational projects for many businesses. It is important that you should be able to identify projects that are likely to attact support, and the schemes which provide that support.

ACTIVITY

1 Choose either a real organisation in your locality, or one of the organisations mentioned in the case studies, activities and assignments in this book.

2 Establish the level of priority the organisation would receive as a result of its geographical location.

3 Establish the level of priority the organisation would receive as a result of the industrial sector it belongs to.

4 Put together outline proposals for three projects that might attract government or EU support within the framework of assistance described in this chapter.

5 Find out what local agencies would be available with the expertise to identify specific schemes from which the project might obtain funds, and the expertise to prepare good-quality applications.

Part Five
EUROPE IN CONTEXT

17 A wider and deeper Europe

OBJECTIVES
1 To introduce the concepts of 'widening' and 'deepening' in relation to EU membership and integration.

2 To consider the criteria for accepting new members into the EU, and how they are being applied to EFTA countries and the central and eastern European states.

3 To analyse proposals of closer integration within the EU, including those in the Treaty on European Union, giving special attention to economic union and the development of common foreign and security policies.

Since the creation of the European Economic Community (EEC), and its subsequent development into the European Community (EC) and its transformation to the European Union (EU), the number of member states has increased, and the degree of co-operation and integration has extended. This process is often referred to as the 'widening' and 'deepening' of the EU. The significance of these developments for 'business within Europe' lies both in the extra opportunities for trade in new markets, and the effects they have on existing markets.

A wider Europe

As countries outside the EU recognise the benefits to be gained from entry, and come to fear the consequences of being left out, more and more of them apply for membership. The EU has to consider the applications very carefully to ensure that new countries have the commitment and resources to play their part in fulfilling the EU's goals.

The following basic criteria have been established for assessing applications; both must be met before the EU will consider admitting a country.

1 The country must have a democratic government.

2 It must be economically sound.

For example, Spain, Portugal and Greece were unable to join initially because their governments were not democratic. Special transitional arrangements were then needed to help them cope with the pressures of entry because they had relatively weak economies – a single market increases competition. Moreover the implications of admitting a weak state into the Community is well illustrated by the reunification of Germany. Germany, undoubtedly the strongest economy in the EU, has found difficulty coping with the pressures of absorbing East Germany, which had an economy considerably weaker than any of the other EU countries. The differences have resulted in pressure on the social security system, unemployment, racism, high levels of migration of workers, and other adverse factors.

At the Copenhagen summit, the EU heads of government confirmed their intention to admit Austria, Finland, Norway and Sweden to the Community by 1 January 1995. However, it was recognised that this was a tight timescale, given that the level of support for such a move within these countries' popula-

Table 17.1 Characteristics of the EFTA countries

		Austria	Finland	Iceland	Norway	Sweden	Switzerland
Area	sq km x 1000	84	338	103	387	450	41
Population	million	7.6	5.0	0.3	4.2	8.4	6.6
Pop density	people/sq km	90.0	15.0	2.0	11.0	19.0	161.0
GDP	ECU x billion	110.0	90.0		75.0	135.0	146.0
GDP per capita	ECU x 1000	14.5	18.2		17.9	16.1	22.1
GDP by sector							
Agriculture	%	4.7	7.0	n.a.	3.5	4.5	3.5
Manufacturing	%	26.0	24.0	n.a.	15.0	32.0	25.0
Other industry	%	13.9	10.0	n.a.	16.5	10.0	9.5
Services	%	55.4	59.0	n.a.	65.0	53.0	62.0
Imports	ECU x billion	30	30	n.a.	20	38	47
EU	%	68.0	44.0	n.a.	46.0	56.0	71.0
USA	%	0.0	6.0	n.a.	7.0	7.5	5.5
Japan	%	5.0	7.5	n.a.	0.0	0.0	5.0
Other	%	27.0	42.5	n.a.	47.0	36.5	18.5
Exports	ECU x billion	26	19	n.a.	19	42	43
EU	%	64.0	44.0	n.a.	65.0	52.0	56.0
USA	%	0.0	6.0	n.a.	6.0	10.0	8.5
Japan	%	0.0	0.0	n.a.	0.0	0.0	0.0
Other	%	36.0	50.0	n.a.	29.0	38.0	35.5

Note: Liechtenstein is omitted because of its small size.

Source: Eurostat

tions was unclear, and that several were legally compelled to put the issue of membership to a referendum.

At the same summit, enlarging the EU to include Bulgaria, the Czech Republic, Hungary, Poland, Romania and Slovakia was considered 'a long way in the future'. Nevertheless, a formal commitment was made that these six countries, all of which already have 'association agreements' with the EU, would be admitted once they had fulfilled conditions in five areas: a stable democracy; a market economy capable of coping with competition; rule of law; human rights; and protection of minorities. The EU promised to help the six separately towards this goal, setting-up institutional frameworks, training lawyers and managers, and providing extra money for infrastructure projects that cannot be funded in any other way. Poland, Hungary, the Czech Republic and Slovakia have so far been the most successful in moving towards market economies. Bulgaria and Romania have moved more slowly.

Regular consultative summits would be held twice each year and eastern European diplomats would be regularly updated on EU proposals and decisions. A commitment was also made to phase out customs duties on products such as cars and chemicals over a two-year period, and for 'sensitive' products, such as textiles and steel, over four to five years. Tariffs on agricultural products would be halved. There was no commitment, however, to remove quotas, which the eastern European states considered to be the biggest barriers to trade. Yet even without membership, the eastern European states were building a stronger trading relationship with the EU. Between 1989 and 1993 exports to the EU rose by 22 per cent per year. Imports from the EU went up even more – by 30 per cent per year. To an extent this trade was forced on the former Comecon countries. After the 1989 revolutions intra-Comecon trade, which previously had accounted for 50 per cent of the total, declined to less than 20 per cent. But expectations that there would be heavy western investment in eastern European countries were not fulfilled. The investment figure of about £3 billion per year is less than 2 per cent of their total GDP. This contrasts unfavourably with other developing countries (e.g. Asia), which made extensive use of international capital markets.

While trade with the EU is more beneficial to ex-Comecon countries than funding from the World Bank, International Monetary Fund or the controversial European Bank for Reconstruction and Development, there is a danger in it being 'too successful'. About 40 per cent of their exports are in 'sensitive' sectors such as food, agriculture, textiles, steel and chemicals, and there have been calls by EU member states for tariffs and quotas to protect EU domestic markets.

The EU and Russia would also like to develop some form of partnership agreement from which both would benefit, but this is considered to be some years off pending further political developments in Russia. Agreements too with the Ukraine and Baltic republics are problematical. The southern EU countries, especially Spain and Portugal, are fearful that their admission would shift

Table 17.2 Characteristics of some of the eastern European countries

		Bulgaria	Czechoslovakia[1]	Hungary	Poland	Romania	Yugoslavia[2]	Turkey
Area	sq km x 1000	238	128	93	313	237	226	781
Population	million	23.2	15.5	10.6	37.9	23.2	23.6	50.6
Density	people/sq km	98.0	121.0	114.0	121.0	98.0	104.0	65.0
GDP	ECU x billion	44.0	36.0	19.0	180.0	82.0	51.0	65.0
GDP per capita	ECU x 1000	4.9	2.3	1.8	4.7	3.6	2.3	1.3
GDP by sector								
Agriculture	%	n.a.	8.0	10.5	n.a	n.a	n.a	n.a
Manufacturing	%	n.a.	71.0	47.5	n.a	n.a	n.a	n.a
Other industry	%	n.a.	n.a.	n.a.	n.a	n.a	n.a	n.a
Services	%	n.a.	21.0	42.0	n.a	n.a	n.a	n.a
Imports	ECU x billion	n.a.	5	5	n.a	n.a	n.a	n.a
EC	%	n.a.	11.0	24.0	n.a	n.a	n.a	n.a
USA	%	n.a.	40.0	25.0	n.a	n.a	n.a	n.a
Japan	%	n.a.	38.0	20.0	n.a	n.a	n.a	n.a
Other	%	n.a.	11.0	31.0	n.a	n.a	n.a	n.a
Exports	ECU x billion	n.a.	5	5	n.a	n.a	n.a	n.a
EC	%	n.a.	10.0	23.0	n.a	n.a	n.a	n.a
USA	%	n.a.	43.0	28.0	n.a	n.a	n.a	n.a
Japan	%	n.a.	36.0	18.0	n.a	n.a	n.a	n.a
Other	%	n.a.	11.0	31.0	n.a	n.a	n.a	n.a

Source: Eurostat, OECD

[1] Now the separate countries of Slovakia and the Czech Republic

[2] Now divided into several independent states

the 'pivot' of the EU towards the north and east, away from them, and that they would suffer substantially from a change in priorities in structural funding.

Another factor that makes it more difficult to agree on a widening of the EU is the current level of unemployment in existing member states – only 60 per cent of the population of the EU of working age is in work, compared with 70 per cent in the USA and 75 per cent in Japan. So, with unemployment in the EU likely soon to exceed 20 million, with the EU spending over 50 million ECU per year on measures to combat unemployment, and with member states spending 75 billion ECU per year on unemployment benefit, it could be argued that efforts should be concentrated on solving existing problems rather than possibly adding new ones by increasing the size and complexity of the Union.

ACTIVITY 17.1

Select one EFTA country and one country from central or eastern Europe and compare their geographic and economic characteristics with the 12 EU countries (refer to Chapters 4 and 5).

The European Economic Area (EEA)

The agreement for the creation of the European Economic Area (EEA) was signed in May 1992. The aim of the EEA is to strengthen trade and economic links between the EU and EFTA countries, extending the Single European Market to a total of 19 countries, and thus creating a single market comprising over 375 million consumers, and a GDP of about £4700 billion, accounting for 30 per cent of world production and 40 per cent of world trade. Its implementation was originally planned for January 1993, but its rejection (49.7 per cent in favour, 50.3 per cent against) by the Swiss in a referendum in December 1992 disrupted this plan.

As well as adopting the principle of freedom of movement for goods, services, capital and labour, the EFTA countries must conform to single market rules on competition, restrictive practices, monopoly abuse, mergers and takeovers, and state aid. The EEA is a dynamic agreement with the intention that new EU legislation will be applied to the whole of the EEA. EFTA is consulted on the development of new EU legislation but has no voting or veto rights. It does have the right to accept or reject the legislation once it has become law in the EU.

The EEA agreement establishes an EEA Council, comprising EU and EFTA ministers and European Commissioners, responsible for policy-making. An EEA Joint Committee, comprising EU and EFTA officials, is responsible for agreeing new EEA rules, ensuring consistent interpretation of the rules, and resolving disputes. Enforcement of EEA regulations is undertaken by a surveillance authority and court.

Free trade agreements in the early 1970s achieved tariff-free trade in industrial goods, and some agricultural goods. The EEA agreement takes this further, but retains protection on some types of fish (which are vital to Icelandic and Norwegian economies). The new agreement also reduces, and will eventually eliminate, non-tariff barriers to trade. These include harmonised technical and safety regulations, prohibition of discriminatory tax and duty, an opening-up of public procurement, and simplified procedures. However, the agreement does not remove border controls between the EU and EFTA countries, nor does it affect tariffs between EEA countries and the rest of the world.

Companies and individuals resident in the EEA are free to provide industrial, commercial and professional services throughout the EEA. EU rules apply throughout the EEA. Furthermore, freedom of movement of capital throughout the EEA offers investment opportunities. Previously several EFTA countries had operated very restrictive inward investment policies.

Nationals of all EEA countries have the right to work (as employees or self-employed), and to set up businesses and subsidiaries under the same conditions as local companies. There must be no discrimination between nationals of the EEA countries in recruitment or pay and conditions.

The EEA provides for increased co-operation in research and development, environmental protection, regional assistance, and access to fishing grounds.

Finally, it should be recognised that the seven EFTA countries are at least as diverse – in culture, economy, outlook, and so on – as the 12 EU countries.

Austria

Austria is a federal republic with nine *Länder* (provinces) and a population of about 7.5 million. It is land-locked and shares borders with the former Czechoslovakia, Germany, Hungary, Italy, Liechtenstein, the former Yugoslavia, and Switzerland. Over 70 per cent of the country is mountainous. The capital, Vienna, has a population of 1.6 million and lies on the river Danube, which is one of Europe's largest inland waterways. Austria has close links with Germany, and the official language is German.

It is a country of small businesses – with fewer than 150 companies employing more than 1000 people, and 95,000 companies employing fewer than 50 people – and has a high standard of living.

Austria also has a trade surplus. Chief exports are machinery, automotive supplies, chemicals, and semi-finished products. Principal imports are clothing, electronic and telecommunications products, medical equipment, security equipment, confectionery, gardening equipment, carpets and toys. Over 70 per cent of its trade is with EU countries.

Finland

Finland became independent from Sweden in 1917, but there is still a close link between the two states. It is one of the most sparsely populated countries in Europe, with almost 10 per cent of the population of 5 million living in the capital, Helsinki. The other towns are small by comparison; Tempere, the largest, has a population of only 170,000.

After growing in 1988 and 1989, the economy declined sharply in 1990 and 1991. Although inflation remained relatively low, unemployment reached a very high level. Nevertheless, Finland has a high per capita income, providing demand for consumer and luxury goods.

Finland's chief exports are paper, pulp, metal and engineering products. The main sources of Finland's imports are Germany, Sweden, the CIS, the UK, Japan and the USA.

Of particular importance to Finland is the independence from the former USSR of the Baltic states, especially Estonia. Here, Finnish companies are involved in very many joint ventures.

Iceland

Iceland is a relatively small island, located in an isolated spot, but one which has in the past had strategic significance. Over one-third of the population of 250,000 live in the capital, Reykjavik. The country has a high incidence of volcanic and geostructural activity, which is reflected in the 'tortured' appearance of much of the interior.

Iceland has a high standard of living, but it is heavily dependent on imports of consumer goods. Unemployment has always been, and remains, low. However, GDP has fallen each year since 1988, mainly because of cuts in the fishing quotas forced upon the government by depletion of fish stocks.

Iceland is heavily dependent on fish. It provides almost 70 per cent of visible exports, although only 13 per cent of the population is employed in fishing and fish processing. Over 30 per cent is employed in the service sector, 15 per cent in manufacturing, and 9 per cent in construction.

Geothermal energy is Iceland's only other natural resource. It is self-sufficient in energy and has sufficient spare capacity to build smelting and other mineral extraction plants.

Liechtenstein

This is a land-locked country lying on the upper Rhine between Austria and Switzerland. It is less than half the size of the Isle of Wight and has a population of about 28,000. It has a high standard of living and little unemployment. The official language is German. Liechtenstein is closely linked with Switzerland, whose currency, postal and customs services it uses.

Liechtenstein lacks natural resources and is dependent on imports of energy and raw materials. Industrial sites are concentrated round the capital Vaduz. Main industries are precision instruments and machinery, textiles, ceramics for dental purposes, and pharmaceutical and chemical products. Of the workforce, 40 per cent is employed in industrial concerns.

The country is an important banking centre and location for investment, holding and 'off-shore' companies. This sector represents 40 per cent of employment and 60 per cent of GDP. Of the workforce, 60 per cent are not nationals of Liechtenstein, and half of these travel daily into and out of the country.

Since 1923 Liechtenstein has had a customs union with Switzerland. Trade and customs treaties between Switzerland and other countries automatically apply to Liechtenstein.

There is no airport, but the capital is only 90 minutes from Zurich by road.

Norway

Norway has a population of about 4 million. It is a mountainous country, with considerable distances between the large towns. The principal cities are the capital Oslo, Bergen, Trondheim and Stavanger.

It has a relatively strong economy based on natural resources such as oil and gas, hydroelectric power, fish, forests, and mineral oils. The per capita GDP is almost twice that of the UK, with low inflation but with unemployment currently at a 15-year high point.

The largest single manufacturing sector is food products. However, high costs make it difficult to compete in world markets, and Norway is increasingly dependent on the oil and gas industry. Norway's main export markets are Sweden, Germany and the UK.

Environmental protection is a key issue in Norway, where forests suffered badly from acid rain in the late 1980s.

Switzerland

Switzerland is a federal republic of 26 autonomous cantons (provinces), set in a very mountainous (70 per cent) terrain. Although Bern is the capital, Zurich is the principal financial and commercial centre. It has a population of about 6.9 million, of whom over 16 per cent are resident foreigners. There are three official languages – Swiss German (65 per cent of the population), French (18 per cent) and Italian (12 per cent).

Switzerland has few natural resources. However, it is the world's fourteenth largest exporter. The per capita GDP is one of the highest in the world, and, despite a recent decline and an increase in inflation, the country still has a strong economy. The main industrial sectors are finance, machinery, pharmaceuticals and chemicals, construction, telecommunications, foodstuffs and tourism. Hydroelectricity provides about 12 per cent of the country's energy needs. Switzerland's main trading partners are Germany, France, Italy, the USA and the UK.

Sweden

Over 85 per cent of the population (8.5 million) is concentrated in the south of the country, in and around the capital, Stockholm, and the other principal cities – Gothenburg and Malmo.

Traditionally, Sweden has had a strong economy and a high standard of living. Wages and prices are high by comparison with many other European countries. After prosperous years in the 1980s the economy went into recession in 1991, with rising inflation and unemployment. The current government is committed to reducing public expenditure, privatising state-owned companies, and encouraging small businesses.

The principal export markets for Swedish goods are Germany and the UK. Sweden imports mainly from Germany, the USA and the UK. In fact, Sweden is the UK's third largest market.

Sweden has always operated a liberal trading policy, with low import duties, except in the agriculture sector, which was highly protected.

ACTIVITY 17.2

Language and culture are the two largest hurdles to be overcome in transnational trading. What additional official languages does the EU need in order to accommodate the entry of EFTA countries? Identify similarities and differences between various EU and EFTA countries' cultures.

Deepening the EU

Moves towards 'deepening' of the EU have often aroused passions and highlighted differences of opinion over their consequences. This is typified by the debate surrounding the Treaty on European Union (Maastricht Treaty).

The Treaty on European Union

The Treaty brings new policy areas within the scope of the European institutions.

- It introduces the concept of European citizenship.
- It proposes a procedure for achieving a single currency as part of movement towards economic and monetary union.
- It sets up a framework for developing a common defence policy and common foreign policies.
- It establishes a legal basis for 'subsidiarity'.

The Treaty is divided into seven 'titles':

Title 1 sets out the goals of the Union, describing the Treaty as a 'new stage in the process of creating an ever closer union between the peoples of Europe'.

Title 2 is the core of the Treaty and includes 86 amendments to the Treaty of Rome. The main provisions are as follows:

1 Articles 2, 3 and 3a define the agenda for achieving European union. They include a commitment to non-inflationary growth, high levels of employment, social protection, raising of the standard of living and quality of life. There is a timetable for completing measures that ensure the Single European Market will function effectively.

2 The concept of subsidiarity is dealt with in article 3b. It states that the Union will take action only if the objectives of a proposal cannot be achieved by the member states but can be achieved by the Union.

3 Although the concept of European citizenship has far-reaching implications, it received very little publicity during the debate on the Treaty. Articles 8 to 8e state that every citizen of a member state shall be a citizen of the Union and enjoy the rights implicit in this. These include the right to move and reside freely in any member state, to vote and stand as a candidate in municipal elections, and to stand as candidate as a member of the European parliament in the country of residence, regardless of birthplace or nationality.

4 The most important theme in title 2 relates to 'a single economy', chiefly dealt with in articles 102 to 109. They call for 'irrevocable fixing of exchange rates leading to the introduction of a single currency (the ECU) and the definition and conduct of a single monetary policy and exchange-rate policy, the primary objective of both of which shall be to maintain price stability'.

5 Member states are required to 'regard their economic policies as a matter of common concern' and to co-ordinate them within the Council of Ministers. Economic policy will be determined by qualified majority. Member states must 'avoid excessive governmental deficits'. If a member state refuses to comply, the Council may 'invite the European Investment Bank to reconsider its lending policy towards the state concerned'.

6 A European System of Central Banks (ESCB) is established to implement monetary policy, conduct foreign exchange operations, and manage the official reserves of the member states. The European Central Bank (ECB) will have the exclusive right to authorise the issue of bank notes.

7 There are transitional provisions for a smooth changeover to a single economic policy. Key dates are:
   (a) 1 January 1994: creation of European Monetary Institute to oversee the move to a single currency; and
   (b) 31 December 1996: meeting of heads of state to decide, by qualified majority voting, whether a majority of member states fulfil the conditions for adopting a single currency; member states who do not qualify for movement to a single currency will have their voting rights to the council suspended.

The UK secured an 'opt-out' clause allowing them not to participate in this aspect of European union.

8 The Treaty calls for the development of a European dimension to education. In particular, the Council of Ministers will have powers to issue directives 'for the mutual recognition of diplomas, certificates and other evidence of formal qualifications'. There is encouragement for language teaching, for the mobility of students and teachers, and for co-operation between educational institutions.

9 Article 128 pledges the Community to respecting national and regional diversity, and at the same time 'bringing to the fore' the common cultural heritage.

10 There is a commitment to work towards preventing diseases and reducing drug dependency, by research into the causes and transmission of diseases.

11 The Treaty addresses the issue of democratic accountability of EU institutions. It gives the European Parliament powers of co-decision with the Council of Ministers, allowing it to reject proposals in areas that include single market legislation, policies for research and development, trans-European networks, training and education, culture, health and consumer affairs.

12 The Parliament is allowed to 'request' the Commission to prepare and submit proposals where it believes new legislation is required. The European Commission will be more accountable to the European Parliament.

Titles 3 and 4 deal with technical aspects of the Coal, Steel and Atomic Energy treaties.

Title 5 deals with foreign and security policies, and looks ahead to 'common defence'. The main provisions are as follows:

1 Where joint action is agreed upon, it is binding on the member states to support that action. Member states are required to safeguard the independence and security of the union and to preserve peace in accordance with the UN charter. Member states must support the Union's security policy 'unreservedly in a spirit of loyalty and mutual solidarity' and 'refrain from any action which is contrary to the interests of the Union'.

2 Decisions on joint action are subject to qualified majority voting.

3 Member states are allowed to continue to meet their obligations arising from membership of North Atlantic Treaty Organisation (NATO) and/or the Western European Union (WEU).

4 The European Parliament has no direct control over foreign and security policy, but the Commission must 'consult' the Parliament to 'ensure that the views of the European Parliament are duly taken into consideration'.

Title 6 identifies areas where the power of the European Commission may be extended, and new areas to which qualified majority voting will apply in the Council of Ministers. If 'the objectives of the Union can be attained better by joint action than by member states acting individually', then the Council of Minsters may take decisions by qualified majority voting in the areas of asylum policy, immigration policy, combating drug addiction, and tackling fraud and other criminal activities.

Title 7 defines the procedure for ratifying the treaty.

There are many 'protocols' at the end of the main Treaty. Some deal with specific aspects of the Treaty (e.g. transitional powers for the European Central Bank) and others relate to specific countries (Denmark, France, Portugal, and the UK). Those specific to the UK relate, first, to UK opt-outs, which include:

- The UK shall not be obliged to move to the final stage of economic and monetary union without a separate decision to do so by its Government and Parliament.
- The UK shall retain its powers in the field of monetary policy according to national law.
- The UK shall have no right to participate in the appointment of the president, the vice-president, and the other members of the executive board of the European Central Bank.
- Non-acceptance by the UK of the Social Chapter's provisions.

If the UK decides not to proceed to the final stage of economic and monetary union, then it would be excluded from:

- irrevocable fixing of exchange rates;
- avoiding excessive government deficits;
- participation in the European System of Central Banks (dealing with management of foreign reserves);
- authorisation of issue of bank notes by the European Central Bank; and
- liability to fines and other penalties for failing to comply with the obligations associated with the final stage.

The UK's voting rights are suspended on all aspects of EU policy associated with the areas of exclusion.

The protocols also deal with the Social Chapter, the stated objectives of which are: to promote employment; to improve living and working conditions; proper social protection; dialogue between management and labour; the development of human resources with a view to lasting high employment; and the combating of exclusion. The Social Chapter declares that the measures to achieve these objectives will 'take account of the diverse forms of national practices, in particular in the field of contractual relations and the need to maintain the competitiveness of the Union's economy'.

ACTIVITY 17.3

The possibility of a 'two speed' Europe is increased when policies are adopted that exclude one or more member states. Would it be better to adopt only policies that are agreed by all?

Threats to progress towards economic union

The target date for a single currency given in the Maastricht Treaty was 1997. However, by September 1993, the chances of attaining this goal were already considered poor.

Table 17.3 EU VAT rates, January 1993

	Rate (%)			Zero rate
	Standard	Increased	Reduced	coverage
Belgium	19.5	none	1.0, 6,0, 12.0	minimal
Denmark	25.0	none	none	minimal
France	18.6	none	2.1, 5.5	none
Germany	15.0	none	7.0	none
Greece	18.0	none	4.0, 8.0	none
Ireland	21.0	none	2.7, 10.0, 12.5, 16.0	wide[1]
Italy	19.0	38.0	4.0, 9.0, 12.0	minimal[2]
Luxembourg	15.0	none	3.0, 6.0	none
Netherlands	18.5	none	6.0	none
Portugal	16.0	30.0	5.0	none
Azores	12.0	21.0	4.0	none
Spain	15.0	28.0	6.0	minimal
UK	17.5	none	none	wide[3]

[1] A variety of goods, accounting for 25% of consumer products.

[2] Dependant territories excluded from VAT.

[3] A variety of goods and services.

The European commissioner on economic affairs, Henning Christophersen, declared that the deepening German economic crisis was undermining the ability of the other EU states to meet the required conditions. He felt, however, that the fall-back date of 1999 was still feasible amd that levels of inflation could be brought down to the target levels, but was less optimistic about budget deficits.

Prospects had also been damaged by the widening of the ERM's exchange rate bands to 15 per cent in July 1993. There needed to be a clear political determination on the part of all the EU member countries to co-ordinate their economic policies, and this was far from certain.

The disparity between the economic policies of EU member states is clearly illustrated by their VAT rates (*see* Table 17.3). They were a long way from being harmonised even seven years after the Single European Act was passed.

ACTIVITY 17.4

Discuss with colleagues the desirability and feasibility of progressive movement towards economic union.

Instability in central and eastern Europe

The EU has, for some years, been working towards common policies on foreign affairs and security. It has been made difficult by the special relationships that various EU member states have with outside countries. The UK, France, Spain and Portugal have links with ex-colonies, the Netherlands has strong trading relationships, and so on.

Probably the biggest challenge to the EU's ability to agree on a common foreign policy has been the war in the former Yugoslavia. During the 45 years that followed the Second World War it seemed that Europeans had learned the lesson that negotiations, however difficult and complicated, were preferable to forcibly imposed solutions and war.

Wars did take place, and EU member states were involved in them, but they were in far-away places. It was a shock, therefore, to see death and destruction in popular holiday spots such as Dubrovnik. Even more shocking was the return of detention camps, and policies of mass appropriation and extermination, labelled 'ethnic cleansing'.

In 1992–3, Slovenia became a separate entity without too much damage or loss of life. The war in Croatia was bloody, but ground to a halt. In Bosnia however it was bloody and long-lasting. The EU was faced with a difficult decision. In hindsight, its decision to recognise Bosnian independence in April 1992 may be criticised. Some argue that it triggered the start of a civil war and the displacement of hundreds of thousands of people. However, the alternatives were equally horrific.

There was no prospect of a quick in-and-out operation by external forces. The USA was unwilling to commit American troops. The UN imposed an arms embargo in May 1992. The UN took on the task of providing an umbrella of humanitarian relief. Canada, France, Spain and the UK provided troops to escort food convoys under the UN flag. Several countries accepted refugees, notably Germany. Cyrus Vance and Lord Owen, acting on behalf of the EU and UN, attempted to find a peace formula.

The biggest danger of all is that the conflict will spread. Albania might become involved because of its close ties with Kosova. Greece fears that the former Yugoslav republic of Macedonia refuses to change its name because it has ambitions to annex the Greek region of the same name. Turkey and Bulgaria could also become involved.

ACTIVITY 17.5

Write an up-to-date situation report on the principal areas of Europe where ethnic and other reasons are causing instability.

Uncertainty in the CIS

Four years after the collapse of communism, Russia's armed forces were engaged in three wars in seven republics within the former Soviet Union. Since the West was no longer perceived as a threat, it was the Islamic East to which Moscow looked with concern as it tried to maintain political cohesion and defend the rights of 25 million ethnic Russians scattered across the vast array of states that were the USSR. The trouble spots were:

- Georgia, where Russian troops were backing Abkhazian separatists seeking union with Russia.
- Naorno-Karabakh, where troops were assisting Armenia in its war against predominantly Muslim Azerbaijan.
- The border region between Tajikistan and Afghanistan, where Russian troops were struggling to maintain the authority of the Moscow-supported government.
- Transdnestr, a break-away region of Moldova where the army was providing back-up and support for the Russian nationalists.
- The northern Baltic states of Estonia and Latvia, where large Russian minorities were protected by Russian troops.
- The Crimea, potentially one of the most dangerous areas because it would involve the Ukraine, apart from Russia, the most powerful state in the former USSR. Although the Russian parliament only claimed Savastopol and the Black Sea fleet, many Russians felt that the Ukraine should return the whole of Crimea to Russia.

Within Russia itself, Boris Yeltsin found it difficult to proceed with the changes he wished for.

The 'new Russia' is a harsh place, full of inequalities. The majority of the population remains poor. Indeed, with high price-inflation, poverty is more common and the social security systems are less able to provide support. In addition, Russians are facing a new deprivation – unemployment. In the previous, communist, state, jobs were made available for everyone. The poverty contrasts with the huge and rapidly acquired wealth of a tiny minority, many of who have links with organised crime. Corruption is rampant. Law and order seems to be collapsing. Figures released in July 1993 showed a 50 per cent increase in the murder rate compared with the previous half-year.

At the time of writing Russia is very much a country in a state of transition. The question is – to what?

ACTIVITY 17.6

Prepare an up-to-date situation report on Russia and the CIS. What effect do uncertainties have on potential for trade with them?

SUMMARY

1 Two basic criteria are applied when considering applications for membership of the EU – the country must be an economically sound market economy and have democratic government.

2 The European Economic Area offered an opportunity for EFTA countries to

move towards membership of the EU that was acceptable to all except Switzerland.

3 Four of the EFTA countries are moving a stage further – Austria, Finland, Norway and Sweden – are accepted as full members of the EU.

4 The criteria for membership applications has been made more specific in the case of the central and eastern European states, where transition to market economies and democratic government is very recent and in many of which stability has not yet been attained.

5 The two areas in which further European integration is proving difficult are economic union and common policies on foreign affairs and security.

6 The EU has proved that it can accommodate differences of opinion as to the extent and pace of 'deepening' but there is a possibility that this could lead to a 'two-speed' Europe.

Assignment 17

BACKGROUND

There is a considerable amount of trade between EU and non-EU European countries, and it is rapidly increasing. Association agreements and membership provide a massive boost to trade. Assessing the nature of the changes that arise from a country gaining association or membership is important to businesses already involved in trade between the countries and to those who want to enter the market.

ACTIVITY

1 Obtain DTI market reports on two non-EU countries (choosing ones that have significantly different characteristics such as Switzerland and Albania).

2 Derive a market strategy that takes account of the changes arising from them moving to a closer association with the EU (e.g. membership).

3 Be specific about how the changes affect the strategy.

18 Europe in a world context

OBJECTIVES 1 To trace the progress of the EU in developing international links and agreements.

2 To explain the nature of competition in world markets and identify the EU's main competitors.

3 To describe the relationships between the European 'independent territories' and the EU.

4 To name, and briefly describe, the aims of, the chief world organisations and groups concerned with finance, trade, security, health, international relations and other matters.

5 To explain the nature of government intervention in international trade.

6 To describe the characteristics of a multinational company and explain how they are of benefit to the organisation.

7 To explain the workings of financial and non-financial barriers to international trade, and how they relate to the EU.

The development of international links

The EU is large enough to be a real force in world affairs. However, it is much 'younger' than Japan and the USA and is still growing as more countries join it. It is understandable, therefore, that its primary concern has been to get the relationships between member countries right, and to establish organisations that democratically determine policy and deal with regional differences and difficulties.

The EU's history as an economic grouping of countries has meant that this side of affairs naturally led the way when it began to take an international role.

Table 18.1 World trade comparisons, 1989

		EU	USA	Japan	USSR (CIS)
Area	sq km x 1,000	2,261	9,373	378	22,403
Population	million	325	246	123	284
Density	people/sq km	144	26	325	13
GDP	ECU x billion	4,000	4,244	2,290	948
GDP per capita	ECU x 1,000	12,308	17,252	18,618	3,338
Exports	ECU x billion	910	280	233	n.a.
Imports	ECU x billion	945	400	165	n.a.
Exports (% of GDP)		22.75	6.60	10.17	n.a.
Imports (% of GDP)		23.63	9.43	7.21	n.a.
Exports per capita		2,800	1,138	1,894	n.a.
Imports per capita		2,908	1,626	1,341	n.a.

Source: DTI

In the GATT (General Agreement on Tariffs and Trade) and in the North Atlantic Fisheries Organisation the EU (through the Commission) speaks on behalf of the member countries. It also negotiates, on behalf of the member countries, on customs procedures, franchises, import quotas, protection against unfair foreign competition, and export credits.

The EU's share of world trade is 19 per cent compared with the USA's 17 per cent and Japan's 10 per cent. The EU has had agreements with the European Free Trade Association (EFTA) countries (Switzerland, Austria, Sweden, Norway, Iceland and Finland) since 1973. Trade with the EFTA countries accounts for about 25 per cent of EU trade.

International trade is currently the most important basis for the EU's external relations, but not the only one. The EU has views on research, science and the environment. It also contributes to the development of the Third World.

Because member countries retain sovereign control over their foreign policies it has been difficult to develop a common policy and a single voice on topics such as defence and human rights. Progress was made by consultation to reach a European foreign policy on human rights in South Africa, on the Palestinian problem, Afghanistan, Central America, disarmament and terrorism. However, the suddenness of the Gulf War of 1990 and the attempted *coup d'état* against President Gorbachev in the USSR in August 1991 made it clear that a quick response was often needed by the EU in response to such problems and that the EU's procedures were too cumbersome to achieve this. Nevertheless, there are frequent high-level talks with developed countries such as Canada, the USA, Japan, Australia and New Zealand, and with state-controlled countries like the People's Republic of China, and the EU's links with the central and eastern European states have assisted them in their move towards democratic government and the development of market economies.

Competition in world markets

The greatest competition to EU companies comes from Japan, North America, and the Pacific basin.

Japan

Japanese companies have the global scale and the determination to succeed in dominating high-technology industries. Leading Japanese companies have adopted the concept of total quality management (TQM) and also managed to achieve high productivity, so that lower production costs are not at the expense of quality. Large Japanese companies operate on lower rates of return, and longer payback periods on their investments. They tend to be highly geared, avoiding short-term pressures from shareholders.

In response to the rising Yen, and to avoid trade barriers, many Japanese companies have located in Europe. Companies like Mazda have established research and development in Europe, as well as production. The Japanese are adept at utilising the local labour market, with Japanese nationals in only the very top management positions. They have also established a large number of joint ventures and collaborative agreements. Toshiba established links with Siemens and GE for example, Honda with British Leyland, Nissan with Volkeswagon.

Japan tends to have a high profile in car-making, watches, cameras, electronics. But, in sectors like food processing, chemicals, metal processing and aerospace, they are far less competitive. Their retailing, distribution, airline and insurance industries have lower productivity than many European and US companies.

North America

Nearly 40 per cent of the world's largest companies are North American – the USA has 345 and Canada has 35 – many of which have operated in Europe for a long time, including IBM, Proctor and Gamble, Nabisco, Ely Lilley, and Caterpillar. The style of North American companies contrasts with that of the Japanese. They tend to aim for a quick return on investments to meet the demands of shareholders and to maintain their share price.

There is considerable unease in the USA that the EU will adopt a 'fortress Europe' policy. It has been much more vociferous in its calls for 'free markets' than Japan, but at the same time has been keen to develop its presence within the EU and to emphasise the 'European-ness' of many of its products.

Pacific basin

Pacific basin countries like Korea, Taiwan, Singapore and Hong Kong have followed the Japanese model for expansion. Malaysia, Thailand, Indonesia and the Philippines are beginning to adopt similar strategies, exploiting the advantage of their low labour costs.

They are particularly successful in original equipment manufacture (OEM) – providing components that can easily be assembled into the final product. Mother-boards, disk drives and power supplies made in the Pacific basin, for example, can quickly and easily be assembled into personal computers in the EU and the USA, and labelled with the brand name of well-known computer companies.

Other markets

The two largest nations in the world – India and China – are at present dormant in terms of world trade importance. In 1997 Hong Kong becomes a province of China and offers this country with a billion people a gateway for entering world markets.

Sydney's success in securing the Olympic Games for AD 2000 offers Australia a wonderful opportunity to raise its profile as a primary influence in world trade. Best known previously for its extractive industries, during the late 1980s Australia established a presence, notably by acquisitions in Europe and the USA, in brewing and the media.

ACTIVITY 18.2

The competitive advantage of countries like Taiwan, Thailand, and Korea is their low labour cost. Competition from Japan and the USA is quite different.

1 Identify the nature of their competitive advantage.

2 What strategies must EU companies adopt to meet the challenge of competitors from each of these trading blocks.

Table 18.2 EU trade with its trading partners

	1970			1980			1990		
	% of imports	% of exports	exports/ imports ratio	% of imports	% of exports	exports/ imports ratio	% of imports	% of exports	exports/ imports ratio
EFTA	17.4	25.1	1.26	17.0	25.5	1.15	22.4	25.7	0.98
USA	21.7	18.0	0.73	16.9	12.8	0.58	18.6	16.8	0.77
Japan	3.4	2.6	0.68	4.9	2.2	0.34	10.5	5.2	0.43
Eastern Europe[1]	6.4	7.3	1.00	7.3	8.0	0.84	7.0	7.5	0.92
ACP countries[2]	8.9	7.6	0.75	7.3	7.9	0.82	3.9	3.8	0.83
Mediterranean basin[3]	9.4	10.3	0.96	8.3	13.4	1.23	8.8	10.8	1.05
OPEC	16.3	7.5	0.40	27.2	18.1	0.51	9.5	9.3	0.84
Asian NICs[4]	1.5	2.1	1.19	3.5	2.7	0.58	6.2	6.1	0.84

[1] Eastern Europe comprises CIS, GDR, Poland, former Czechoslovakia, Hungary, Romania, Bulgaria, Albania.

[2] ACP comprises 68 African, Caribbean and Pacific countries.

[3] Mediterranean basin comprises Malta, Yugoslavia, Morocco, Algeria, Tunisia, Libya, Syria, Israel, Jordan, Gibraltar.

[4] Hong Kong, South Korea, Singapore, Taiwan.

Source: Eurostat

Independent territories

There are several parts of Europe which have a special relationship with the EU for customs and trade purposes. Some of these are independent territories and some are dependent or associated territories which have developed closer geographical and historical links with a particular member state.

The **Channel Isles** have a special position in relation to the EU. They are part of the EU for customs purposes, outside it for VAT purposes, and part of the UK for Eurostat (EU statistics). An SAD is required for goods that are subject to excise duty and/or import/export restrictions.

The **Isle of Man** is part of the EU for customs, VAT and excise purposes. It is part of the UK for statistics purposes.

The **Balearic and Canary Isles** are provinces of Spain. The Balearic Isles are part of the EU for customs, VAT, excise, and statistics, but the Canary Isles are only part of the EU for customs purposes.

Madeira and the Azores are districts of Portugal. They are part of the EU for customs, VAT, excise and statistical purposes.

Mount Athos (in Macedonia) is a department of north-east Greece. It is a holy community of monks. Men require a permit to visit it, women are not admitted. It is a part of the EU for customs and statistics, but outside it for VAT and excise purposes.

Table 18.3 EU imports and exports by commodity type

SITC	1970			1980			1990		
	% of imports	% of exports	exports/ imports ratio	% of imports	% of exports	exports/ imports ratio	% of imports	% of exports	exports/ imports ratio
0, 1, 4	18.7	8.2	0.39	9.9	8.7	0.67	8.1	7.7	0.82
2	18.8	2.4	0.11	10.6	1.8	0.13	6.7	1.9	0.24
3	17.1	3.0	0.15	34.4	4.5	0.10	14.4	2.5	0.15
5	5.0	10.6	1.84	4.2	10.3	1.89	6.6	12.0	1.57
6	18.3	23.0	1.10	12.7	21.8	1.32	14.2	16.9	1.02
7	14.2	40.4	2.50	13.6	37.1	2.10	30.0	40.8	1.16
8	5.0	10.3	1.79	7.4	9.9	1.02	14.9	13.4	0.78
9	2.8	2.2	0.68	7.2	5.9	0.63	5.1	4.8	0.81
65	2.0	5.1	2.27	2.1	3.2	1.20	2.4	3.1	1.10
67	3.3	6.5	1.70	1.8	5.7	2.51	1.7	3.3	1.68
75	1.7	1.5	0.75	1.9	1.4	0.59	5.2	2.5	0.42
76	0.7	2.0	2.45	1.7	1.9	0.87	3.6	1.8	0.44
84	1.2	1.9	1.36	2.4	1.7	0.53	5.2	2.5	0.41

SITC categories:

0	Food products	5	Chemicals
1	Beverages	6	Manufactured goods
2	Crude materials	7	Machinery and transport equipment
3	Fuel products	8	Miscellaneous manufactured articles
4	Edible oils	9	Goods not classified elsewhere

SITC subcategories

65	Textiles and fabrics
67	Iron and steel
75	Office machinery and computers
76	Telecommunications equipment
84	Apparel and clothing accessories

Source: Eurostat, OECD

Andorra is a small, mountainous co-principality located between France and Spain. It is counted as part of the EU for customs purposes but is outside it for VAT, excise and statistics purposes.

French Overseas Departments, which include French Guiana, Guadeloupe, Martinique and Reunion, are part of the EU for customs purposes, but outside it for VAT, excise and statistics.

Monaco, in the south of France, is a part of the Marseille department and for most purposes is classed as a part of France. The main differences are in the registration and regulation of companies..

San Marino is the smallest republic in Europe. It is located in the Apennines, forming an enclave in Italy. It is considered to be part of the EU for customs, excise and statistical purposes, but is outside it for VAT purposes.

Jungbolz in the Tirol, is a tiny part of Austria which is only accessible, by road, from Germany. There are no customs formalities. It uses German currency. **Mittelberg** is also a tiny mountain area which belongs to Austria but is surrounded by German territory. Both are considered to be part of Germany, inside the EU, for customs, VAT, excise and statistical purposes, although they are part of Austria.

Gibraltar was a British crown colony until 1969. Although covered by most EU legislation it is considered to be outside it for customs, VAT, excise and statistical purposes.

The **Vatican State City**'s independence was recognised by the Italian government in 1929. It is considered to be outside the EU for customs, VAT, excise and statistical purposes.

World finance groups

The World Bank

Its prime role is to lend to developing countries to promote economic development and to revitalise their infrastructure.

The **International Development Association** is an affiliated body which obtains long-term (e.g. 50 years) loans from the World Bank, with very favourable interest rates for large government projects for energy, utilities and transport. It operates only on behalf of the poorest countries.

The **International Finance Corporation** is another affiliated body. It invests in private enterprise projects in developing countries, raising capital in the international money markets.

The European Development Fund

This is used to help those countries that are members of the Lomé Convention in Africa, the Pacific and the Caribbean.

The European Bank for Reconstruction and Development

The institution was formed in 1991 with capital of 10 billion ECU. Its function is to finance programmes of infrastructure rebuilding and market privatisation in the former Communist countries of Europe.

International trading groups

European Free Trade Association (EFTA)

This organisation comprises seven countries – Austria, Finland, Iceland, Liechtenstein, Norway, Sweden and Switzerland. Its objectives are to establish free trade in industrial goods between its members, and to negotiate other trade agreements on behalf of its members.

The Organisation for Economic Cooperation and Development (OECD)

The aims of the OECD, established over 30 years ago, are to co-ordinate economic policy, expand trade, and encourage sustainable growth, full employment and higher standards of living in its member countries. It also aims to provide aid to developing countries and provides a code of conduct for multinational companies. The OECD comprises the EU and EFTA countries, together with Canada, the Czech Republic and Slovakia, Japan, Malta, New Zealand, and the USA. It is based in Paris.

General Agreement on Tariffs and Trade (GATT)

Trading relationships between most free-market countries are negotiated within the framework of GATT. In working towards agreements, GATT has to take note of the national laws and regulations of the member countries, and to aim to achieve fair competition, expand multilateral trade, reduce import tariffs and quotas, and prevent preferential trade deals. It has been possible to reduce the average level of tariffs from 40 per cent to 5 per cent since GATT began in 1947. Over 95 per cent of world trade is governed by GATT agreements, signed by 117 countries. GATT is based in Geneva, but the real action takes place in 'rounds' of negotiations.

Progress in the earlier rounds was substantial but not controversial. Easily agreed issues were decided first. As round succeeded round, the problems became tougher, and the length of the round increased.

In the Uruguay round, which started in 1986, agriculture and services were included for the first time and it proved very difficult to reach agreement. The round should have ended in 1990 but it was extended to 1992, and then again to 1993. Agreement was finally reached at the end of 1993.

Key points for UK companies include:

- On average, tariffs on trade in goods between the USA and EU is halved.
- On average, Japanese tariffs on goods from the EU are cut by 35 per cent and import duties on whisky and pharmaceuticals are completely removed.

Table 18.4 GATT rounds

Title	Year
Geneva	1947
Annecy	1948
Torquay	1950
Geneva	1956
Dillon	1960–61
Kennedy	1964–67
Tokyo	1973–77
Uruguay	1986–93

- Developing countries have agreed to make large tariff cuts and dismantle non-tariff barriers.
- The new GATS (General Agreement on Trade in Services) introduced in the Uruguay round is especially attractive to the UK, as services account for about 23 per cent of UK trade and exports of services were worth £32.9 billion in 1992.
- More negotiations are planned to liberalise the telecommunications, shipping and financial service sectors.
- Over time, agriculture will operate in a fairer and more market-oriented trading system. Worldwide restrictions on agricultural imports will be converted to tariffs. Over a period of about five years there is to be a cut of at least 15 per cent in tariffs, at least 5 per cent of every country's domestic market in agricultural produce will be open to imports, and subsidies will be cut by between 20 per cent and 35 per cent.
- The system of bilateral quotas in textiles and clothing is to be ended, while rules to deal with unfair trade are to be strengthened.
- Agreement on intellectual property rights will help to reduce the level of counterfeiting. The UK will be able to patent pharmaceuticals in many countries for the first time.
- Anti-dumping rules are to be clarified and strengthened and there are to be stricter constraints on subsidies.

ACTIVITY 18.3

Assess the significance of the GATT Uruguay round for some of the industries studied in previous activities and case studies.

The Group of Seven

Economic summits are held periodically by the heads of state and senior finance and foreign ministers of the seven member countries – Canada, France,

Germany, Italy, Japan, the UK, and the USA. The aim is to co-ordinate economic and foreign policy.

Other significant international groups

The Council of Europe

Twenty-five countries, all of which are parliamentary democracies, make up the council. Other countries, including those of the CIS, wish to join.

It acts as a forum for discussion of issues that affect Europe and surrounding areas. Its aim is to encourage unity and facilitate economic, cultural and social development. It is particularly involved in education, environmental health, consumer protection, youth activities, and social services. Almost 100 conventions and agreements have been signed by its members, including a Convention on Human Rights. It is based in Brussels.

United Nations (UN)

This is perhaps the best-known international organisation, and most countries of the world are members. The UN is based in New York, where the General Assembly meets for three months each year to make recommendations. Each country has one vote.

The key organisations within the UN are:

- Security Council.
- International Court of Justice, at the Hague.
- International Monetary Fund (IMF), a key source of world finance.
- UN Education, Scientific and Cultural Organisation (UNESCO).
- UN International Children's Emergency Fund (UNICEF).
- World Health Organisation (WHO).
- International Labour Organisation (ILO).

ACTIVITY 18.4

The UN was quick to endorse military action when Iraq invaded Kuwait. Why do you think it initially confined itself to humanitarian aid in the former Yugoslavia?

North Atlantic Treaty Organisation (NATO)

NATO was established in 1949 with the aim of safeguarding the peace and freedom of its member states – the EU countries, Canada, Iceland, and the USA. Its headquarters are in Brussels.

The Western European Union

This is a defence policy organisation which works closely with NATO. Its principal members are Belgium, France, Italy and Luxembourg.

Conference on Security and Cooperation in Europe (CSCE)

This is a negotiating body on human rights, scientific, social and environmental issues. Participants include the EU, EFTA and other European countries, and the USA, a total of 34 countries.

ACTIVITY 18.5

The security situation in western Europe has changed dramatically as a result of the collapse of the USSR as a military power bloc in 1991.

1 How realistic was it to expect there to be a 'peace dividend' – diversion of spending on arms to other things – and what effect did the changing situation have on the arms industry in the UK and France (the countries of the EU with the largest arms industries)?

2 To what extent has the situation changed now?

Government intervention in international trade

Many countries adopt policies that encourage, or discourage, businesses seeking to establish a base there. Incentives include: *government development grants; tax relief on investment*; and *preferential duties*. Other control mechanisms available to governments include:

- *Tariff barriers*   Higher or lower barriers can prevent or encourage foreign investment.
- *Visas and work permits*   These prevent or restrict the duration that foreign nationals can work within the country.
- *Foreign staff restrictions*   Some countries make it mandatory to have local directors, a specific minimum proportion of local staff, or a maximum level of foreign staff.
- *Quotas*   These restrict the quantity of goods flowing into (or possible out of) the country.
- *Currency controls* These limit the flow of the local and other currencies into and out of the country.
- *Restricted goods* Certain goods may not be allowed into the country.

There may also be hidden controls. For example, there may be onerous safety or quality-checking regulations, or the number of customs staff involved in documentation procedures may be deliberately kept low. Both these effectively restrict the volume of goods that can flow into the country.

Multinational corporations

In our studies of EU countries some company names have occurred regularly. Shell, Unilever, Renault, Philips are just a few of them. These companies have carried transnational trading to such lengths that it is meaningless to consider them as 'belonging' to one country and importing or exporting to others. They have marketing and production organisations in many countries, and the flow of goods and financial transactions forms a complex network. The nature of their ownership, sources of finance, and legal framework also involve many countries without any single one being dominant. They are truly multinational.

The level of representation in the countries makes it possible for them to take advantage of, circumvent, and even influence the formulation of government policies. Thus, they are no longer 'foreign' companies.

The Japanese quickly recognised that the development of the EU presented a potential threat to the import of Japanese goods into EU countries. Many Japanese companies have established production plants within EU countries and developed marketing and sales organisations as well. Consequently the value added of many 'Japanese' cars – the difference between the value of the imported materials and components and the final value of the car – is greater than those of so-called 'domestic' cars (i.e. manufactured by EU-based companies), for which many major parts, such as engines, gearboxes and even body shells, are imported. In this sense, so-called 'Japanese' cars are more 'European' than 'domestic' cars.

ACTIVITY 18.6

Choose a multinational corporation that has a presence in your locality and investigate its geographic spread and range of products.

Tariffs and quotas

With the full implementation of the Single European Act the movement of goods between the UK and other EU countries cannot truly be considered as import or export. Thus we should really refer to goods leaving the country, destined for another EU country simply as *despatches*, while goods entering the country from another EU country are *acquisitions* or *arrivals*.

The change is exemplified by the abolition of the Single Administration Document (SAD) for the movement of goods between EU member states. However, the document, introduced to simplify the movement of goods between countries, is still needed where goods move into the EU or out of the EU.

Although a substantial part of transnational trading by companies based in the EU countries is with customers or suppliers who are also within the EU, there is a significant amount of external trading (i.e. genuine exports and imports). The geography of the EU also results in a considerable movement of goods through non-EU countries, even though both source and destination are in the EU.

The importance of origin

Barriers to trade can be grouped into two categories.

Financial

A government may subsidise producers or industries, making it possible for these businesses to offer their products at an artificially low price. This can have an adverse effect on the indigenous companies of a country to which these goods are exported. In the extreme, this is called 'dumping'.

A government can protect its industries by imposing tariffs on certain imported goods. These tariffs make the price of imported goods artificially higher and it is consequently easier for indigenous companies to compete. In the extreme tariffs have the effect of excluding imports.

Non-financial

A government may also protect its industries by banning the import of certain goods, or by imposing a quota – a quantity or value limit.

Sometimes a ban is indirect – environmental or safety standards may be introduced that discriminate against the characteristics of the import. A more insidious method is to insist on special checks as goods arrive, effectively delaying their distribution and adding to the importer's costs. Japan has frequently been accused of this tactic.

The key factor in determining whether goods can be imported and at what cost is the country of origin. For example, tomato puree imported into the UK from Cyprus attracts 18 per cent duty, but if it comes from Italy there is no duty. For most goods there is no restriction on the flow of goods to the EU from the USA and Japan, but duties are payable. By contrast, the volumes of goods that can enter the EU from China are restricted by quotas.

Negotiations are continually taking place to regulate trade between countries, resulting in preference agreements of origin. These agreements relate to the reduction or removal of financial and non-financial barriers to trade. The EU has agreed reciprocal preference agreements with the members of the

European Free Trade Association (EFTA), and it has similar agreements with Cyprus, Israel and Malta. The African, Caribbean and Pacific States (ACP) and Overseas Countries and Territories (OCT) also have preference agreements with the EU.

Goods may enter the EU free of duty, but exports from the EU are subject to a duty of 150 per cent, in the case of the following: the Faeroe Islands; Egypt, Jordan, Lebanon, and Syria; Algeria, Morocco, and Tunisia; the West Bank of Jordan and Gaza; and the 'General System of Preferences' countries, which include Brazil, Mexico and India.

Status

Goods that are classified as 'in free circulation' can move between countries without duties being applied in the destination country. Goods are in 'free circulation' if they are produced in the EU, or if they have been imported into the EU and customs duty has been paid.

The concept of 'free circulation' can sometimes be used to advantage by an importer. Each EU country will have its own quota on products from a country to which EU non-tariff barriers apply. If the UK has reached its quota it would still be possible to import the goods, if, for example, Italy had not reached its quota. The goods would be imported into Italy from the country of origin and duty would be paid there. The goods would then be in 'free circulation' and could be transported to the UK without hindrance.

Tariff classification

Whenever goods are transferred between EU and non-EU countries they need to be classified. According to this classification:

1 Licensing and quota controls are applied.
2 Customs duties are determined.
3 Import and export statistics are compiled.

It is the trader's responsibility to classify correctly the goods on the customs documentation. Failure to do so will result in delay, and may lead to a fine and/or confiscation of the goods.

There are several publications to assist traders, including *Customs and Excise Public Notice 600 – Classifying your imports and exports*; and guides specific to textiles, fruit and vegetables, audio and video equipment. Since 1989, the Tariff and Statistics Office in Southend has been responsible for tariff classification policy and represents the UK at EU meetings.

The key information needed by traders, and obtainable from tariff classification documents, comprises:

- Detailed description of the goods.

- The harmonised commodity code.
- Specific provisions on quotas and ceilings (i.e. maximum quantities and how they are allocated).
- Units of quantity.
- The full rate of duty incurred on imports from non-EU countries.
- Preferential rates and the origins to which they apply.
- VAT rate.

The commodity code

Although traders have an obligation to describe correctly the goods to be transferred between countries, it is sometimes the case that alternative codes are equally acceptable. The state of the goods may also affect the classification. For example:

Good	Commodity Code	Duty (%)
Fresh or chilled sardines (*sardina pilchardus*)	0302.62.10.0	23
Fresh or chilled sardines (*sardinella*)	0302.81.30.0	15
Frozen sardines	0303.71.10.0	23
Canned sardines	1604.13.11.0	25

Transferring goods as assemblies rather than as a finished product can sometimes be advantageous. For example, a cathode-ray tube (CRT) has a rate of duty between 1 per cent and 3 per cent, according to its resolution. However, the duty on a computer incorporating a CRT is 4.9 per cent and on a television (which also incorporates a CRT) the duty is 15 per cent. However, high labour costs in the destination country could easily erode the saving and would have to be considered in deciding where to carry out assembly of the final product.

Choosing between alternative materials can also affect the duty. PVC hose is rated at 12.5 per cent, while unhardened vulcanised rubber is rated at 4.9 per cent. If both are equally fit for the purpose, the cost inclusive of duty should be considered and will depend on the country it is destined for.

Goods clearance

The importance of correct documentation, and especially the correct tariff classification, cannot be overemphasised.

For an organisation that frequently imports or exports goods these achieve the following benefits.

1 Swift clearance and hence reduced storage costs.
2 A happy customer because delivery promises are kept.
3 Credibility with Customs and Excise.

SUMMARY

1 The EU now has a larger share of world trade than either the USA or Japan.

2 The EU represents its member states in negotiations with other groups of countries and concludes agreements on behalf of the member states.

3 The EU has found difficulty in adopting a common approach to some aspects of foreign affairs and defence. The nature of its institutions, and the need to consult each member state, makes it difficult to react quickly to world events.

4 The EU's chief competition in world markets comes from North America, Japan, and the Pacific basin. India and China have tremendous potential for impact on world markets, particularly because of their low labour costs.

5 Many businesses based outside the EU have established collaborative arrangements or based their production and other functions within the EU. In many cases the large amount of 'value added' within the EU and the extent of their presence make it impossible to describe them as 'foreign' businesses.

6 A number of small principalities and other 'independent territories' exist within and peripheral to the EU and have special arrangements with the EU for taxation, VAT, duty and statistical purposes.

7 EU member states are represented individually and collectively on all the international organisations that influence international affairs.

8 Government policy can have a profound effect on the extent to which foreign companies can penetrate that country's market. Covert barriers to trade can exist even when the country is party to agreements on free trade. Multinational companies benefit by being able to circumvent government restrictions and, because of their size, may even be able to influence government policy.

9 The origin of goods determines their liability for tariffs and quotas.

10 Free circulation of goods can take place inside the EU once the conditions with regard to the tariffs and quotas associated with their origin have been satisfied.

11 The tariff class of goods is determined by a commodity code. Sometimes a product can be assigned one of a number of valid alternative commodity codes to the advantage of the importer.

Assignment 18

BACKGROUND

Tariffs and quotas have an important influence on market-entry decisions. They may make it totally impossible to enter the market in specific countries, or make it impossible to achieve the economies of scale for profitable operation.

ACTIVITY

1 Choose one of the companies investigated in earlier assignments, and determine the commodity codes for the products of this company.

2 Investigate the possibility of alternative commodity codes, bearing in mind that different classifications can attract quite different quotas and tariffs. It may be necessary to consider different uses for the product (e.g. exporting it as components).

3 Determine what tariffs, quotas and other restrictions (if any) apply to these goods when they are imported from various countries outside the EU.

4 Conduct a similar investigation with regard to export to various countries.

5 Write a short report for senior management identifying which markets are affected by trading barriers, and what market-entry strategy you would recommend.

Glossary

A

'Add on'. Additional to.

Agrichemicals. Chemicals associated with agriculture.

Annual percentage rate (APR). A notional interest rate, derived from the actual charges and interest payments due on a loan, which makes it possible to compare the financial costs of different types of loans.

Audio conferencing. Discussion between three or more people who are geographically separated and who communicate by a telephone system where each can hear and talk to all the others.

B

Back-load. Goods to be transported on the journey back to the vehicle operator's home country after a load has been delivered abroad.

Bilateral trade agreement. A commercial arrangement between two companies or countries.

Biotechnology. Applied science involving living things (plants or animals).

Black economy. Business activities undertaken surreptitiously to avoid taxation, etc.

Business culture. Pattern of human behaviour, beliefs and social norms within a business organisation.

C

Capital (finance). The value of the long-term assets of a business – initially the amount of money put into a business by its owners.

Capital adequacy. The extent to which the capital of a business is sufficient to ensure its viability.

Carnet. Set of documents, usually in a folder or wallet.

Clearing bank. A bank that participates in a clearing house system for settling claims and accounts.

Clearing house. An establishment maintained by banks for the mutual settling of claims and accounts.

Comecon. The countries that, prior to the political upheaval and re-shaping of eastern Europe, formed the Council for Mutual Economic Assistance, which comprised Bulgaria, the former Czechoslovakia, the former East Germany, Hungary, Poland, the former USSR, and the former Yugoslavia, together with Vietnam, Mongolia and Cuba.

Command economy. An economy with a high degree of government intervention and in which production and commerce between individuals and privately-owned organisations is discouraged or prevented.

Conglomorate. A widely diversified company.

Copyright. Exclusive legal right to reproduce, publish and sell a literary, musical or artistic work.

Coup d'état. Violent overthrow of the legitimate government.

Critical path analysis. Method of calculating the duration of a project and identifying those tasks that cannot be extended or delayed without extending the project duration.

D

Destination principle. VAT liability is determined by destination. Goods to be exported are zero-rated in the exporting country and VAT is paid in the country of destination at the rate that applies in the destination country.

Digital exchange. A telephone exchange which represents voice and data as discrete pulses for transmission. Digital exchanges have almost replaced older exchanges based on analogue technology.

Direct trader input. This is a computer-based system for entering and recording details of shipments. It avoids the need for customs officers to process documentation at the frontier.

Directorate-General (DG). Most of the staff employed by the European Commission work for one or other of the DGs. Each DG is concerned with implementing one aspect of EU policy – agriculture, regional policy, competition policy, etc.

Distortion of competition. Anything which interferes with organisations' freedom to compete with one another, e.g. quotas, subsidies, or tariffs.

Distribution node. Points from which several delivery routes originate or at which they converge. Usually they are locations at which goods are stored, or transferred from one type of transport to another.

'Dumping' – Export of goods at much reduced prices, usually supported by government subsidies in the exporting country, when there is over capacity in the industry.

Duty free. Goods on which no payment (excise duty, VAT, etc) is due to the government.

E

Eco audit. An investigation to establish the extent to which a product or process is 'environmentally friendly'

Eco-labelling. Information on product labels which indicates the extent to which they are 'environmentally friendly' (i.e. not harmful to the environment).

Electronic data interchange (EDI). Transfer of information, particularly financial and other commercial data, between computers connected by telephone or satellite communication links.

Electronic funds transfer (EFT). A way of making payments that involves electronic communication between computers, rather than the use of documents.

Encryption of data. Coding or scrambling of information so that it cannot be understood by unauthorised persons.

Enterprise society. A political, legal and economic framework that encourages entrepreneurial activity.

European Economic Area (EEA). An association between the seven EFTA countries and the 12 European Union countries.

European Free Trade Area (EFTA). An arrangement to trade in industrial goods without restriction made between Austria, Finland, Iceland, Liechtenstein, Norway, Sweden and Switzerland.

European Guidance and Guarantee Fund (EAGGF). One of the European Commission's regional funds, aimed at tackling regional disparities.

Eurostat. A part of the European Commission which collects and publishes statistical information about the European Union.

Extractive industry. An industry that extracts raw materials and minerals from the earth, sea or air. An example would be coal mining or oil extraction.

F

Factoring. The factoring agency carries out debt collection activities on behalf of a supplier. The factoring agency charges a fee for its services, based on the debt value. The supplier receives the value of the debt, less the fee, immediately. The contractual obligation between supplier–customer is unchanged.

Fibre optic. A cable that uses fine threads of glass to pass information optically, rather than employing electrical pulses along wires.

Flag of convenience. Applied to vessels registered in countries where the levels of taxation, wages, and/or safety legislation are now making it possible for them to be operated more cheaply than ones registered in other countries. Since all vessels must fly the flag of the country of registration they are easily identified.

Forfaiting. A term used in exporting. A forfaiting agency purchases deferred trade debt from the exporter, paying an amount slightly less than the full value of the debt. The forfaiting agency subsequently collects the full amount of the debt from the customer. The contractual obligation changes from supplier–customer to agency–customer.

Franchise. The right granted to an individual or organisation to market a company's goods or services in a particular territory.

Free market economy. An economy in which businesses are allowed to operate in competition with one another with little or no constraint by the government.

G

Gearing. The ratio of loans to share capital. An organisation is 'highly geared' if it has a high level of loans compared with its share capital.

General Agreement on Tariffs and Trade (GATT). An organisation that arranges rounds of talks on international trade, committed to achieving fair competition, expansion of multilateral trade, reduction in import tariffs and quotas, and the prevention of preferential trade deals.

'Green' exchange rate. A notional exchange rate, used within the EU, to determine prices, subsidies and other payments within agriculture and the agricultural products industry.

'Greenhouse' gases. Gases, produced principally by motor vehicles and production processes, which deplete the ozone layer and expose the earth's surface and people to radiation from space.

Gross domestic product (GDP). The UK's GDP is the total value of the output of all the production industries and services in the UK.

Gross national product (GNP). The UK's GNP is the total value of the GDP plus interest, profits, and dividends produced by UK-owned resources located abroad.

H

Hard currency. A currency which has a relatively stable exchange rate against other currencies, and which is generally acceptable as a currency in which transnational trading deals are negotiated.

Harmonised base rate. The base rate is a guideline for the setting of bank interest rates within a country. If there are harmonised (i.e. similar) base rates in several countries there is little incentive for speculators to switch funds between those countries to gain increased income from interest payments.

Hazardous substances. Substances that are potentially harmful to people, animals or the environment. They include many gases, inflammable liquids, and toxic, corrosive and radioactive products.

Human resource management (HRM). Activities arising from the recognition that people are a major business resource and so aim to optimise the effectiveness and efficiency of employees.

I

Indigenous company. A company registered in a country is indigenous to that country.

Information technology (IT). A combination of computer and telecommunication technologies.

Infrastructure. The underlying structure or basic framework.

Inland clearance depot system. A computer-based system that makes it easier to identify the source, destination, and current location of goods that are in transit.

Input tax (VAT). The VAT paid on purchases. It may be reclaimed from Customs and Excise or offset against output tax (collected on sales) by a VAT-registered organisation.

Insider dealing. Trading of shares based on knowledge derived from persons with privileged access to company information. Insider dealing is illegal.

Integrated services digital network (ISDN). A telecommunications network capable of carrying a wide variety of services.

Intellectual property. Ideas, especially business concepts, innovative methods of working, etc may be registered as being owned by their originator to prevent them being copied by others.

Interactive. Communication between two people, or between a person and a computer, where the actions of each have a direct and immediate effect on the actions of the other.

Inter-personal skills. Skills associated with communicating and working with other people.

Inventory. Another word for goods held in stock to avoid problems arising from unplanned fluctuations in supply and demand.

Investors in People status. Companies that can demonstrate they have a high level of commitment to staff development and training are able to gain this award from the Department of Trade and Industry.

J

Joint venture. A formal arrangement between two or more companies to carry out some activity together. It usually occurs where the resources and expertise of the participants are complementary to one another.

Just in time techniques (JIT). A management technique which involves obtaining goods 'just in time' for them to be used. It contrasts with the practice of keeping stock – 'just in case' unexpected events disrupt the business's plans. JIT demands a very good relationship between the user and the supplier, with good communications and good transportation arrangements.

M

Maastricht Treaty. The Treaty on European Union, signed by the 12 countries of the

European Community in December 1991, and ratified during 1993, is popularly known as the Maastricht Treaty. One of its effects was to change the name of the Community to 'the European Union' (EU).

Management buy-out. A scheme whereby managers employed by a company gain ownership by buying a majority of its shares from the previous owners.

Management Charter Initiative (MCI). A UK scheme, strongly backed by government and employer organisations, which allows experienced but unqualified managers to gain recognition of their competence as managers by providing a portfolio of evidence. The evidence must demonstrate their personal effectiveness as well as their competence to manage people, finance, operations and information.

Market share. Every company aims to increase its market share, i.e. to increase the proportion of the total volume of sales in a particular product or market (achieved by all companies) that is represented by the company's sales.

Mass marketing. Advertising and selling methods directed at large numbers of people, rather than targeted at specific individuals or companies.

Monetary compensation scheme. Certain payments made to farmers and food producers within the provisions of the Common Agricultural Policy (CAP).

Monopoly. A product or service for which there is only one supplier.

Mother board. The principal part of a micro-computer, housing the microprocessor and memory.

N

Negotiated procedure. A method of performing a task that is agreed by discussions between interested parties.

Niche marketing. Advertising and sales directed at a specific, usually fairly small, part of the total market for a product or service.

Non-registered individual. A person who is not registered with the Customs and Excise for VAT purposes. Below a particular level of sales, individuals are not compelled to register, although they may do so if they wish.

Non-taxable institution. An organisation, such as a charity, that has special tax exemptions.

O

Open network provision. An arrangement whereby information is shared between individuals or organisations without restrictions imposed by technological or commercial considerations.

Open tender system. An invitation to quote for a contract to provide goods or services that is not restricted to certain potential suppliers.

Origin principle (VAT). A system in which VAT liability is based on the origin of goods and services rather than their destination.

Output tax (VAT). The VAT collected on sales and payable to Customs and Excise on a quarterly basis by a VAT-registered organisation. The amount paid may be reduced by the amount of input tax paid on purchases.

Ozone layer. A portion of the earth's atmosphere that protects its inhabitants from radiation. Depletion of the ozone layer in certain regions leads to 'global warming' and climatic changes.

P

Packet-switched data services. A method of transmitting data from one location to another across a telecommunications network in which each part of a message may travel by a different route to optimise transmission speed and utilisation of the network.

Patent. A product or process may be patented (i.e. registered) in order to prevent others from making or using it without the permission of the owner of the patent.

Payback period. The period it takes for an organisation to receive in income the amount it has invested.

Pension fund. An organisation that administers an occupational pension scheme. It collects contributions from employees and employer, makes investments to maximise the value of the available funds, and makes payments to retired employees covered by the scheme.

Per capita. Per person.

Petrochemicals. Chemicals involved in the refining of crude oil to provide petroleum products.

Piggy-backing. Use of standard articulated semi-trailers that drive straight onto lightweight rail cars.

Planned economy. The economy of a country where commercial activity is restricted and the levels of supply of goods and services are planned and controlled by the government.

Point of sale. The place at which a member of the public pays for goods in a retail store. Point of sale terminals at the 'check out' serve a multiple purpose – price goods, print till receipt, check the status of a credit card, act as a repository for cash and cheques, calculate the amount of change to be dispensed, and record details of the sale.

Pre-entry customs clearance. A system where formalities associated with transnational trade are carried out before the goods cross the frontier, rather than at the frontier crossing point.

Preference agreement of origin. An agreement between countries, whereby goods can be transferred free of tariffs or quota restrictions.

Price sensitive. Products or services for which demand changes rapidly in response to relatively small changes in price.

Priority services. Services that are considered to have a higher than average level of importance.

Promissory note. A document that legally commits an organisation to make a payment, usually on a pre-determined date.

Prospectus. A document that sets out plans (often business or financial plans) and invites participation.

Public limited company (plc). A company of limited liability, the shares of which can be bought and sold without restriction.

R

Radio-pharmaceuticals. Drugs and similar substances associated with radio therapy (X-ray and other radiation treatment).

Risk exposure. The extent to which an individual or organisation is at risk from unplanned events. Risk exposure can be reduced by avoiding risk situations, and by insuring against the financial loss.

S

Second-tier management. The lowest level of supervision or management within an organisation is often known as 'first-level management'. Those who manage these managers are known as 'second-tier managers'.

Sector specific. The total market for goods and services may broken down into a number of 'sectors' on the basis of industrial classification, customer type, etc. Anything that is sect specific is aimed at a particular sector of the market.

Segmented marketing. Advertising and selling activities directed towards particular group of customers, often identified by their age, gender, social status or economic background.

Semi-conductor. A substance, such as silicon, with properties that make it suitable for use in the construction of electronic devices such as computers.

Single Administrative Document (SAD). A document introduced in 1988 to simplify the transfer of goods between countries. Prior to its introduction there was a multiplicity of documents covering the official, financial and commercial needs of the supplier, shipper and customer. The SAD is no longer required for trading between countries committed to the Single European Market (SEM).

Single European Act (SEA). This Act, passed by the European Council of Ministers in 1987, committed the European Community (as the European Union was then called) to remove all barriers to the movement of people, goods and services, and finance by the end of 1992.

Single European Market (SEM). An area of Europe without internal barriers to the movement of people, goods and services, and finance, brought about by the SEA.

Small to medium-sized enterprise (SME). Businesses in this category, defined by turnover or number of employees, are considered, by the European Commission, to have special importance in the creation of employment and wealth, and attract financial and other support.

Sole agency. The appointment of an individual or organisation to act on behalf of a company (e.g. to undertake advertising and sales activities) on the understanding that no other agency agreement will be undertaken in the same geographic or product area.

Solvency ratio. The extent to which an organisation is able to settle its short-term liabilities. A business may have considerable assets – buildings, equipment, etc – but may still lack solvency because it is not able to turn these into cash to meet immediate debts.

Spot rate. The rate of exchange that will be obtained by a business that wishes to make an immediate transfer between currencies.

Spreadsheet. A very common type of general-purpose computer program that is used to carry out calculations.

T

Takeover. Gaining control of a business by acquiring enough shares to overcome any opposition from the other shareholders.

Tariff. A tariff is a surcharge imposed on certain goods when they cross national borders as imports or exports. They are used to control the volume of imports and exports, to raise revenue for the government, and to protect local industries producing similar goods.

Tax paid. Once all liabilities to pay tax and excise duty have been fulfilled, the goods become 'tax paid'.

'Third country' shipping company. A shipping company based in a country other than the one from which the goods originated or to which they are destined.

TickIT. An accreditation scheme denoting that the activities of a computer department are of a high quality.

Title to goods. Legal ownership of goods.

Total quality management (TQM). A systematic approach by the management of a business to improve quality standards on a continual basis.

Treaty of Rome. This treaty, signed in March 1957, created the European Economic Community (EEC), which was the forerunner of the European Community (EC) and European Union (EU), as well as the European Atomic Energy Community (EURATOM).

V

Value-added service. A service, involving a close relationship between provider and customer, from which the customer perceives that the benefits (e.g. increased competitiveness) are significantly greater than those directly attributable to the service and significantly more valuable than the cost of the service.

Value-added tax (VAT). A tax calculated as a percentage of the selling price. The amount of VAT a UK business has to pay quarterly to Customs and Excise is calculated by deducting the amount of VAT it has paid out on its purchases from the amount it has collected on its sales. The tax is, therefore, effectively applied to the value added to the goods by the business, hence the name.

Value analysis. A technique involving the comparison of the cost of incorporating a feature into a product or service with the amount by which its selling price can be increased if the feature is incorporated.

VAT-exempt trader. Traders with a turnover below a certain threshold, and certain other organisations whose goods or services are mainly exempt from VAT (schools, for example).

Video conferencing. A technique, using video cameras and telecommunications, whereby a number of people, geographically separated, can see and talk to each other almost as easily as if they were located in the same room.

W

Weighting (statistical). A technique used to give greater or lesser significance to the scores associated with some of the assessment criteria. The technique is used in education; for example to give greater significance to coursework (60 per cent) than to the examination (40 per cent) rather than giving each equal significance (50 per cent each).

Z

Zero rated (VAT). Throughout the EU, goods and services are assigned a classification for VAT purposes. Most goods are 'standard rate', some are 'higher rate' and some are 'zero rate'. The VAT applied to 'zero rate' goods and services is zero per cent.

Index

Accreditation of prior learning	264
Active exporting	183
Aerospace	134
Agents	156
Agricultural development	278
Agriculture	9,25,134
Aims of the European Union	6
Air freight	219,226
Air transport	90
Airway bill	238
Animal and plant health	216,233
ATA Carnet	240
Austria	4,70,78,99,113,216,218,290,294
Banks	131
Belgium	4,9,220,222,225,229,254,257,261
Bill of exchange	237
Bill of lading	237
Biotechnology	39
Blacklist exemption certificate	240
British Overseas Trade Board (BOTB)	275
BS5750	201–3
Bulgaria	54,225,279,291,292,302
Bus transport	90
Cabotage	218
Canada	306,307,312,313
Capital movements	66
Carriage, Insurance Freight (CIF)	241
Carriers	227
Central Europe	301
Certificate of origin	237
Certificate of quality	239
Chamber of Commerce	275,284

Channels of distribution	167,230
Chemicals	135
China	306,308
CIS	302,306
Coal, support for	280
Commercial documentation	235
Committees in the European Parliament	15
Commodity type	310,319
Common Agricultural Policy	24,25
Common position	18
Communications	85
Company law	67
Competition	148,307
Competition Policy	6,9,47,68
Computers	136
Conditions of employment	266
Conference on Security & Cooperation in Europe	315
Confirming finance	246
Consultation procedure	17
Consumer protection	54
Containerisation	214
Cooperation procedure	18
Copyright	199
Council of Europe	314
Council of Ministers	8,16–18,298
Counter-trading	175
Court of Auditors	8
Court of Justice	8,17,48–9
Cultural and social issue	282
Currency accounts	247
Currency management	247–8
Customs procedures	215,233,251
Cyprus	6
Czech Republic	291,312
Czechoslovakia (former)	291,292,302
Dangerous goods	240
Data protection	58
Decision making in the European Union	8,9
Deepening the European Union	297
Delivery terms	242
Democratic deficit	18,299
Denmark	4,9,57,78,99,113,224,254,257,261,300

Department of Trade and Industry (DTI)	274,284
Development aid	283
Direct exporting	170
Directives	9,17,47
Directorates General (DG)	9–11,17,49
Distribution	137
Distribution and transport legislation	214
Distribution systems	213
Documentary advances	246
Documentary credits	245
Documentation	50
commercial	235
financial	235
official	233
Domestic road transport	218
Eastern Europe	301
Economies	95–9
Education	281
Electrical products	136
Electricity	135
Electronic data interchange (EDI)	93
Electronic funds transfer (EFT)	93
Electronics	136
Employee consultation	268
Employee protection	267
Employment grants	278
EN29000	201–3
Energy	39
Engineering	136
Equal opportunities	270
EU Budget	22–4
EU structural funds	276
EU support schemes	275
European Agricultural Guidance & Guarantee Fund (EAGGF)	24,34,276,278
European Bank for Reconstruction and Development	311
European Business Information Service	188
European Central Bank	298
European citizenship	298
European Commission	8–9,17–18
European Currency Unit (ECU)	40,66
European Development Fund (EDF)	283,311

European Economic Area (EEA)	293
European Economic Union	300
European Free Trade Association (EFTA)	4,216,290,293,306,309,312
European Information Centre	190
European Investment Bank (EIB)	279,284,298
European Monetary System (EMS)	66
European Monetary Union (EMU)	39
European Parliament	8,11–5,17,18,19
European Regional Development Fund (ERDF)	34,276,278
European Social Fund (ESF)	34,37,276,278
European Union membership	4
Excess capacity	148
Exchange programmes	262
Exchange Rate Mechanism (ERM)	41,66
Exchange schemes	281
Excise duty	215,234,250,251
Export Credit Guarantee Department (ECGD)	275
Export factoring	247
Exporting	146
External protection of agriculture	27
External relations policy	9
External trade policy	53
Factoring	247
Field research	186
Finance	9
Financial documentation	235
Financial services	67
Finland	4,70,224,290,294
Fishing	31
Flexibility in industry	256
Food	134
Food law	60
Forfaiting	247
Forward exchange contracts	248
France	4,9,35,79,100,114,217,222,224–5,229,254, 259,261,263,266,300–2,313
Free circulation principle	318
Free on board (FOB)	241

Gas	135
General Agreement on Tariffs & Trade (GATT)	53,306,312
Geographic diversification	149
Germany	4,9,35,57,68,79,101,116,222,224–5,254, 257,259,261,263,268,290,313
Goods clearance	318,319
Government intervention in international trade	315
Government support schemes	274
Greece	4,9,25,29,66,80,103,119,224,257,259, 261,290,302
Group of Seven	313
Harmonisation	47
Health	60
Health and hygiene	60
Health and safety	64,204
Health and Safety audit	206–7
Health and Safety policy	205
Holidays	267
Hungary	6,54,70,225,279,284,291,292
Hygiene	60
Iceland	4,70,290,295
Importing	173
Incoterms	241
Independant territories	309
India	308
Indirect exporting	170
Industrial democracy	268
Industrial relations	254–5,271
Industry	134
Information – background data	184
Information – specific data	185
Information gathering	183
Information sources	184,189,190
Information Technology (IT)	38,59
Inland waterways	89,225
Innovation	194
Innovation funding	196
Innovation, support for	280
Insurance	67,131
Insurance documents	239

Integrated delivery services	227
Intellectual property rights	57
International links	305
International marketing opportunities	155
Internationalism	150
Intervention in agriculture	27
Invoice	237
Ireland	4,9,35,80,103,120,224,254,257,263
ISO9000	201–3
Italy	4,9,26,35,81,104,120,224,254,259,261,313
Japan	44,70,292,306–7,309,312–3
Job vacancies	259
Language	63
Letter of credit	245
Liechtenstein	295
Loans for economic development	279
Lobbying	19
Logistics	167,229
Lome Convention	283,311
Luxembourg	4,9,81,105,121
Maastricht Treaty	*see* Treaty of European Union
Malta	6, 312
Management Charter Initiative (MCI)	264,265
Market entry strategies	156
Market infrastructure	151
Marketing data selection	187
Marketing mix	163
Mass production	255
Medicines	61
Members of the European parliament	11–3,14,18,19
Methods of payment	245
Mining	136
Morocco	6
Moving goods out of the EU	236
Moving production abroad	171
Multinationals	316
Negotiating a deal	171
Netherlands	4,9,57,82,106,122,217,220,222,225,254,257,261,263,301

New Zealand	312
North Atlantic Treaty Organisation (NATO)	299,314
Norway	4,70,89,290,295
Official documentation	233
Oil	135
Open account	245
Organisation for Economic Cooperation & Development (OECD)	54,312
Origin of goods principle	216,317
Overdrafts	246
Pacific basin	308
Patents	198
Payment in advance	245
Pharmaceuticals	61,135
Poland	54,284,291,292
Politics in the European Parliament	14
Population	149
Portugal	4,9,25,29,35,68,82,106,124,234,261,290, 291,300,301
Prices	28
Pricing	166
Privatisation	138
Product life cycle	146
Product policy	164
Promotion	169
Protecting products and ideas	197
Public purchasing	52
Purchasing power	149
Qualifications	63,263,298
Qualified majority voting	298,299
Quality concepts	200
Quality standards	201
Quotas	316–7
Railway consignment note (CIM)	238
Railways	87,224
Recommendations and opinions	9
Recruitment	261
Regional aid	277
Regional Enterprise Grants	196–7

Regional Policy	32,37,70
Registered Excise Dealers and Shippers (REDS)	234
Regulations (EU)	8,17
Representation in the European Parliament	13
Research and Development	38,70,281
Retail	128
Risk management	244
Risk types	244
Road consignment note (CMR)	239
Road transport	222
Roads	85
Romania	54,225,279,291,292
Russia	54,291,302
Sea transport	89
Selling methods	170
Service provision abroad	171
Service sector	132
Shipbuilding	136
Shipping	219,226
Short term financing	246
Single Administrative Document (SAD)	50,215,234,317
Single European Act (SEA)	4,46–7
Single European Market (SEM)	4,44–6
Slovakia	291,312
Small exporters	157
Small or Medium Sized Enterprise (SME)	139
Social Charter	34,64,221,253,259,266
Social issues	282
Social Policy	34,64,70
Social security	269
Spain	4,9,29,35,68,83,107,124,224,234,261, 263,290,291,301,302
Spot rate	248
State ownership	138
Steel, support for	280
Subsidiarity	297
Support for business	279
Support for SMEs	280
Sweden	4,70,225,290,295
Switzerland	70,216,218,225,290,295

Tariffs	316,317,318
Taxation	67,269
Technology	38
Telecommunications	38,57,92,136
Temporary employment	262
Trade marks	198
Trade statistics	217
Trade unions	268
Training	269,281
Training & Enterprise Council (TEC)	284
Training grants	278
Tram transport	90
Transit countries	218
Transport	9,51,137
Transport system, liberalisation of	217
Transport, environmental issues	221
Transport, harmonisation of regulations	220
Treaty of European Union	4,37,297
Treaty of Paris	3
Treaty of Rome	3,37
Turkey	6,70,292,302
TV and radio	58,93
UK legislation	18
Underground	90
United Kingdom	4,9,25,35,57,83,108,217,220,222,254,259, 263,300,301,302,313
United Nations (UN)	299,314
Unsolicited orders	182
USA	44,70,292,302,306,307,309,312,313
Value Added Tax (VAT)	47,50,215,234,250,301
Vehicle manufacture	137
Voting in EU institutions	8,13,47,298,299
Water	135
Western European Union (WEU)	299,315
Wider Europe	289
Working in other countries	62,260
World bank	311
Yugoslavia (former)	218,225,292,302